leeds
metropolitan
university

Mouse Morality

University of Texas Press
Austin

Mouse Morality

The Rhetoric of
Disney Animated Film

Annalee R. Ward

Foreword by Clifford G. Christians

The material in Figure 6.1 is from *The Great Wall in Ruins: Communication and Cultural Change in China,* by Godwic C. Chu and Yanan Ju (page 244, figure "Five Categories of Traditional Values"). Reprinted by permission of the State University of New York Press © 1993, State University of New York. All rights reserved.

Material in Chapter 2 originally appeared as "The Axiology of the *Lion King*'s Mythic Narrative: Disney as Moral Educator," in *The Journal of Popular Film and TV,*" Winter 1996. Reprinted with permission of the Helen Dwight Reid Educational Foundation. Published by Heldref Publications, 1319 18th Street, NW, Washington, DC 20036-1802.

COPYRIGHT © 2002 BY THE UNIVERSITY OF TEXAS PRESS

All rights reserved

Printed in the United States of America

First edition, 2002

Requests for permission to reproduce material from this work should be sent to Permissions, University of Texas Press, P.O. Box 7819, Austin, TX 78713-7819.

⊗ The paper used in this book meets the minimum requirements of ANSI/NISO Z39.48-1992 (R1997) (Permanence of Paper).

LIBRARY OF CONGRESS CATALOGING-IN-PUBLICATION DATA

Ward, Annalee R.
  Mouse morality : the rhetoric of Disney animated film / by Annalee R. Ward ; foreword by Clifford G. Christians.—1st ed.
    p.   cm.
Includes bibliographical references and index.
  ISBN 0-292-79152-6 (alk. paper) — ISBN 0-292-79153-4 (pbk. : alk. paper)
  1. Animated films—United States—Themes, motives. 2. Walt Disney Company. I. Title.
  NC1766.U52 D5925 2002
  791.43′3—dc21

                                   2001008475

CONTENTS

Our analysis of morality in entertainment is limited and stylized at present. Violence in the media is a major concern, and we research it relentlessly. Pornography in cinema and virtual sex on the Internet are routinely condemned. Blatant consumerism in advertising and commercial entertainment is increasingly offensive. Racial stereotyping and gender typecasting are on everyone's short list. But our treatments are typically moralistic and academically superficial. *Mouse Morality* illustrates a complex, multilayered, and well-informed content analysis that the field needs and will welcome.

The author's worldview framework is *Mouse Morality*'s golden strategy. It accomplishes exactly what Professor Ward intends, that is, opening up both the moral and the cognitive domains rather than isolating the moral and reducing it to emotivism. With worldview as the book's interpretive axis, the author articulates a strong version of Disney as a moral educator and, in the process, avoids simplistic conclusions about its animated films either in terms of market sales or family values. Through the worldview perspective, this book comes to grips with the incongruous moralities in Disney. It enables both parents and educators to gain a critical understanding of Disney content without being judgmental or promotional for the wrong reasons.

Gaining an inside perspective on human life is exactly what Wilhelm Dilthey intended when he developed weltanschauung as an analytic tool for the humanities in late 19th-century Germany. The prevailing scientism of his day sought deterministic causal explanations that were empirically testable by quantifiable means. Because of stupendous gains vis-à-vis the natural world, the mechanistic motif overwhelmed the study of human beings and society as well. But Dilthey insisted that positivistic science could not give us truth about the whole of reality: "We explain nature; we understand (Verstehen) the life of the soul" (*Gesammelte Schriften,* vol. 6). The humanities have a different logic from that of physics. Our lived experience is irreplaceable and inexhaustible. Human forms of consciousness and expression are situated historically. People act on the basis of beliefs and attitudes about the world, not according to formal laws, as, for instance, the planets are governed by gravity. Human understanding for Dilthey included a pretheoretical world picture (Weltbild); our lived experience, which we orient historically; and a systematic worldview, which gives meaning to our consciousness. Through understanding rooted in life itself and a holistic humanness, this successor to Hegel at Berlin laid the foundation for interpretive studies until today.

Professor Ward follows particularly the anthropological version of Clifford Geertz, who defines worldviews as our "comprehensive ideas of order, . . . pictures of the way things in sheer actuality are." She highlights Walsh and Middleton's philosophical version of worldviews as "a model *of the world* which guides its adherents *in the world.*" Jürgen Habermas is used approvingly also—worldviews, in his terms, "lay down the framework of fundamental concepts within which we interpret everything that appears in the world." Professor Ward stitches worldview thinking into rhetorical theory through Burke's "equipment for living" and "terministic screens," through which humans frame their interpretations. And out of these contemporary configurations of Dilthey's interpretive legacy, Professor Ward formulates her own definition for unearthing Disney: "A worldview is the means by which experience and belief are merged and organized and by which values are prioritized."

Bringing rhetorical criticism into its own through worldview analysis is particularly impressive for examining popular culture. The global mass media are not neutral purveyors of information but creators and shapers of culture. They are institutional agents of acculturation. The media sketch out our world for us, organize our conversations, engage our everyday language, and locate time and space for us. They provide a common body of symbols for enabling our public rituals. In Jacques Ellul's formulation, communication technologies represent the meaning-edge of our cultural habitat. Communication is the connecting tissue in culture building. Values, signification, and meaning are thus congenital to the lingual domain. If cultures are sets of symbols that orient life and provide it with significance, then cultural patterns are inherently normative. With ordering relations recognized as a constituent part of symbolic environments, we can begin putting content into the normative, asking what authentic social existence involves. Thus worldview analysis takes hold of cultural forms on their presuppositional level through asking systematically what definitions of humanness, society, and epistemology are revealed in the text.

Worldview analysis within the interpretive paradigm differs fundamentally from the conventional study of morality in entertainment, where ethical principles are extrinsic. Human action and conceptions of the good are not separate domains, with the latter an external apparatus for judging the former. Rhetorical criticism in worldview terms works from the ground up and inside out. It is Geertz's thick description, resonating in depth with the ways human language symbolizes our emotionality, orientation, and purposiveness. Rather than privileging thin abstractions, moral order is positioned close to the bone, in the creaturely fabric of everyday life. Rather than presuming a dualism of two orders, moral values are investigated as intrinsic to a community's ongoing existence and identity.

E. G. Guba and Yvonna Lincoln argue that the fundamental issues in the liberal arts must ultimately be engaged at the worldview level: "Questions of method are secondary to questions of paradigm," defined as our "basic belief system or worldview" (*Handbook of Qualitative Research*, p. 105). *Mouse Morality* meets that challenge for popular culture. In media criticism, political economy and critical theory have been seen traditionally as more convincing and intellectually stimulating than rhetorical critique. But in my judgment, this book matches the quality and sophistication of those perspectives, feeding off the commodification of global media and hegemony but establishing an explicit rhetorical analysis overall. *Mouse Morality* is a pleasure to read and discuss in itself but also shows the pathway to media criticism of the first order.

Clifford G. Christians
Research Professor of Communications
University of Illinois—Urbana

Disney continues its yearly release of an animated feature film. The company hasn't missed a year since *The Lion King* (1994), a commercial hit that keeps on giving to its parent company through its merchandising and its continued success on video, on DVD, and onstage. As I write this, *Atlantis* (2001) has been released to mixed reviews, and I expect the next animated feature film will also get mixed reviews. Why?

The place of Disney in American culture—and, increasingly, worldwide culture—has grown to be both a dominant and a powerful fixture on the contemporary landscape. But because of its image as a family-oriented corporation, audiences expect to trust the messages in its films. The films, however, in trying to please the largest audience possible, send inconsistent messages, mixing moral values in ways that offend various people.

The films discussed in this book represent successive releases. Each of the films examined from *The Lion King* to *Mulan* reflect changes or lack of changes that Disney makes as a result of cultural influences and critical response from earlier films. With each film, I have used a different critical approach to uncover the moral messages taught. In so doing, I am trying to demonstrate that it is possible to understand these films from any number of angles. But in the final chapter, I add these messages together and ask some questions about a Disney worldview, a Disney understanding of what is important, what is valuable to teach the Disney audience, for description and analysis without evaluation stop short of completing the critic's task.

It is my hope that students of rhetoric, of film, of ethics, and of Disney will find this book useful. But I also hope parents and all those concerned about creating a moral society will also find this book of interest. It may require a bit of work to get through some of the theoretical language, but my goal in using such language is to ground the conclusions well.

As you read through the orientation of Chapter 1 and the critical analysis of the five films, perhaps you will see Disney through a different lens. Perhaps you will find the discussion of worldview in the last chapter to be helpful in sorting out what you believe about Disney and moral values. And perhaps it may even lead you to question what worldview you live by or what you teach your children or allow them to be taught.

ACKNOWLEDGMENTS

Thanks are due to many people. I could not have completed this project without their encouragement and critiques.

Regent University in Virginia Beach has been a constant source of support. This book is based on my dissertation from Regent. There I had the privilege of working with Michael Graves as an advisor. He embodies a scholar and a gentle teacher. His encouragement and insights enabled me to pursue this subject with enthusiasm. Dennis Bounds, Rodney Reynolds, and Kathy Merlock Jackson provided helpful references, suggestions, and clarifications. These contributions make the scholarly endeavor a rich experience.

Maureen and Paul Flanagan made my studies at Regent University possible by providing unlimited hospitality and friendship.

I would also like to acknowledge the support and challenges of colleagues both at Regent and at Trinity Christian College. These colleagues often acted as sounding boards and helped me over difficult hurdles. Trinity Christian College provided me the peace of an office and has supported me in this process.

Finally, I want to thank my husband, Mark Ward, who willingly made time to read each chapter and give insight and kind criticism. I could not have done this without him.

● ● ● *Mouse Morality*

ONE

Disney, Film, and Morality

A BEGINNING

Storytelling is vital to every society as a way of searching for and sharing truth, but the role of storyteller in culture has changed, affecting what is told. Today, popular film has become a central storyteller for contemporary culture. It communicates myths and fairy tales, entertains, and educates the audience for better or worse. One company in particular has had tremendous audience appeal and enjoys brand-name popularity: Disney.[1]

The Walt Disney Company is a powerful economic and cultural phenomenon[2] known throughout the United States and the world as a provider of family entertainment (Maltin 1, 308).[3] Its media and entertainment holdings establish it as a central communicator in contemporary life.[4] Yes, the Walt Disney Company has become the "Stories R Us" store, particularly for children. As such, it provides many of the first narratives children use to learn about the world. In light of Disney's popular appeal[5] and pervasiveness, and given a cultural climate that issues frequent calls for evidence of a moral society, I take Disney's presence as being worthy of serious consideration. Thus in this book I am going to closely examine five animated films to unearth the messages—particularly the messages about how we ought to live, about morality—that are being taught to the audience. In order to look for not only the obvious but also the more subtle lessons on life, I approach this from the perspective of rhetorical criticism. My understanding of that approach is to carefully study which messages are embedded in the text by describing what I see, to use theories to help orient the descriptions, and finally to draw some evaluative conclusions about those messages.[6]

DISNEY AS MORAL EDUCATOR

Generations are now raised on Disney fairy tales, and original story lines are forgotten or dismissed as not the real thing. Disney rewrites the original tales for its particular version of American values. For example, *Disney's Hercules* creates an amalgamation of myths that confuse the original story of Hercules' parentage, exploits, and motivations. Or consider *Disney's Pocahontas*. The movie changes Pocahontas's age, looks, and accomplishments from the few historical facts that we do have to a romanticized beauty. Disney is a central storyteller in our society, aiming its messages at families with children. And families have responded with overwhelming acceptance of Disney products and, by implication, Disney messages. William Powers of the *Washington Post* writes,

> Here is where we reach the absolute center of Disney's power. It begins with the children, for whom Disney's products are so powerful; they teach life's lessons (think of Pinocchio's nose) and they build dreamscapes. Children grow into adults, who are fond of Disney because it shaped the way they think about the world. (G1)

Disney helps shape children's views of right and wrong, their morality.

The Walt Disney Company's animated films established Disney in the cultural mainstream, beginning with the 1937 release of *Snow White*, and they continue to make a vital contribution to Disney's financial success. Blockbuster films provide additional characters for Disney theme parks and a plethora of material for merchandising. The popularity of home videos and DVDs means that the messages can be heard repeatedly—almost propaganda-like. Henry Giroux, in a critical article, makes the following observation:

> [There is a] largely unquestioned assumption that animated films stimulate imagination and fantasy, reproduce an aura of innocence and wholesome adventure, and, in general, are good for kids. . . . [O]ne of the most persuasive [roles] is the role they play as the new "teaching machines." . . . [T]hese films inspire at least as much cultural authority and legitimacy for teaching specific roles, values, and

ideals [as] more traditional sites of learning such as public schools, re-ligious institutions, and the family. ("Animating" 24–25)

The extreme popularity of these films and associated merchandise pro-pels them into the critical spotlight. For if millions of children are view-ing these films once or even repeatedly, what messages might they be internalizing? John Taylor in *Storming the Magic Kingdom* observes, "The [Disney] company's executives saw Disney as a force shaping the imagi-native life of children around the world. It was woven into the very fab-ric of American culture. Indeed, its mission—and it did, they believed, have a mission as important as making money for its stockholders—was to celebrate and nurture American values" (viii). Media critic Michael Real argues the point: "Disney instructs through morality plays that structure personal values and ideology" (*Mass-Mediated* 48). Similarly, Benjamin Barber argues in the *New York Times,* "Whether Disney knows it or not, it is buying much more than our leisure time. It has a purchase on our values, on how we feel and think and what we think about" (15). Disney films are a significant force in children's moral education.

CONCERN FOR MORALITY

In recent years we hear an increasingly loud call for a return to valuing morality as an end in itself. From Bellah et al.'s discussion of virtues in *Habits of the Heart* and *The Good Society* to Alan Wolfe's *Moral Freedom: The Search for Virtue in a World of Choice,* William Bennett's collection of virtuous stories in *The Book of Virtues,* and Stephen Carter's plea for people of integrity in *Integrity,* many people criticize current morality and argue for better moral education. The Chicago Public School system, for ex-ample, developed a new curriculum that interweaves values into a vari-ety of subjects (Rossi, "Schools" 8). Moral education is a concern for so-ciety. That concern naturally raises questions about the messages of a popular cultural phenomenon like Disney. Do its films contribute posi-tively to children's moral education?

Kenneth Burke, in discussing literature, observes Disney's power to provide "equipment for living" (*Philosophy* 253–262). I like this phrase and find that expanding it describes well one of the goals of this book: seeking to discover how Disney films provide equipment for *moral* living and what equipment that might be. Given the growing concern for moral awareness, there is a certain exigency to which Disney, in its desire to provide family entertainment—entertainment that is not morally offensive—is responding with its animated films.

A UNIQUE AUDIENCE

Because Disney aims its films particularly at children, additional issues are involved in its persuasive role. Always challenged by the perception of manipulation, persuasive attempts must be ready to justify both the means and the ends—particularly with an audience of children who are still forming their moral vision. Robert Coles in *The Spiritual Life of Children* reflects, "How young we are when we start wondering about it all, the nature of the journey and of the final destination" (335). Children are concerned about moral issues.

For Disney, the issue faced is that children "are more vulnerable, more persuadable, than adult audiences" (Schrag 221) and therefore require greater care. If, as Coles believes, movies help both adults and children "try to figure out the moral significance" of their lives, Disney has a great burden to present a responsible moral vision (*Moral Life* 90).

The fact that film not only has dialogue but also uses visuals and music to add to its potential power is an observation of which Disney is well aware. Cochran states, "He [Disney executive Jeffrey Katzenberg] works entirely by instinct when it comes to the animated stuff—it's all about 'is this telling the story, is it holding together, is there an emotional core to this thing?' He's a great emotional foil. If it moves Jeffrey, it'll move other people" ("Hans Zimmer" 34). Disney wants powerful emotions at work in its films. Cochran also comments on the visuals: "What intrigued Hans [composer Hans Zimmer] was that animation, especially animation with animal characters, works its audience magic on a purely subconscious level." For, Cochran observes, "what animation does is present emotional truth, not 'realistic' truth" ("Hans Zimmer" 35). Not only do the words and the visuals combine to tell the story, but the music is also a conscious part designed to follow "the emotional structure of the story itself" ("Hans Zimmer" 36). Cochran gives the following example:

> Zimmer composed a theme for Mufasa which he believed should not be played after he died—except when he appears in the sky. "You hear this theme when Mufasa explains the kingdom and responsibility to Simba, but it basically dies with Mufasa, and doesn't return un-

til Mufasa reappears as a ghost. But it isn't linked to Mufasa. It's linked to the whole idea of being King, and Simba has to earn the right to have that theme, because he has forgotten all about responsibility and his role in life." ("Hans Zimmer" 37)

Film is a powerful storyteller; employing narrative, visuals, and music enhances its power to communicate a vision of moral living.

Hence, the implication for Disney is that it needs to take extra care in what it does, because its tools are powerful, and it is working with a vulnerable audience. As Robert Schrag concludes in a narrative analysis of Saturday morning television, "[T]hese first stories are not subjected, in the minds of those young children who view them, to the test of narrative fidelity. These children are in the process of constructing the criteria against which they will judge the narrative fidelity of other stories" (231). The stories children are exposed to will form the standards for testing the truth of other stories later in life. Consequently, charges of racism, sexism, misrepresentation of history, and so on, particularly in children's films, are not something to be taken lightly. If children believe that what they see represents a true picture of life, then the potential for cultural change and growth is diminished.

There is another side to this picture of film as moral educator, however. While acknowledging that it plays a role, Coles concludes that other factors are equally important in forming the moral life of children. The child "doesn't forget what he's learned in school, learned at home, from hearing people talk in his family and neighborhood" (*Moral Life* 80). In other words, it is possible for negative messages to be overridden by other influences in a child's life, as long as those other influences are both positive and strong. That those messages are there in the first place, however, raises warning flags.

As narratives, Disney films delight children while revealing insights into living. Those narratives reveal perspectives on morality, for, as historian Hayden White asks, "Could we ever narrativize *without* moralizing?" ("Value" 23). The popularity of Disney animated films and the growth in their production and rereleases[7] affirm Disney animated films as significant communicators in the public sphere that beg to be examined more closely. Disney's influence in society is powerful. It can shape the way children think about who they are and who they should be. Understanding the values espoused by Disney as implied or overtly communicated in its films is vital for the conscientious viewer and parent.

METHOD OF RESEARCH

This book focuses on five consecutive Disney animated films that represent diversity in story origination and reveal differing dimensions or perspectives of Disney morality. This study could fruitfully be applied to other texts, but these were chosen to provide both continuity over time and diversity in audience appeal. *The Lion King* (1994), one of the top ten films ever released, is an original story[8] and focuses on a male hero. Because of that male focus, Disney tries hard to balance its releases to provide identification with the female gender. *Pocahontas* (1995) is loosely based on historical narrative and features a female lead. *Disney's The Hunchback of Notre Dame* (1996) is loosely based on Victor Hugo's novel and includes both male and female characters as the heroes of the film. *Hercules* (1997) is a melting pot of Greek myths designed to appeal to young boys (Tucker 38). *Mulan* (1998) is based on a treasured Chinese legend and highlights the courage of a young girl.

To identify the morality or moralities in these films, I use tools of the rhetorical critic that support a close reading. These tools enable me to go beyond a superficial glance at what the film teaches about right and wrong to a depth that unearths more messages, some that may even contradict each other. I uncover what understanding(s) of morality the texts invite, and I conclude by discussing how Disney's version(s) of morality signifies a Disney worldview. Note the word *invite*. Rather than testing one theory and applying it to every film, I begin with a close look at the film and then find the right tool to help open the text up. In this way, I take each film on its own terms. I ask questions of the films such as, What is the overall theme or moral message? How does Disney communicate that? What other messages are coming through? Are the messages contradictory? The answer to the "how" question then leads me to use theoretical tools only as they mesh with what Disney says it wants to communicate and with the obvious ways it does communicate. Some of the tools could have been usefully employed more than once, but I found that, by applying a variety of methods, I could show how moral messages reveal themselves in diverse ways.

DEFINITIONS

In questioning the text for Disney's messages, I've tried to focus on questions about right and wrong. In so doing, I use a number of terms. To clarify those terms, I offer several definitions. *Moral,* as I use it, refers to right or virtuous behavior, and *morality* thus means the principles of that virtuous behavior or conduct. Here, morals and morality differ from social mores in that *mores* are based on social customs of unique groups. Morality is related to ethics in that *ethics* is the systematic study of morals and values. *Values* are ideals that are important to a person or a society. They can include morals but can also include things such as being on time to work, exercising craftsmanship, getting a journalistic scoop, and so on. Occasionally I may use the terms *morality* and *values* interchangeably, in which case I am referring to the moral dimension of values.

Focusing on the morality espoused by Disney animated films necessarily leads to questions about how Disney sees the world—what assumptions does it make in the messages it sends? Chapter 7 looks back at the five Disney films studied and tries to make sense of Disney's moral messages. Questions of assumptions, of presuppositions, lead to questions of worldview. Another way of describing that worldview is to use Kenneth Burke's language of "terministic screen" (*Permanence* 7) or "frame of interpretation" (*Attitudes* 92–93), meaning that these assumptions create a "trained incapacity," or limit how a person is able to see the world. Each of these terms encompasses the way people think about their world and how their thinking shapes every part of their life. I particularly like Brian Walsh and Richard Middleton's definition of *worldview:* "A world view, then, provides a model *of the world* which guides its adherents *in the world.* It stipulates how the world ought to be, and it thus advises how its adherents ought to conduct themselves in the world" (32). In seeking to understand what morality or moralities Disney films advocate and how they do so, I will be examining Disney's worldview—something that is frequently overlooked when parents recommend Disney films to their children.

Worldview should not be neglected, because it has the power to shape attitudes and values, as well as the ability to determine what is important in cultural and individual living. Disney's influence on our culture is pervasive and powerful. Understanding its value system, particularly its worldview as implied in its perspective of morality, is a necessary ingredient for the conscientious viewer's understanding of its influence.

Finally, I also use the terms *rhetoric* and *rhetorical.* Numerous perspectives on the meaning of *rhetoric* exist. For the purposes of my research, I rely on Kenneth Burke's understanding of *rhetoric* as "the use of symbols, by one symbol—using one entity to induce action in another" (*Rhetoric* 46). Burke sees persuasion, identification, communication, and rhetoric all as interrelated. In addition, Burke emphasizes the moral dimension of rhetoric when he observes, "Such considerations [that 'a man can be his own audience' (38)] make us alert to the ingredient of rhetoric in all *socialization,* considered as a *moralizing* process" (39). In that Disney films communicate to or identify with an audience, they use persuasion, which necessarily involves a moral process.

The Disney films studied here are examined as separate texts. Defining those texts has come to be a controversial task in and of itself, given the divergent views on rhetorical criticism held by people like Michael Leff and Michael McGee.[9] The method for this study can best be defined by what it is not. It is not a broad cultural study in the tradition of McGee. It is not a "cookie-cutter" application of one textbook method to all of the films. It is, however, a rhetorical criticism in the historical-critical model of research.[10]

READING THE TEXTS

In this book, each film is studied for what the moral messages might be and how they are being communicated. The book draws on rhetorical, sociological, philosophical, and moral development theories to facilitate the unearthing of the Disney morality portrayed in these films. It also involves a close reading in "Leff style" to understand how the individual parts of the film contribute to the whole message. In some senses, my method leans toward John Campbell's "House of the Middle Way" (346), in that I seek to understand the variety of critical responses and the cultural moral context in which the films participate. For that reason, I begin studying each film by looking at critics' responses to get a sense of the film's reception. In addition, I study the film itself through a variety of theoretical tools to uncover how and what it communicates regarding morality. Those tools, however, are secondary to the interrogation of the text itself, for they are meant to shine light on the results rather than to determine what may or may not be examined.

In each of the next five chapters, I use a different theoretical grounding to illuminate what and how the particular film teaches. After examining the film and the critical response, I have ideas about what themes emerge. As I begin to study the film more closely, I find that using a theoretical approach to questioning the text opens it up for greater understanding.

Using different theories, then, I interrogate the text for its moral messages to better understand what Disney is teaching its audience about what is right and wrong, good and bad, valuable and worthless. The different narratives lend themselves to different approaches.

Chapter 2 demonstrates how *The Lion King* acts as a mythic moral narrative that taps into spiritual consciousness by drawing on biblical myth, universal archetypes, and sacred rituals. Chapter 3, on *Pocahontas,* identifies the messages sent by Disney's disrespect of history and uses symbolic boundaries of moral order to reveal Disney's attitudes about right and wrong, or acceptable and deviant behavior. Disney's version of *The Hunchback of Notre Dame,* studied in Chapter 4, overlays a comic frame on Victor Hugo's tragic story, requiring a morality that is clearly defined in terms of virtue and vice. Chapter 5 focuses on how Disney changed historical legend in *Hercules* to create moral identification through characters' actions, visual images, music, and symbolism. *Mulan,* the film studied in Chapter 6, is an intercultural text that incorporates both Eastern and Western values. Finally, Chapter 7 is a metacritical perspective on the work of the previous chapters that builds on the identified morality to construct a Disney worldview.

Much of recent Disney criticism (see particularly Bell, Haas, and Sells) is cultural criticism from a critical studies perspective of neo-Marxism and/or feminism. Although this is helpful in identifying the cultural dominance or hegemony of Disney productions and products, it can also be limiting. Consequently, I find myself approaching these texts on the narrow ridge of fence sitting. I do not wish to assume that Disney films are "only good entertainment," which many are, nor do I wish to assume that Disney is a "hegemonic, capitalistic structure" that manipulates the minds of children, which might also be true. Disney is a very real, very significant part of contemporary culture. As such, it functions rhetorically, influencing perspectives of morality either explicitly or implicitly. The research demonstrates what Disney's understanding of morality is and how it, as the dominant "Stories R Us" store, sells, through its films, its lessons on moral life.

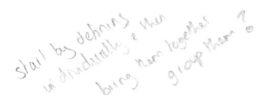

The Lion King

MORAL EDUCATOR THROUGH MYTH, ARCHETYPE, AND RITUAL

FILM BACKGROUND

We live, we die. The children live and die—all part of the great "circle of life," as *The Lion King*'s theme song implies. A Disney animated film aimed at children, *The Lion King* features a cast of animals who represent a society in harmony, then in a struggle for survival, and finally in a climactic battle resulting in renewed peace for the lion kingdom. More specifically, the story focuses on the life of lion cub Simba, son of Mufasa, the king. But it is also a story that relies heavily on myths, archetypes, and rituals as rhetorical means to communicate moral values.

In recent years, the Disney conglomeration has emerged as a significant storyteller of our cultural myths. At one time the sources for myth were diverse but almost always included religious institutions. Now that is less common, and people turn to popular culture to satisfy spiritual hungers. For increasingly harried parents, Disney serves brightly packaged, nutritious, "safe food" in convenient locations, including their own home (in the form of videos). *The Lion King* in particular, however, invokes transcendent elements as it entertains.

The Lion King has achieved tremendous popularity at the box office, in merchandising, and in home video sales. It grossed $312.9 million domestically, making it seventh on the list of top-grossing films ("Worldwide"). According to Sallie Hofmeister, "analysts estimate that *The Lion King* represents $1 billion in profit for Disney over two to three years," producing revenue from box office, home videos, and merchandising (37). Disney expects the home video release to sell 27 million copies before they put on a moratorium. That would make it the "biggest selling video of all time" and would generate "nearly $450 million in revenue" (Hettrick 1). Capturing two Oscars and two Grammies for its music (Honeycutt 13; Jolson-Colburn 5), this movie works through catchy songs, rich animation, and a diverse cast of voices that add depth to the pathos in the animals' eyes—not unlike other Disney animated films.[1] Yet this film has grossed significantly more than earlier popular films such as *The Little Mermaid, Aladdin,* or even the first animated film to be nominated for an Oscar for Best Picture, *Beauty and the Beast.*[2]

At the same time, *The Lion King* managed to bring out the rage of many critics who assert that it is a racist, sexist, homophobic, stereotyping, and violent film. Those are strong charges, especially in the present environment of politically correct concern. This kind of criticism of Disney films is not new, however.[3]

Nevertheless, the question emerges, why did *The Lion King* receive such intense response, both positive in light of the box office receipts and negative? I believe that the answer lies in the movie's use of mythic narrative, which employs archetypes and rituals and, by its nature, advocates a morality. Given the postmodern proclivity for the relativity of values, as Alasdair MacIntyre has observed, many might respond negatively to the advocacy of particular values. By the same token, because the film taps into cultural myths, it strikes a deeper chord than other narratives might, which in turn evokes strong responses.

In this chapter I will examine the natures of mythic narrative, archetypes, and rituals and the appearances of each in *The Lion King;* how they work as communicative tools; and how the film acts as moral educator. It is to the topic of mythic narrative that I now turn.

MYTHIC NARRATIVE

A Definition of Myth

The statement that *The Lion King* is mythic needs clarification. Because definitions of *myth* vary, I will summarize several of the more significant approaches to understanding myth. Examinations of myth are usually included in narrative criticism or even subsumed under psychoanalytic criticism. The difficulty of constructing a uniform definition of *myth* can be seen in some examples of differing approaches.

Michael Real defines mythic activity as "the collective reenactment of symbolic archetypes that express the shared emotions and ideals of a given culture" (*Mass-Mediated* 96). This definition comports well with psychoanalyst Carl Jung's belief in the primacy of archetypes: "Archetypes create myths, religions and philosophies that influence and characterize whole nations and epochs of history" (Jung and von Franz 68). The psychoanalytic approach to criticism is common to literary criticism, film criticism, and rhetorical criticism, which is my focus.[4] An example of rhetorical criticism can be seen in the work of Janice Hocker Rushing and Thomas Frentz, as well as of Robert Davies, James Farrell, and Steven Matthews. According to Rushing and Frentz, "the historical text that unites singular public expressions into a narrative is called a 'myth'" ("Frankenstein" 64). In *"The Wizard of Oz* and Other Mythic Rites of Passage," J. Scott Cochrane uses psychoanalytic language in summarizing the depths to which myth resides in people: "Myths are not . . . in any superficial sense created, but rather bring to expression the deepest values present in the collective human psyche" (79).

A useful survey of theories of myths, *The Message of Television*, provided by Roger Silverstone, summarizes the commonalities of theorists Ernst Cassirer, Lucien Levy-Bruhl, and Mircea Eliade in these words: "[The theorists lay] their stress on the world view that myth generates and in which it participates. . . . [The mythic, the] world of mystery and imagination, of feeling, participation and transformation is involved in the creation of order and of a secure reality out of the darkness of the unknown" (57–58). Historically, myth has been associated with the sacred because of its ability to touch mystery in a timeless manner. Silverstone also examines Claude Lévi-Strauss's view of myth as structural and concludes: "The myths are basically answers to questions, and the questions and to a degree the answers also, are the universal ones of human existence" (60). Concluding that myth has often been related to magic, to ritual, and to fairy tales, Silverstone summarizes by broadening the concept of myth to mythic, with the following definition:

> The mythic dimension of culture contains traditional stories and actions whose source is the persistent need to deny chaos and create order. It contributes to the security of social and cultural existence. The mythic is a world apart, but it is also close at hand. It acts as a bridge between the everyday and the transcendent, the known and the unknown, the sacred and the profane. (70)

In building that bridge, Eliade observes, myths touch a mysterious reality: "Myth is bound up with ontology; it speaks only of *realities,* of what *really* happened, of what was fully manifested" (*Sacred* 9).

Myths carry truths—not always literally but essentially. They are closely related to the transcendent, spiritual dimension of life and necessarily entail an axiology, a theory of values. That axiology is communicated by myths through narrative.

Myth as Narrative

Narrative is an extremely popular topic today—no longer the sole purview of literary theorists or folklorists. Philosopher Alasdair MacIntyre advocates narrative as part of the solution to the contemporary problem of ethical relativity. Theologians Stanley Hauerwas and L. Gregory Jones link narrative to both theology and ethics. Communication scholar Walter Fisher develops narrative as a paradigm for human communication, also linking it to morality. Taking the argument further, historian Hayden White holds that narrative by definition moralizes ("Value" 23). In a later critical response, White observes, "Story forms not only permit us to judge the moral significance of human projects, they also provide the means by which to judge them" ("Narrativization" 253). White continues, "Narrative has the power to teach what it means to be *moral beings* (rather than machines endowed with consciousness)" (253).

Mythic narrative is found in every culture, enabling people to organize the meaning of their lives. Joseph Campbell argues that not only do all people use myths, but also those individual myths are variations of universal myths: "[A]ll [communities] have been built from the one fund of mythological motifs—variously selected, organized, interpreted, and ritualized according to local need, but revered by every people on earth" (20). Some of the more common myths deal with creation, the origins of humankind, the nature of evil or suffering, heroes, and cataclysmic destruction.

When a narrative that moralizes builds on myth, the result is axiological advocacy; the story, although it may entertain by virtue of its being a narrative, promotes certain values over others. It does so by linking the common cultural ideals to the power of mystery that includes references to the sacred, spiritual, or transcendent, which in turn is supported by a truth value.

Myth as Sacred

The link between the sacred and myths is important to this study, for the primary myths from which *The Lion King* draws are religious, with roots in biblical stories. They include the stories of paradise, the fall, desert wandering, the reign of Satan, the need for a savior, and the cataclysmic destruction of the earth, followed by the return of the savior who restores peace and the beginning of his full reign as rightful king.

Even the creators at Disney admit that they were trying to do something deeper, something "allegorical" in this film. Critic Perri Klass observes that *The Lion King* "is an interesting mix of *Hamlet, Bambi,* and *The Jungle Book,* all shot through with some contemporary sensibility about men who can't grow up" (1). I believe there is more to it than this and that the creators' desire to add depth to the film is reflected in the use of biblical myths, relying on archetypes and ritual to raise spiritual consciousness. In most instances this consciousness relates to traditional spirituality, but as Klass notes, New Age messages are also included. Director Rob Minkoff is quoted by Jamie Bernard about the film's spirituality: "the movie attempts 'a level of spirituality, something slightly metaphysical'" (G4).

That the director chose to add a spiritual dimension raises questions of intent. Davies et al. offer one possible explanation: "The heroes and gods, or god-like beings, of the mythic fantasies . . . may well be efforts to fill a psychic void created by the rational emphases of modernity" (342). Real observes that "myths reflect and make sacred the dominant tendencies of a culture, thereby sustaining social institutions and lifestyles" (*Mass-Mediated* 103). Most likely, following in the Disney tradition, the film aspires to offer a positive lesson for children about behavior that Disney values by associating itself with deeper myths; in a sense it is sacralizing Disney's (some would say American) values.

Myths in *The Lion King*

The first myth to which *The Lion* King alludes is the biblical narrative of life in paradise before the fall into sin. The movie begins with a diverse group of animals that normally prey on one another, joyfully meeting together at Pride Rock to witness shaman Rafiki's blessing of Simba, the new cub of lion king Mufasa and queen Sarabi.[5] The king—Mufasa here, God in the Bible—rules the beautiful land, and all appear to be happy and at peace.

A second reference to the Garden of Eden myth comes when Simba is a frisky lion cub. Just as Adam and Eve are forbidden to eat of the fruit of one tree, Mufasa places a limitation on Simba. He says, "Everything the light touches is our kingdom" (16).[6] When Simba asks about the "shadowy place," Mufasa replies, "You must never go there, my son" (16). The allusion continues when a tempter, in this case jealous Uncle Scar, suggests that "only the bravest of lions" go to the land of shadows (21).

In a 1990s feminist reversal, Simba, the male, is tempted and recruits his best friend, female Nala to go with him, as opposed to Eve's recruitment of Adam. Both know it is wrong. Both proceed. And the consequences are that it is the beginning of the downfall of nature's operating in harmony and the inauguration of the reign of evil, for, unknown to Mufasa and Simba, Scar has hatched a plan with his evil cohorts, the hyenas, scavengers of the shadow land who periodically prey on Pride Land animals. They intend to kill both Mufasa and Simba, thus allowing Scar to ascend to the throne.

Their plot succeeds in that Mufasa is killed saving Simba from a wildebeest stampede. Scar manages to convince Simba that he is guilty of causing his father's death and tells him he must leave Pride Land and never return; Simba is in essence banished from the beautiful Garden of Eden. Scar then takes over, allowing the hyenas to roam freely. The result is nature out of balance and destruction of the land. In the biblical narrative, that means that evil is in the world and Satan is alive and at work, a reality in which Christians believe.

The route by which Simba leaves is the desert. Aimlessly running until exhaustion and thirst take over, Simba would probably die if it were not for the care he receives from Pumbaa the warthog and Timon the meerkat. This part of the narrative resembles biblical stories of desert wanderings or journeys. Perhaps the most common is the story of Moses, who fled to the desert after killing an Egyptian and was there ministered to and taken in by the family of Jethro (Genesis 2). Another biblical desert wandering is the story of the nation of Israel. God and Israel covenanted together, each with responsibilities to fulfill, but Israel frequently disobeyed and did not live up to its obligations. In the same way, Simba, in taking up life with Timon and Pumbaa, fails to live up to his obligations to his father and to the Pride Land.

While Simba lives his carefree life in the jungle, things grow worse for the animals at home, and Nala finally runs away to the jungle, where she finds Simba. With the help of the ancestral spirit of Mufasa in the sky and the work of mystic Rafiki, Nala succeeds in convincing him that he is the rightful king and must return to Pride Rock.[7] Mufasa appears in the sky, calling to Simba to take his "place in the Circle of Life," to "remember who you are" (Ingoglia 79). Compare this event to God's speaking directly to Moses out of the burning bush. God reminds Moses of his ancestors and of his care for the oppressed people of Israel, and he sends Moses back to Egypt to lead Israel (Genesis 3).

When Simba returns to the Pride Lands, he encounters a bleak, desperate land. Ingoglia describes the sight:

> Everything had been touched by the drought. The trees were almost leafless. Starving giraffes, stretching as high as possible, had eaten the branches bare. The enormous ancient baobabs were stripped, their stringy bark devoured by desperate, hungry elephants.
>
> The dry wind picked up, and threatening clouds gathered overhead. . . . A blinding lightning bolt scorched the earth, and the dry grasses caught fire. (83–84)

Not only has the land suffered, but Zazu, Mufasa's faithful servant, is also confined to a cage; the hyenas, having exhausted the herds meant for the lions are about to riot; and Scar is trying to stop a rebellion by the starving lionesses.

Compare this description to the one in the book of Matthew, telling of "the last days" before the return of Christ. Christ tells his disciples:

> You will hear of wars and rumors of wars. . . . Nation will rise against nation, and kingdom against kingdom. There will be famines and earthquakes in various places. . . . Immediately after the distress of those days "the sun will be darkened, and the moon will not give its light; the stars will fall from the sky, and the heavenly bodies will be shaken." (Matthew 24:6–7, 29)

Once again the use of biblical myth is evident.

The final comparison is to the biblical description of the savior's rescuing humanity through the conquering of Satan, and Christ's reign over a new heaven and a new earth as the rightful king. The story of *The Lion King* concludes with Simba, the victor of the battle with Scar, vindicated of responsibility for his father's death. Jung observes, ". . . the myth of the hero is the most common and the best known myth in the world. . . . The essential function of the heroic myth is the development of the individual's ego-consciousness—his awareness of his own strengths and weaknesses—in a manner that will equip him for the arduous tasks with which life confronts him" (Jung and von Franz 101). In one possible stage of the heroic myth, the hero becomes the culture's savior (104). Simba is the hero of Pride Land, for he has saved its inhabitants from chaos and possible extinction.

In the final scene, it is dawn, the Pride Lands have been restored to beauty, the animals once again have gathered in harmony to witness the blessing of a new cub—this time Simba and Nala's—and the circle of life continues. As Eliade observes, "The myth of the end of the world is a universal occurrence; . . . This is the myth of the periodic destruction and re-creation of worlds, the cosmological formula of the myth of the eternal return" (*Myths* 243). This has obvious references to New Age philosophy in its beliefs in cyclical history, in the intimate relationship of nature and culture, and in ancestors' life after death; all things are related in the "circle of life." But the cyclical understanding of life is present in biblical myth as well. For example, the Christian understanding of salvation is based on understanding birth, life, death, and rebirth. Biblical descriptions of the end of time include a new heaven and new earth, with a tree of life in the new Jerusalem. Northrop Frye's work on myths and archetypal criticism also confirms the presence of "cyclical movement" in myth (158 ff.). *The Lion King* speaks in sacred myth to communicate its message. In so doing, it relies on archetypes.

ARCHETYPE

A Definition of Archetype

Because myth depends on archetype, identification of the archetypes used in *The Lion King* illuminates the rhetorical force of the film as mythic. Examples of this kind of rhetorical criticism of film with a psychoanalytic emphasis are found in the research that Rushing and Frentz have done, which frequently relies on Carl Jung and archetypal analysis.[8] They observe that Jung believed the cinema to be a significant expression of archetypes, for, as Jung put it, it "enables us to experience without danger to ourselves all the excitements, passions, and fantasies which have to be repressed in a humanistic age" ("Frankenstein" 64). Archetypes as part of the "collective unconscious," states Jung, "manifest themselves in fantasies and often reveal their presence only by symbolic images" (Jung and von Franz 58). Archetypal analysis is growing in popularity as a tool that cracks open the narrative structure, enabling deeper insights into the psychological power of film.[9]

Although archetypal criticism looks to Jung as its father, others have expanded the definition. Northrop Frye defines "archetype" as "a symbol which . . . helps to unify and integrate our literary experience"; it is a "typical or recurring image" that acts as a "mode of communication" (99). Chesebro, Bertelsen, and Gencarelli provide a detailed description of archetypal criticism, setting forth the following characteristics: they are "recurring," and they are based on principles of "human constructivism," "conventionality," "ambiguity," "epideictic understanding" (or being emotionally tied to the community), and "reduction" (260–261). These repeating images, they argue, are "indispensable to human beings" and help in "explaining human experiences" (271).

Although a more Platonic approach to archetypes might take issue with Chesebro et al. over the human constructivism and conventionality characteristics, all approaches agree that archetypes are universal symbols. For example, Eliade even compares Jung to Plato: "The world of the archetypes of Jung is like the Platonic world of Ideas, in that the archetypes are impersonal and do not participate in the historical Time of the individual life, but in the Time of the species—even of organic Life itself" (*Myths* 53). Archetypes act metonymically, as a kind of symbolic shorthand for universal experiences.

A final characteristic of archetypes, argues Rushing, is that they are "changing over time, co-varying with the development of human consciousness" ("Evolution" 2). This last aspect is helpful in clarifying how some of the mythic stories have changed in recent years yet retain their communicative power.

Archetypes in *The Lion King*

A number of archetypes have already been alluded to in the description of the myths, but there are more. The film begins with the song "Circle of Life." The song is clarified by the visuals of all different animals coming together in a loose circle around Pride Rock, where we see a new life, Simba. Historically, records Aniela Jaffe, circles represent "ultimate wholeness" and "the cosmos in its relation to divine powers" (266, 267). They are some of the strongest sacred archetypes and frequently appear as mandalas throughout history.

Next, Rafiki represents the medicine man or shaman or priest. His job is to somehow "baptize" the new cub with his blessing and to watch over him. Simba's birth is an important event in Pride Land, for he represents the birth of a new king, ultimately a savior. The significance is highlighted by the film's archetypal use of dark and light at the moment Rafiki finishes the blessing and holds Simba high:[10] ". . . the clouds parted, and a shaft of sunlight broke through, shining down on the future king. The animals fell silent and bowed" (8).

As was mentioned above, Simba and Nala represent Adam and Eve, who were tempted by the snake, in this case, Scar. Here the forbidden fruit is an elephant's graveyard, the shadow lands—an archetype for death. Once again, light and dark are used significantly. Scar's mane is black, whereas Mufasa's and Simba's are golden. The forbidden land is dark and shadowy. The hyenas are dark gray and black.[11] The only other animals in the land to have any black coloring are the wildebeests with black manes who inadvertently kill Mufasa.

Another important archetype is that of the family. It is in this context that feminine and masculine are usually defined. Although in a number of places *The Lion King* makes concessions to a newer definition of femininity, it is here that what have been considered traditional archetypal feminine roles are reinforced to the extent that many critics have objected to the film's stereotyping.

As a child, Nala, chosen to be Simba's wife when they mature, is portrayed as being quicker and stronger than Simba and his best friend. But as an adult her role is to get Simba to be her king. She succeeds and bears his child. Her role is strictly that of helpmate. The feminine archetype has regressed to stereotype.

Likewise, the role of the mother, for example, is of one who submits to her husband; otherwise her role is almost nonexistent. Other than Narabi's token presence at the ritual, in "bed" in the cave, gossiping with her friend, or serving Scar, she has little significance to the plot. Klass observes, "Most Disney cartoon features have not included mothers at all; the title character in *The Little Mermaid* has only a father, as do Princess Jasmine in *Aladdin* and Belle in *Beauty and the Beast*" (1).

By the same consideration, the father's role in each of these movies is very important. Mufasa's father role is that of the archetypal "90's-style . . . involved dad," says Klass, unlike Bambi's "archetypal distant father of the 1940's" (1). Here the relevance of seeing the archetype as an evolving symbol is apparent, for the father's role has changed over time.

Nevertheless, the father figure is significant. Not only is Mufasa father of his immediate family, but he, as king of the Pride Lands, is responsible for the circle of life on his land; he is a father figure to the Pride Lands. W. Lloyd Warner cites the example of the African Bantu people, who see their king as father of their people; interestingly, the Bantu also "worship their ancestors" (31–32). That we see an emphasis in *The Lion King* on the important guidance provided by the ancestors in the sky demonstrates the centrality of the family archetype to the film. Warner states strongly the significance of family: "all symbol systems, in different ways, are related to the family structure" (41).

The family is a significant archetype, and the familial relationships are an important part of this film. Gerhardus Oosthuizen summarizes the centrality of family to African religions.

> Humanity in Africa is basically family, basically community, with a strong emphasis on the traditional religion and its symbiotic union with ancestors and spiritual entities in the metaphysical world. In the traditional religious context, all the acts from birth to death and thereafter bind the person as a communal being to everyone around themselves. . . . The person is the center of existence—not as an individual, but as family, as community. (41)

The Lion King also emphasizes the importance of family, but in community, and the appearance of Mufasa in the sky demonstrates the "symbiotic union" of Simba with his father.

Another significant archetype is that of the journey that nearly leads to Simba's death. (I will expand on the discussion of journey below as part of the section on ritual.) Simba tries to cross a vast desert frontier. Images of past archetypal frontiers such as the sea and the American frontier are elicited.[12] Befriended by Pumbaa and Timon, Simba recovers and matures during this time, as well as cements the bonds of friendship. These friends advise him to live for the moment and to forget worries and responsibilities. That is not quite possible, however, when Nala appears and reminds him he is king. The film returns to archetypal imagery when he struggles over what to do—at night. Osborn describes the suggestive power of light and dark as one of the strongest archetypes: "Light . . . relates to the fundamental struggle for survival and development. Light is a condition for sight. . . . In utter contrast is darkness (and the night), bringing fear of the unknown, discouraging sight. . . . One is reduced to a helpless state" ("Archetypal Metaphor" 117). Simba agonizes over who he is and what he should do, during a sleepless night. Rafiki appears, however, encouraging him to look at himself. Ultimately, Simba sees his father in the light of the stars and is encouraged to take up his rightful role.

He returns to Pride Rock to fight Scar to the death. The fact that Simba must ascend to the highest point on the land to do battle and ultimately achieve his goal is also symbolic. Frye suggests that the "mountaintop" experience, the highest point between heaven and hell, also acts as archetype (203). During the fight, the grasslands catch on fire. The scene is one of deathly darkness interrupted by the destructiveness of fire, an archetypal fire of "a purifying force," as Osborn describes it (123). It is an apocalyptic vision of a struggle with the powers of darkness. When it seems that Simba is about to lose to Scar, Scar brags about how he killed Mufasa in a similar manner. That confession exonerates Simba from his guilt, renewing his strength and enabling him to overcome Scar. Scar falls to his death, serving as food for the hyenas. As Simba and Nala rejoice, the fire is quenched by rain—rain that ends the famine and stands as an archetypal image of renewal and rebirth.[13] The image is completed in the next scene—a colorful, lively picture of the revived Pride Lands. The king has returned, nature is restored, and life is in rightful balance. *The Lion King* concludes with the dawn of a new day, literally and figuratively. The animals gather again to witness the blessing of a new cub. The circle closes.

RITUAL

A Definition of Ritual

In intimate relationship to myth and archetype is ritual, for myths are built on archetypes and ritual. Defining *ritual* is a difficult task. As professor of performance studies, Richard Schechner observes, "The writings about ritual are voluminous" (264), and the term "has been so variously defined—as concept, praxis, process, ideology, yearning, experience, function—that it means very little because it means too much" (228). As I use the term, I understand it to be repetitive action identified with the sacred or as symbolic experience. Either usage relates it to myth and archetype and is an important dimension in understanding myth.

Rituals in *The Lion King*

BAPTISM In *The Lion King* two rituals in particular play primary roles in furthering the mythic power of the narrative. The first is the ritual of baptism performed at the beginning and the end of the film. Much is made of the ceremonial nature of the occasion and its importance to the lion family but also to the broader culture. Rafiki, the representative of the spiritual, gathers the cub in his arms, shakes a gourd over his head, then cracks it open to loose the sticky substance (perhaps symbolizing life) inside. Next he smears the gourd's contents on Simba's forehead and sprinkles dust (perhaps symbolizing death) over Simba's back. It is a careful orchestration of a performance that has been given before, Rafiki notes, when Mufasa was born, and will be given again to Simba's cub. The ceremony concludes with Rafiki holding Simba high in presentation to the cheering kingdom and to heaven. Heaven responds positively with a shaft of light falling on Simba. The "people" respond solemnly in silence and worship as they bow to Simba. It is a sacred ritual, part of the structure of the community.

This scene alludes to both the Christian ritual of baptism and the West African ritual of the naming ceremony. Baptism is a ritual that signifies the washing away of sins and the new life in Christ. The purifying symbol of water is placed on the head of the person (or in some traditions, people are immersed), much the same way as Rafiki put the contents of the gourd on Simba.

Although many different rituals are exercised by various African people (Mbiti 119), some tribes practice a naming ceremony that has many similar features to the one in the film. The West African Wolof people include in their ceremony red and white kola nuts: "The red kola nuts symbolize long life, and the white ones symbolize good luck. An elderly person rubs hands over the child's head, prays and spits in its ears to implant the name in the baby's head. After that the name is then announced loudly to the crowd . . . " (Mbiti 119). The West African Nupe religion follows a brief private ceremony with a large public ceremony. Nadel observes that "this is done before a gathering of guests as large as the host can make it"; then, traditionally, the grandfather had the important role of stating the name (116–117). *The Lion King* begins with a huge gathering of all the animals. Then, someone who appears to be one of the oldest members of the community, Rafiki, takes over the ceremony.

PILGRIMAGE The second important ritual in the film is that of Simba's journey, or pilgrimage, although he does not recognize it as such. This journey can be considered ritual in two regards: it is a rite of passage, and it is a pilgrimage.

Anthropologist Arnold Van Gennep researched rituals extensively and, in particular, rites of passage. He concludes: "Life itself means to separate and to be reborn. It is to act and to cease, to wait and rest, and then to begin acting again, but in a different way. And there are always new thresholds to cross: . . . thresholds of birth, adolescence, maturity, and old age; the threshold of death and that of the afterlife . . ." (189–190).

He could be describing the plot of *The Lion King*, for it is a story about birth, death, separation, maturity, and even the afterlife. The rite of passage involves an archetype of initiation that forces the individual "to experience a symbolic death." It is a "'rite of passage' from one stage of life to the next . . . ," ending in the realization of self-actualization through symbols of transcendence (123).

Simba experiences a separation, a crossing of the threshold, which in his case is a literal crossing of the desert. In addition, he experiences both a symbolic death, in having to leave all that he knew and loved, and a near physical death. When he recrosses that threshold to reenter society, he has arrived at self-knowledge, with the help of transcendent symbols such as the appearance of his father in his face in the pond and then his father's appearance and voice in the sky. The film concludes with reference to Simba's maturity—another ritual ceremony for Simba and Nala's new cub. Appropriately, the song "Circle of Life" is heard once more.

Victor Turner, drawing on the work of Van Gennep's three distinct phases of rites of passage—separation, transition, and incorporation—focuses especially on the transitional state, also called the liminal. He defines *liminal*, which has its roots in the Latin word *threshold*, as "that time and space betwixt and between one context of meaning and action and another. It is when the initiand is neither what he has been nor is what he will be" (113). This in-between state is characterized by a "blurring and merging of distinctions," which leads to a "leveling" process. Individual identities become meaningless, and people "are pushed as far toward uniformity, structural invisibility, and anonymity as possible" (25).

Yet this anonymity brings a certain freedom with it. In tribal ritual, initiands are beyond the "normative social structure"; participants are "dead to the social world but alive to the asocial world" (26). Turner calls this a kind of "anti-structure." The antistructural tendency of the liminal is, for Turner, a positive function that allows for the development of creative seeds for societal change. Those seeds are germinated in the unique relationships of fellow pilgrims, relationships called "communitas." In this state, argues Turner, "we place a high value on personal honesty, openness, and lack of pretensions or pretentiousness" (48). Hence, the liminal, though a state of limbo, can actually be a time of refreshment, a time to let go of the old and envision the new.

In the film, Simba experiences the liminal state when he joins with Timon and Pumbaa, certainly unpretentious characters, to live the life they advocate through the song "Hakuna Matata." In the words of the song, "It means no worries for the rest of your days. It's our problem-free philosophy, Hakuna Matata." Simba spends his teen years, it implies, living the care-free life, accountable to no one, responsible for nothing. It is an antistructural life lived in a unique community where there are no social distinctions between a lion (normally king of the jungle), a meerkat, and a warthog; it is the life of the liminal, transitional stage for Simba. It is a simple, communal life, and ultimately, with the help of Nala and Rafiki, leads to his self-discovery.

In addition to the view of his journey as a ritualistic rite of passage, it can be understood as a ritual of pilgrimage.[14] Anthropologist Alan Morinis describes the pilgrimage as "a paradigmatic and paradoxical human quest, both outward and inward" (ix), that functions as "a journey undertaken by a person in quest of a place or a state that he or she believes to embody a valued ideal" (4). Morinis adds, "The allegorical pilgrimage seeks out a place not located in the geographical sphere. Some sacred journeys are wanderings that have no fixed goal; the pilgrimage here is the search for an unknown or hidden goal" (4).

Simba journeyed both physically and metaphorically. Although he did not recognize his goal, he was on a journey of self-discovery that began with birth and continued until he took his rightful place as king of the Pride Lands. In addition, Morinis notes that "pilgrims tend to be people for whom the sacred journey is a limited break from the routines and familiar context of an ordinary, settled social life" (19). Or in Turner's language, it can be a liminal experience.

Having done extensive research on pilgrimage, Victor and Edith Turner identify a number of characteristics that can be seen in Simba's journey. They suggest that pilgrimages have the following attributes: a sense of leaving one's sins behind, voluntariness, penance, ordeal, leveling of statuses, simplicity, community, and self-discovery of one's center

(1–39). All of these factors occurred in Simba's experience, with the self-discovery coming when Simba returns to his rightful place. Morinis observes that the return to society is the test of the success of the pilgrimage. He cites Karen Sinclair as having said, "Salvation and grace depend only partially upon transcendence. Ultimately moral redemption lies in the creation, by whatever symbolic sacred means, of a positive place within the mundane social order" (27). That this kind of message resides in the subtext of a film that uses ritual as a communicative strategy is a positive moral lesson. Whether or not the audience perceives that will be taken up later.

Nevertheless, that the film is aware of itself as a story of pilgrimage is alluded to in the opening and closing song, "Circle of Life," which tells of the movement through cycles of hope and despair. The song suggests that we are all on a journey, seeking to "find our place" in the world.

Viewed as a rite of passage and/or a pilgrimage, Simba's journey has ritualistic implications related to the sacred, to the mythic.

COMMUNICATION TOOLS

The Lion King's communication tools are used to tell a narrative that moves its audience and with which they can identify, despite its lack of human role models. The film transcends the context symbolically to speak to human concerns and experiences.

Myth, Archetype, and Ritual: Rhetorical Tools

Roderick Hart argues that "all rhetoric depends on myth" (318), which he defines as "master stories describing exceptional people doing exceptional things that serve as moral guides to proper action" (315). *The Lion King* draws its rhetorical strength from the use of biblical myths, archetypes, and rituals.

That "proper" actions are easily identifiable has long been a characteristic of Disney. For example, in an analysis of Disney as a morality play (particularly Disneyland), Real interviewed 192 Disneyland visitors and discovered a unanimity about perceptions of what Disney considered virtues and vices ("Disney Universe"). Smoodin observes that even today the Disney "company works diligently to control the manner in which . . . films can be interpreted by modern audiences" (*Animating* 189). Because Disney's audience is primarily children, the company uses these didactic means to clarify and reinforce its lessons. Disney envisions a moral society that embraces traditional myths. Philip Lee comments on the need for the familiar as a tool to communicate the film's message:

> Film makers have to make use of stories that can be generally recognized. Don Cupitt, among others, has identified the themes of these universal narratives. They move from pilgrimage to goal, desire to satisfaction, struggle to success, opposition to mediation, conflict to resolution, confinement to freedom, loss to recovery, problem to solution. They confirm our identity; locate us in time and space; and reassure us about life and death. (23)

The universality of the company's myths and the metonymic nature of archetypes contribute to Disney's communicative strength in *The Lion King*. By using these tools, Disney increases the power of its rhetoric, for it speaks not only to the conscious but also to the unconscious.

Myth, Archetype, and Ritual: Psychological Tools

Malcolm Sillars makes two important points about the human psyche: "Human thought and behavior are products of the interaction of the conscious and unconscious" and "the conscious and the unconscious are the products of childhood" (173–174). In childhood, the individual's core identity is formed. According to David Payne, Walter Ong provides insight into the function of contemporary media as helping in the process of identity formation, necessary because of the "absence of straightforward puberty rites" (37). Payne exemplifies the quest for identity in an analysis of *The Wizard of Oz*, writing, "Just as fairy tales foreshadow and prepare children with lessons for later life experiences, Oz might encapsulate or reflect a particular interest in and experience of identity search, one that can be aroused and fulfilled by viewing the text" (37). The same could be suggested of *The Lion King*. It acts as a sort of fairy-tale, adolescent-identity quest that teaches children the lesson that growing up means accepting responsibility.

Bruno Bettelheim's psychoanalytic approach to fairy tales echoes Ong's voice regarding the role of media in identity formation. Payne summarizes Bettelheim's view of the benefit of fairy tales, a type of myth:

> Fairy tales often picture a child's powerlessness in the adult world, and the narrative creates a world where the child does have power

and is involved directly in choices, actions, and sometimes conquest of adults. Bettelheim thus sees fairy tales providing "equipment for living" in the form of advice or moral lessons about ethical choices and character, about what one encounters in the world, and about childhood foibles such as running away from home. Finally, fairy tales help to bolster the child's sense of importance and self reliance, by providing stories told especially for children where children are central characters and heroes. (29)

The Lion King gives advice for living, by encouraging the "right" choice of accepting responsibility. By confronting children with the reality of parents' mortality and the emotional pain of death, it teaches lessons of life yet frames the lessons in a positive narrative. Children are encouraged to see that friends help, that love continues and life goes on. Through the communicative power of myths, archetypes, and rituals, *The Lion King* provides children with spiritual and psychological "equipment for living."

THE LION KING AS MORAL EDUCATOR

Although Disney's role as moral educator is strong, recognition of that role is limited. For example, in the comprehensive *Walt Disney: A Bio-Bibliography*, Kathy Merlock Jackson cites a number of articles that discuss Disney's role as educator in connection with history or children's literature, but morality is not discussed (162–163). Nevertheless, she does suggest just how powerful an influence Disney has had on our culture: "The Disney vision has permeated our culture; it is recognizable, inescapable" (109).

Michael Real, however, not only believes Disney has influence in culture but also suggests that it acts as a moral educator. In analyzing 200 questionnaires administered to people who had just completed a day at Disneyland, Real concludes that "Disney instructs through morality plays that structure personal values and ideology" ("Disney Universe" 48). Historically, morality plays served a "particular religion," but today the emphasis on multiculturalism and pluralism "prevent[s] the direct teaching of ethics, metaphysics, or theology in the public schools." Real continues, "This leaves a vacuum for students—one not always filled by familial religious-ethnic interpretations of behavior and values. Mass-mediated culture is available to fill the void" ("Disney Universe" 77). Critics are well aware of that media potential and are paying more attention to even children's films. *The Lion King* raised an uproar of both negative and positive response. Understanding the film's role as a promoter of morality then means examining the critical response and identifying its axiology.

Critical Response

While receiving many positive reviews, *The Lion King* also heard much criticism. This criticism found problems of racism, sexism, the stereotyping of gays and Jews, and violence. Foster observes, "Some . . . see not family fun but shocking violence and offensive stereotypes: subservient lionesses, jive-talking hyenas, a swishy Uncle Scar, a father's murder" (3). Citing the *Boston Globe,* Foster observes a Harvard psychologist's beliefs about the film: "The good-for-nothing hyenas are urban blacks; the arch-villain's gestures are effeminate, and he speaks in supposed gay cliches" (3).

Those who perceived the film as racist frequently commented on the hyenas and Uncle Scar. An article by Spark on the criticism cites a Detroit paper that said, "The animators have marked him [Scar] as sinister in a racially insensitive way. Scar's coat seems to have a permanent shadow over it. And although Simba's mane is gloriously red, Scar's is, of course, black" (44). Obviously not all critics viewed Scar in the same way; some saw him as a stereotypical gay.

Criticism about sexism was also strong. For example, Spark cites Ellen Goodman as having said, "The film is a paean to patriarchy. All is well in the world only when princes like Simba are willing to take their rightful place on the throne" (44). Other criticism commented on the minor role of females in the film.

Concern over the violent death of Simba's father, Mufasa, was also voiced, and critics called for "more restrictive ratings" because of it ("Film Censors" 78). Klass compared it to *Bambi* in a positive way but noted that *Variety* "pointed to 'scenes of truly terrifying animal-kingdom violence that should cause parents to think twice before bringing along the *Little Mermaid* set'" (1).

Other criticism includes concern that Timon was a stereotyped Jew because he used the expression *oy.* Spark also observes the objection that the film "is unfair to Africa," stereotyping the continent, and that it has a political agenda of "hierarchical, even monarchical propaganda" (44).

Response to the negative criticism was also strong. Foster quotes the spokesperson for Disney, Terry Press: "These people need to get a life.

It's a story. It's fiction" (3). Spark observes, "They [the critics] are people for whom the very word 'black' has racist suggestion. They sniff out racism and sexism and this discrimination and that discrimination where no reasonable person would ever suspect they existed" (44). He points out that children need to be exposed to some of the realities of life to enhance their coping skills. He uses fairy tales as an example of a positive force in children's growth: "We must not let our own crop of self-righteous crackpots spoil a film which our children will not only enjoy, but which will teach them a good deal about life. Life as it is. Not as the political correctness brigade would like it to be" (44). Lipson echoes the strong criticism of the critics:

> People who think lovely thoughts and find so many nursery rhymes upsetting just won't like this straightforward message [get on with your life]. . . . This message . . . is a tough one for many self-pitying boomer parents raised in a peacetime, surrounded by consumer luxuries and endlessly in recovery from one perceived slight or remembered injury. They are continually mewling about past traumas that now excuse them from this responsibility or that challenge. It's the victim thing, and the movie sets Simba up for the part. (2)

Perri Klass, a pediatrician, is concerned about those critics who would sanitize life: "If children's entertainment is purged of the powerful, we risk homogenization, predictability and boredom, and we deprive children of any real understanding of the cathartic and emotional potentials of narrative" (1). She believes that literature enables children to learn powerful lessons that may be dramatic but are not harmful.

> Do we really want to protect our children from being saddened or scared or even upset by movies—or by books? Do we want to eliminate surprise, reversal, tragedy, and conflict? . . . When we talk about children made sad by a movie, we are talking about children being moved by things that are not really happening to real people, and that is what art and drama and literature are all about . . . that is a giant step toward empathy. (1)

I belabor the critical response to point out that *The Lion King* evokes deep responses on a moral level that involves questions of value—it operates as a mythic narrative that necessarily advocates a morality. Some agree with the dominant message, and others believe that the subtleties are dangerous teachers of a morality with which they do not agree.

The Lion King's Axiology

What values does this film teach? The primary message that *The Lion King* makes central to the story is that Simba, much as he enjoys life in the jungle with Pumbaa and Timon, must live up to his calling. He must accept the responsibility of who he is. Growing up means accepting responsibility. Certainly, few would disagree that Disney is proffering a "prosocial" message here, using Brown and Singhal's definition of *prosocial* as "any communication that depicts cognitive, affective, and behavioral activities considered to be socially desirable or preferable by most members of a society" (90).

A second dominant value is that the survival of the lion kingdom— and by implication, our society—depends on the relatedness of the members. All are part of the "circle of life," posits the theme song. The song teaches the importance of those relationships as part of the food chain, as well as the reality that life and death are part of the same circle. Hence, the third significant message is entwined in the song: birth, death, and new birth are part of creation, and death is not something unnatural. At the same time, life is valuable and precious. The ritual of baptism adds significance to that fact. Again, these are lessons that mirror truth and to which few would object.

Numerous other values can be derived from the story and the use of archetypes and may or may not be observed by the children watching. They include the following:

1. There are mysteries in life that point to a transcendent, spiritual reality. This can be seen in the film's use of biblical myths and, more specifically, in the instances of the mystic Rafiki's participation and of Mufasa's appearance in the sky.
2. Cleanliness is an important part of life (even for animals). This is observed in the fact that Nala could not go with Simba until she had finished her daily bath.
3. Family is family, and it has good and bad members. This is evident in the fact that Scar, though seemingly a good-for-nothing whiner, is not cast out or ignored, and Simba respects and listens to him.

4. Father is the head of the household; mother's role is to feed and clean the family while dad's is to rule. This was the relationship of Simba's family.

5. Fathers should be involved in raising their children. Mufasa took time to teach Simba lessons and had a positive, loving relationship with him.

6. Friendship, surprisingly, is a good basis for marriage. The friendship between Nala and Simba is encouraged and valued. When Simba discovers, however, that they are pledged to be married when they are older, his response is, "I can't marry Nala. She's my friend" (Ingoglia 28).

7. There is good and evil in the world, and they are often associated with light and darkness. Many visuals throughout the film suggest this, as well as the use of the only dark mane on Scar, the darkness for the elephant graveyard, the darkness of the hyenas, the darkness of the land ravaged by Scar's rule, the light of the heavens shining on Simba (and later his son) in a baptismal blessing, and the light on the land under Mufasa's and then Simba's rule.

8. Obedience to one's parents is right. Simba is disciplined—and suffers consequences—for disobedience.

9. Death comes to all—to those who are good as well as to those who are bad. We do not understand it, but it happens. Simba learns this lesson when his good father is violently killed by a stampede and later when Scar is killed in battle.

10. Life goes on even in the face of death. Simba wished he were dead, thinking he was responsible for Simba's death, yet Timon and Pumbaa showed him that life goes on.

11. Guilt can get in the way of who we ought to be and what we ought to do. Simba experienced this and had to be shown that responsibility is greater than guilt (and later discovered his own guilt was unfounded).

12. Life is more than the pursuit of no worries and no responsibilities. Simba wanted to live the easy life but found he had to accept who he was and the responsibility that came with being the king's son. However, it is also possible, particularly for the children who own the video of the film, to get the opposite message by focusing only on the song "Hakuna Matata." One wonders whether or not the audience of children understands

that the liminal stage Simba goes through in the jungle is *only a stage*. Given the upbeat nature of the song, the wider media's attention to the song and its overall attractiveness, children tend to replay this part of the movie more than others. They hear the message over and over again—"no worries for the rest of your days . . . Hakuna Matata."

13. Honesty and openness help truth win out. By hiding his guilt from everyone, Simba could not learn the truth that he did not cause Mufasa's death. When he confessed, the truth came out, and he was absolved.

The majority of these values are noncontroversial, prosocial concerns that provide important lessons about life and especially life lived in community. MacIntyre argues that we need to combat today's moral decline by returning to an emphasis on character, on moral virtue rooted in narrative, practice, and community. *The Lion King* exemplifies the drive toward this kind of morality with its emphasis on Simba's character, the need for him to practice his rule, his responsibility to his community, and the importance that his story and that of his people be told. *The Lion King* is a mythic, moral narrative.

Disney, by grounding its narrative in myth that employs archetypes and rituals and by infusing the story with moral purpose, has chosen to take on the role of a moral educator. In most instances, it raises ethical sensitivity and suggests a positive direction to follow. However, when racism or sexism becomes the norm that appears to represent reality, then Disney has lost its moral high ground.

THREE

Pocahontas

THE SYMBOLIC BOUNDARIES OF MORAL ORDER

FILM BACKGROUND

High on the edge of a promontory, Pocahontas, her long, glossy hair blowing in the wind, studies the sea-blue horizon. With a body like a Barbie doll, the skin of a high-paid model, the sensitive eyes of an innocent child, and the sculpted features of an artist's dream, Pocahontas begins and ends her appearance in the 33rd Disney animated film in this statuelike pose, overlooking the audience, the present, and the past.

Disney's *Pocahontas* is set in 1607 when the English Virginia Company sent out a group of adventurers who hoped to "kill ourselves an injun or maybe two or three"—all for "glory, God, and gold and the Virginia Company." They were under the authority of Governor Ratcliffe but were inspired by the leadership of John Smith, who exercised great heroism in saving his friend Thomas from drowning in a storm. They traveled across the ocean on the flotilla of ships led by the *Susan Constant*. Meanwhile, Pocahontas, daughter of Chief Powhatan and also known as Little Mischief, has had a disturbing dream that leaves her unsettled and wanting to find her true path. Her father interprets it to mean she will marry the warrior Kocoum, but she finds that upsetting as he is "so . . . serious" (Ingoglia, *Disney's Pocahontas* 17). As she sings "Just Around the Riverbend," we hear of her restless search for something more than a steady husband. Her spiritual advisor—Grandmother Willow, a willow tree—encourages her to "listen with her heart" in order to understand the dream. Pocahontas tries to listen but instead sees the ships of the English.

Once ashore, the English adventurers begin to ravish the land in search of gold, lustily singing "Mine, Mine, Mine." John Smith ventures out to explore and discovers Pocahontas and her pet raccoon, Meeko, and hummingbird protector, Flit. Pocahontas and Smith are magically drawn to each other. Pocahontas teaches him about her people and the land through her powerful song "Colors of the Wind." Ultimately she comes to believe that he is the answer to her dream, and he believes that he has found what was missing in his life.

However, relations among others of her tribe and the Virginia Company have disintegrated into plans for war. When she tries to warn Smith, Kocoum, who followed her, is shot by Thomas, Smith's friend. Smith is captured by the Powhatans and sentenced to death. At dawn, with both groups preparing to fight, each singing its own cruel version of "Savages," and with Smith about to be killed, Pocahontas throws herself over him, persuading her father to take the way of peace. Ratcliffe, however, is not convinced and inadvertently shoots Smith as Smith saves Powhatan. The film concludes with the injured Smith being taken aboard the ship to return to England. Pocahontas, torn by her love for him and her loyalty to her people, chooses to stay.

Pocahontas, while not setting the records that *The Lion King* set, did very well for Disney, bringing in more than $141.6 million in the domestic box office ("Top"). Their unusual publicity stunt of previewing the film in New York City's Central Park drew more than 100,000 people (Walt Disney Co., "Year"). And by September 1995, the end of the fiscal year, "*Pocahontas* [had] already generated over $1 billion in revenues on an $80 million investment (a $55 million production budget and $25 million for advertising and marketing)" (Edgerton and Jackson 92).

As with most recent Disney films, *Pocahontas* was received with mixed critical reviews.[1] Frequently cited as "politically correct" (Edgerton and Jackson 90–91; Felperin 58; Kilpatrick; Larson 328), *Pocahontas* is an attempt on Disney's part to respond to past criticisms of racism in *Aladdin* (Kim 24; Sharkey 2) and *The Lion King* (Ward 174–175) or of insensitivity to feminists' concerns, as in *The Little Mermaid* (Trites; Susan White; Sells). This time the controversy arises primarily because the subject of the film was a historical figure, and Disney chose to blend history with legend and entertainment values.

Disney rewrote the historical legend of Pocahontas both to claim it as its own and to ensure a strong bottom line. The choices it made in so doing reveal a Disney orientation on right and wrong, good and evil. Let's examine those choices by looking at Disney's version of Pocahontas in relationship to history and then in the light of symbolic boundaries of moral order. In other words, how does Disney craft the characters, their relationships, and the surrounding cultural phenomena to delineate a moral society?

DISNEY AND HISTORY

Although the actual history of Pocahontas is limited and many "facts" in various accounts are speculation or reconstruction based on the study of Powhatan Indian life, certain elements of the Pocahontas story have been documented. Robert S. Tilton's study of the Pocahontas narrative lists them as follows:

1. Her birth about 1595.
2. The traditional story of her rescue of Captain John Smith in 1607 and her continued relationship with him and help to the people of Jamestown.
3. Her abduction by Captain Argall in 1612 and subsequent captivity at Jamestown.
4. Her conversion to the Christian faith in 1613 while living in Jamestown.
5. Her marriage to John Rolfe in 1614 and the birth of her [their] son [Thomas] in 1615.
6. Her trip to England in 1616 including her success there as an Indian princess. . . .
7. Her death [and burial] at Gravesend in 1617. (8–9)

Rasmussen and Tilton approve of Disney's adaptation of history in their publication for an exhibition in October 1994 to April 1995, commemorating the 400th anniversary of the birth of Pocahontas and sponsored by the Virginia Historical Society (49). In *Pocahontas: Her Life and Legend,* the authors observe that the Disney film focuses on the early part of Pocahontas's life but captures the essentials.

If some of the facts in this story are altered or embellished, the film-makers are simply following the nineteenth-century tradition of making her story their own. The Walt Disney film will again expand the Pocahontas legend and, by including new elements, will further obscure for the public the line where the primary sources end and fiction-alization begins. But viewers of an animated film expect fantasy and may lump invented elements such as the Pocahontas-Smith romance with the fantasy of the "grandmother tree." In any case, the Disney film will succeed in bringing much of the history as we know it to the largest audience that ever has been exposed to her tale. *And it will convey the essential element of the story*—it will demonstrate that Pocahontas was an individual of unusual energy and vision who influenced the course of history. (Emphasis mine.) (50)

The positive spin on the film is perhaps not surprising given that the Walt Disney Company provided partial support for the exhibition through a grant (Rasmussen and Tilton, title page). In Disney's words, "Although the Disney version of the Pocahontas story takes liberties with regard to her actual age at the time she met Smith and speculates about their friendship, it remains true to her spirit and enhances her acknowledged role as a peace keeper" (*Pocahontas: Press Kit* 39). Disney chose to tell not Pocahontas's complete story but only the part in which she rescues John Smith. Although we know she married John Rolfe, speculation that she may have fallen in love with Smith earlier is not uncommon (Rasmussen and Tilton 14; Mossiker 91–92).

The historical Pocahontas was a prepubescent girl most likely between 10 and 12. According to anthropologist Helen Rountree, she was also naked and bald (Connell D1). That picture did not fit Disney's film. And so, as Glen Keane, the supervising animator on the film says, "Jeffrey Katzenberg told me to make her the finest creature the human race has to offer" (Kim 24). But the rendering was an "Anglicized" Native American who has lighter skin than her people and a voluptuous body covered more scantily than any other tribe members (Edgerton and Jackson 95). Most of the critics comment on this Disney version of Pocahontas. For example, Paul Rudnick describes Disney's Pocahontas as a "Rodeo Drive stunner in a fringed one-shoulder minidress, with a microwaist and an infomercial-ready mane" and as "lusciously sexual" (67). Laura Shapiro describes her as a "Native American Barbie" (77). Paula Gunn Allen, a Sioux tribe member and a professor of literature, finds Disney's description of Pocahontas disturbing. She is "troubled that Hollywood's sexual stereotyping eclipses much of the power women ative cultures" (Connell D7).

ising animator Glen Keane defends the change: "This is a love John Smith was about 30. We had to decide between being historically accurate or socially responsible" (Kim 24). It could be argued, however, that they were neither "historically accurate" nor "socially responsible" by turning their historical figure into a sex object.

Not only were the reactions against the film strong over the sexual, romantic depiction, but some people also critiqued other dimensions of Disney's use of history. "The Indian Romance" states, "Disney's writers have merely traded one stereotype for a new polar opposite. The native peoples of America weren't quite the peace-loving, environmentally enlightened sages of cartoon fame. . . . In real life, Pocahontas' father Chief Powhatan conquered and tyrannized 20 other tribes" (74). Kilpatrick cites Disney consultant Shirley Custalow McGowan (Little Dove): "History is history. You're not honoring a nation of people when you change their history" (37). The untold story and the character distortions are significant problems for McGowan.[2]

Similarly, critics Edgerton and Jackson conclude that Disney fails to honor the American Indian culture by giving only another version of the "white man's Indian" (96). S. Elizabeth Bird suggests that Disney "sentimentalizes" the history for an Anglo version (76), and Kent Ono laments that "*Pocahontas* transforms an historical abomination into kid's candy—genocide into a contemporary romance" (21). Disney uses history for its own purposes.

Concern over Disney's willingness to change the historical record to suit its purposes abounds. Stephen Fjellman expresses his dismay: "What Disney does, perhaps, is kill the *idea* of history by presenting it as entertainment. If the truth value of parts of the past is indistinguishable from the truth value of fantasy and futurology, then what is history but crafted amusement?" (62). When one's identity is tied to that history, abuses of the facts would seem particularly offensive.

Although Disney is sensitive to criticism, countering that criticism is not as simple for the company as giving a positive response to something inappropriate; rather, by responding in more politically sensitive ways, the all-important bottom line is likely to be enhanced. Michael Eisner's "Letter from the Chairman" in the Walt Disney Company's *1995 Annual Report* confirms that financial concern is central to Disney animated films. Eisner rallies the stockholders by saying,

> Our goal is to increase wealth for our shareholders. . . . We are fundamentally an operating company, operating the Disney Brand all over the world, maintaining it, improving it, promoting and advertising it with taste. . . . We must, however, not commit to any ven-

ture, no matter how great, unless the project can promise a good fiscal return. (4–5)

In other words, it is a fine thing to respond to criticism, but only if it sells. And this is a central lesson from Disney's *Pocahontas:* Capitalism is the driving morality. If the revenue is solid, that must mean there are enough people who don't care how history is used or abused. Therefore, do what sells.

Cultural critic Henry Giroux believes that Disney's abuse of history signals an ominous trend: "The Disney Company is not ignorant of history, it reinvents it as a pedagogical—and political tool to secure its own interests, authority, and power" ("Animating" 46). Disney uses its version of history to teach lessons that ensure a broad audience acceptance. Since it is widely recognized that even entertainment affects knowledge, development, and actions (Fjellman 62; Giroux, "Animating" 45), concern over the Disney "schoolroom" merits consideration. As Betsy Sharkey observes, "For some children, it [Disney films] is virtually their only literature" (2). If history is story and story moralizes (White, "Value" 1–24), what happens when the story—history—is changed? The result is whatever moralizing the storyteller chooses. Although Disney does not profess to be a historian, its choice of what to include and exclude reveals its boundaries for what it perceives to be right and wrong, good and bad, or for its perception of what its audience believes is an acceptable moral order.

SYMBOLIC BOUNDARIES OF MORAL ORDER

Sociologist Robert Wuthnow concerns himself with the question of how to understand the place of morality in a society in *Meaning and Moral Order: Explorations in Cultural Analysis.*[3] Drawing from the work of anthropologist Mary Douglas, he states that moral order is constructed of "implicit categories that define proper relations among individuals and groups" (58). This latter definition is particularly helpful in looking for distinctions of proper and improper, better or worse, good or bad— distinctions that relate the moral order to ethical/unethical behavior either literally or communicatively.

The communicative dimension functions as an illuminator of moral order. Vernon Cronen adds the emphasis on communication because, he notes, "moral orders emerge as aspects of communication," both verbal and nonverbal. Furthermore, he posits, "The creation of moral orders seems to be one of the few universal features of human societies. All peoples indicate what can be done, what must be done, what is prohibited, and what is beyond their responsibility" (48). The moral order is a universal phenomenon. All peoples have a sense of right and wrong within their society. What constitutes the morality, however, is not necessarily universal.

To determine the particular morality, one would do best to consider the possible choices. In *Risk and Blame*, Douglas contends that the choice of one moral over another, one preference over another, is still a choice and reveals the structure of morality.[4] Douglas argues that "something affirmed means something else denied" (*Natural Symbols* 260–261). For, as Wuthnow observes, "boundaries are often revealed by opposites" (339). Uncovering the moral order, then, can be accomplished by identifying the symbolic boundaries as revealed by the binary opposites of social structure within *Pocahontas*. In the case of Disney's telling of the Pocahontas story, the company chooses to affirm certain symbols of culture, certain values, and certain moral standards over others. The symbols representing those choices indicate the boundaries of morality. The symbolic boundaries act rhetorically to communicate a Disney vision of moral order. To understand what the boundaries are, one looks for what is obligation and what is, to use Douglas's term, "taboo." Cultural values emerge as one studies characters, relationships, and cultural phenomena with respect to the boundaries, the acceptable and unacceptable.

Characters: Villains/Heroes

One of the most common ways to look for boundaries is in the category of heroes and villains. What makes someone laudable and someone else despicable? Who represents the good and evil, and how are they represented?

The Colonists

Disney applies a historically enlightened perspective when it suggests that the colonists are the villains. This delineation marks respect for the American Indians, who were here long before the Europeans. The colonists appear as villains in both what they say and what they do, as well as in the songs they sing. They are portrayed as greedy and ignorant.

Their opening song tells the story of the Virginia Company. It includes lines like, "On the beaches of Virginny, there's diamonds like debris. There silver rivers flow and gold you pick right off a tree." The song ends with these lines: "We'll kill ourselves an injun, or maybe two or three. We're stalwart men and bold of the Virginia Company. It's glory, God, and gold and the Virginia Company."[5] Later in the film, Ratcliffe sings in one particularly telling song, "What can you expect from filthy little heathens? Their whole disgusting race is like a curse." Calling them savages, he continues, "Barely even human. . . . They're not like you and me, which means they must be evil."

The men of the Virginia Company are coming to the new land to become rich and possess the land. If there are Indians, they had better not get in the way or they will be killed. All the adventurers sing the song. All the settlers are represented in group context as having evil intent. However, although the group as a whole is villainized, distinctions are made within the group as to degree of villainy.

Three men of the Virginia Company are singled out and given individuality: Governor Ratcliffe—leader of the expedition, Captain John Smith—adventurer and known Indian fighter, and Thomas—new to sailing and admirer of Smith. While all three share the group culpability, Smith and Thomas are able to redeem themselves by demonstrating that they have learned the lessons Pocahontas taught.

That Ratcliffe is the epitome of villainy is signaled in several ways. His very name, "Rat"-cliffe is negatively charged. His hair and boots are black, and his clothes are trimmed in black. He wears an effeminate dark magenta suit. He is excessively overweight. Disney villains are usually coded by color or shadow (note the darkness of Jafar in *Aladdin* or of Scar in *The Lion King*) or by excess (note Ursula's corpulence in *The Little Mermaid*). He also is the leader of the song "Mine, Mine, Mine," which reveals his motivation as greed and glory for himself. By the end of the film, other characters have grown morally, but Ratcliffe remains a villain to the end.

Several scenes allow the contrasts between Ratcliffe and Smith to distinguish the latter as not really of the same type as Ratcliffe. For example, in looks, Smith is blond and physically fit. The light, be it day or night, seems always to shine on Smith, leaving him in a glow. In words, Smith is cocky, but he is kind to his peers and well liked by them. Even in the opening scene, Smith is set apart from all others so that it is visually evident that he is his own man. Additionally, early in the film, Smith is established as having the character of a hero. When Thomas is washed overboard, Smith dives in the water and manages to drag him back on board, where he brushes aside the men's praise.

That Ratcliffe is ultimately left holding the villainy bag, so to speak, is seen in the end of the film. The men have to choose to follow Ratcliffe or stand up to him as Thomas did. They follow Thomas and bind Ratcliffe up to be shipped back to England.

The third colonist who stands out is Thomas. The film begins by establishing Thomas as a family member bidding his parents and siblings goodbye, thus establishing him within mainstream ideals as a caring son and brother. Wide-eyed, he boards the ship looking for adventure, naively expecting the best, a representative of innocent imperialism. Once in Virginia, he is a loyal company member who does whatever he is ordered to do by Ratcliffe or by Smith. When that leads to his shooting Kocoum, to the dismay of both Pocahontas and Smith, he looks troubled. In the climax scene, he finally refuses to obey Ratcliffe and puts his gun aside.

Because of the sympathetic treatment of Thomas, the audience is led to understand that he is not responsible for his attitude toward the Indians; he was part of an unenlightened group. However, by the end of the film he comes to see the error of his thoughts and actions and willingly steps forward from the crowd as someone who will not continue to stereotype the Indians as all bad. He is rewarded for his learning, we discover in the final scene, by becoming the leader of those who will stay in the new land. The implication is that although all these company members are guilty of wanting to kill Indians, it was guilt due to ignorance. Once they have seen the light (as discussed below), their guilt is removed; the villainy of Smith and Thomas is temporary, and they ultimately emerge as heroes.

Contrast Thomas, as Smith's "second," to Ratcliffe's second, Wiggins. Wiggins functions only to serve Ratcliffe and expresses little personality other than echoing his boss's displeasure. However, even Wiggins arrives at the conclusion that Ratcliffe is never going to amount to anything and shifts his allegiance away from him. For Ratcliffe is the epitome of evil and therefore remains guilty to the end. As supervising animator, Duncan Marjoribands observes, "Ratcliffe carries the racism and greed of the movie" (*Pocahontas: Press Kit* 45). Ratcliffe is the ultimate villain.

What do these boundaries reveal about Disney's moral order? First, that behavior and attitudes exhibiting racism and greed are wrong. Second, a Disney moral order requires a boundary of evil to clearly delineate what is inappropriate.

The Native Americans

In contrast, Pocahontas and her people are presented as the antithesis of the colonists. As a group, the Indian nation lives in harmony with nature and is not abusive of it. Their homes are made of natural materials; they are respectful of the spirits of the earth and of their lives. Their opening song, "Steady as the Beating Drum" (after opening and closing the song with an Indian-language chant), sums their philosophy of life as living in balance with the seasonal changes and respecting the "ancient ways." The Native Americans are represented as a civilized, sensitive, and ecologically smart people. They respect their environment and honor their "mother earth" and the "Great Spirit."

Similarly, Pocahontas lives out that philosophy. The animals are her friends; her advisor is an old willow tree. She studies the river and marvels in its changing nature, wondering always what is "just around the riverbend." As the daughter of the chief and as his favorite, she holds a place of honor among her people. But she is an individual who expresses herself as she pleases (her name means "Little Mischief" [Ingoglia 42]) and, because of her status, has the freedom to do so.

Pocahontas is the unquestionable heroine of the story. It is she who enlightens John Smith about the errors of his attitudes. It is she who suggests to her father talking instead of making war. It is she who rescues Smith from death and lectures her father on "where the path of hatred has brought us," challenging her father to choose the path of peace (Ingoglia 88). The reason she saved Smith, however, was not because of her wish to encourage peace but because she loved him.

The boundary line of the heroic blurs for a time when Powhatan and the warriors are convinced that they need to do battle. They too sing a version of the song "Savages," calling the colonists "just a bunch of filthy, stinking savages" and saying, "Destroy their evil race." The villainous role is short-lived, however, because Pocahontas helps them redeem their evil ways of war and consider peace.

Before the conversion, though, Pocahontas's father, Powhatan, while portrayed as a loving father, is also stubborn and misguided. He chooses a husband for Pocahontas whom she does not want. He prepares the village for war without trying to talk to the colonists, and he is willing to kill Smith without listening to Pocahontas. Only after Pocahontas lectures him does he come to an "appropriate" position. His response to her follows: "My daughter speaks with a wisdom beyond her years. We have all come here with anger in our hearts. But she comes with courage and understanding. It is that spirit that will guide us to a place of peace" (In-goglia 88). Powhatan shows his "true" heroic character.

Similarly, Nakoma, Pocahontas's friend, is portrayed as basically good, but misguided when it comes to the colonists. It is she who reveals to Kocoum that Pocahontas has left the village to meet Smith. Ultimately, Kocoum is killed because he follows after Pocahontas. But Nakoma, too, comes to redeem herself when she later lies to those guarding Smith in order to get Pocahontas in to see him one last time. Just as Smith and Thomas emerge on the heroic side, so do Powhatan and Nakoma. Kocoum's character is not developed. He is portrayed simply as the lead-ing warrior, honorable enough to marry the daughter of the chief, but boring—"so . . . serious"—so like the steady, beating drum (Ingoglia 17). This complaint is stated first to Pocahontas's father, and then Grand-mother Willow repeats it. That Disney finds the serious, steady members of a society too boring to be considered heroic is cause for concern.

True heroes, Disney seems to be saying, have lively personalities, are willing to stand up for what they believe in by facing authority, and are willing to take the consequences. Both Smith and Thomas ultimately refuse to follow their leader. Pocahontas and Nakoma ultimately refuse to obey Powhatan's commands. And Powhatan himself demonstrates the heroic quality of being willing to admit he was wrong. Pocahontas also takes a hero's stance at the end when she finally stops following her heart and chooses to stay with her people.

But the film raises the question of her motivation. Does she do it out of a noble desire or out of guilt? Nakoma says to her, "I know what you are thinking. But remember, dear Pocahontas, the fighting has stopped because of you. Who knows what will happen if you leave?" (Ingoglia 94). For Disney, motivation does not influence the morality of her choice. She does the right thing; that is enough. The implication remains, how-ever, that her choice is the act of a martyr—she gives up her happiness found in Smith, but she chooses to always hold him in her heart.

Native Americans Versus the Colonists

The boundaries between good and evil are accentuated by the sharp contrast between the goals of the Native Americans and those of the colonists: harmonious life versus gold. Because the characters are painted with broad strokes as groups, notwithstanding the individuals mentioned above, the audience easily reads who the good characters are and who the bad ones are. And because the structure of each group is roughly parallel, the contrasts are easily drawn.

Pocahontas and John Smith, each representing their own people, express the differing philosophies. Smith describes how his people intend to develop the land into cities to improve "the lives of savages" (Ingoglia 44). When Pocahontas is offended, he tries to correct it to "people who are uncivilized" (Ingoglia 44). Pocahontas then lectures him about all that her people know that his do not. The theme song of the film, "Colors of the Wind," encapsulates one of the central moral themes: Do not stereotype; racism is wrong. That this particular song is vital to carrying the message is undisputed by Disney. The *Press Kit* says that the song "best sums up the entire spirit and essence of the film." James Pentecost, the producer, stated it even stronger: "This song was written before anything else. It set the tone of the movie and defined the character of Pocahontas. Once Alan [Menken] and Stephen [Schwartz] wrote that song, we knew what the film was about" (*Pocahontas: Press Kit* 51–52).

The lyrics describe how ignorant Smith really is. Pocahontas takes offense at being called savage and points out that the earth isn't a thing to be conquered; rather, it is full of life. She challenges Smith to look at the world through someone else's eyes, to walk in someone else's shoes. The song continues with descriptions of nature and the statement that all of nature are her brothers, her friends, and all are part of a never-ending circle. The circle theme, very strong in *The Lion King,* emerges again here and represents part of the symbolic boundary that separates the Native American from the colonist.

Many other characters are contrasted. Probably the most obvious are the father figures for each group—Powhatan and Ratcliffe. Although both are leaders and both have war in their hearts, Powhatan is presented as rational, willing to listen, and respectful of others. Ratcliffe is selfish, racist, and single-mindedly greedy. Although good and evil are obvious in these characters, because Powhatan does seek war, he is a more complex and consequently more believable character. That believability furthers the moral lesson by example.

Closely related to the hero/villain boundary in the film is the group stereotype. Disney is to be commended for its attempts to point out the fallacies involved in stereotyping. The argument in "Colors of the Wind" for the benefit of being open to people different from oneself is an important moral message for children to learn.

At the same time, however, the very demands of the Disney formula call for broad stroking of good and evil. In this case, the implication is clear that early explorers and settlers were all guilty of stereotyping the Native Americans as savages. White descendants of those people bear that implied guilt today and need to be taught the lessons that Pocahontas teaches Smith.

Disney walks between tensions in encouraging, on the one hand, collective guilt about what contemporary culture has generally deemed inappropriate or immoral, such as racism, gender typing, and stereotyping in general. On the other hand, fearful of alienating audiences, Disney also must provide a way of escape from guilt.

In *Pocahontas,* both the characters of Thomas and John Smith alleviate the collective guilt implied by the white "invaders" through sympathetic portrayal and conversion experiences. Smith and Thomas, along with the other men of the Virginia Company, are villainized as a group. Thus, the Indian killing that Smith had done and Thomas wanted to do—and eventually does—is not something they are personally responsible for. Rather, it is a group guilt. When they choose to no longer be a part of that group, they assume the moral status of the heroes. Thus the boundary between guilt and innocence exists for the collective.[6]

Relationships

MALE/FEMALE RELATIONSHIPS The Disney tradition of animated storytelling requires a romance and, until this film, a romance that ends "happily ever after." However, the studio had been considering doing a *Romeo and Juliet,* and this film fit that vision (*Pocahontas: Press Kit* 37). That romance is an expectation of a male/female relationship has been established in past Disney films but is reaffirmed in this story. Young men and women are never just friends but establish a romantic dimension to their relationship.

The central characters of this romance are defined as the heroes by their stunning appearance, another requirement of the romantic relationship. Disney's design of Pocahontas, which includes big eyes, lots of hair, and an unrealistic figure, reveals a male fantasy. Because Pocahontas is billed as the heroine, the sexual image sends the message that "good" girls and women are characterized by looks as well as deeds. Smith, too, is drawn as a macho, swaggering, blond with handsome features and a fit body. His proportions, however, are not as unrealistic or impractical as Pocahontas's. That these two exceptionally good-looking characters are both the heroes and the subjects of the film's romance indicates a moral vision that equates good looks with good character, as well as suggesting that people are right for each other when they are equally attractive. Pocahontas was not attracted to Kocoum, and Smith was not attracted to Nakoma. Kocoum and Nakoma were not drawn to look as dramatically beautiful.

Another significant boundary in relationships for Disney is sex. Although Disney has no trouble casting the lead figure as a very well developed, sexy young woman, any suggestion that romance gets beyond a kiss is forbidden. Peter Biskind notes that "during production, it became apparent to then Disney studio chief Jeffrey Katzenberg and the filmmakers that the material had an unusually strong live-action feel to it." That posed a danger for Disney because "with realism . . . comes sex, a no-no in the Disney universe." At one point the animators had drawn a scene of John Smith kissing Pocahontas in which Smith had no shirt on. "It was very steamy," Biskind notes. "At first the executives loved it; then they started to worry that it would be read as a prelude to 'a night in the sack,' as Pomeroy [Smith animator] puts it. 'They were afraid that this would turn off the audience,' and out it went" ("American" 85).

Note that the reason for the boundary, however, is not a fear of encouraging premarital sex—something traditionally seen as a moral boundary—but of offending the audience. Audience offense is taboo because it is the audience who buys the movie tickets, the videos, and the tie-in products. For Disney, a major determinant of its view on morality is the concern for the bottom line, for money. By the same token, because Disney still wishes to see itself as oriented to family values, it has a secondary concern for traditional morality when it comes to sex.

PARENT/CHILD RELATIONSHIPS Parent/child relations establish lines of power and control. Russell Means, the voice of Powhatan the father, appreciated Disney's version of the film, especially in this regard: "I like the father-daughter relationship. It's a two-way street. They listen to each other" (Davis 8). For Disney to highlight the relationship with Pocahontas's father and then to allow Pocahontas to become her father's teacher in the way of peace is a radical thought to American traditional family roles. However, it was not unusual for Native Americans to have strong women in their society. Means asserts, "To my people, society is matriarchal, the women are the most important. They are powerful, the strongest, the most influential" (Davis 8).

Nevertheless, Powhatan arranges for Pocahontas's marriage and fully expects her to accede to his wishes like an obedient daughter would. That Disney's Pocahontas contradicts her father reflects a contemporary American belief in the individual's right to choose the marriage partner and reflects a feminist emphasis of asserting one's rights—especially against patriarchal attitudes. Powhatan compares her to the wild mountain stream, encouraging her to join the big steady river (by marrying Kocoum). She later ponders that thought: "She had always followed his wishes, but this time was different. She did not *want* to marry Kocoum" (emphasis mine) (Ingoglia 18). The description implies that she obeyed only because it was something she already wanted to do. She concludes, "Rivers aren't steady at all. They're always changing" (Ingoglia 18).

At this point, Grandmother Willow's advice to "follow your heart" takes over tradition. Given the individualism in American society and its emphasis on romantic love, this seems like a logical option. Pocahontas continues to choose her own path, disobeying her father's orders to stay in the village. Her actions led to Kocoum's death, which, rather than sending the message of dreadful consequences for disobedience, secretly delights the audience. Kocoum is now out of the way, and Pocahontas will not have to marry him. She will be free to pursue Smith. The result is a moral vision that says obedience to parents is fine when it fits with what the young person wants; otherwise, the message is "follow one's heart." Legitimate authority remains with the parent only as long as the child agrees with the decisions made on his or her behalf.

GROUP/LEADER RELATIONSHIPS Extending the category of relationships to the authority figures for each group of people, one sees strict authoritarianism associated with the villain, Governor Ratcliffe. He fully expects his orders to be carried out without regard to rationality. When Smith tries to explain that the Indians do not have gold, Ratcliffe's response is an order to shoot every Indian seen. Powhatan, on the other hand, respects his people, rewards his brave warrior Kocoum with a feast in his honor, and speaks to his people before announcing the course of action. His behavior suggests a more democratic approach. The message is conveyed that blind obedience is wrong. People (like the Virginia Company) need to think for themselves and do what is right despite orders.

That same message comes through with respect to Pocahontas's actions but is complicated by the fact that she is disobeying her father and that she is motivated by her heart. The film sends mixed messages about authority. The overriding one is, "do what you have to in the name of love; follow your heart and do what you think is best." Teaching children to think for themselves is valuable, but to teach that concept without also teaching respect and obedience for authority could lead to problems.

Cultural Phenomena

LIGHT/DARK METAPHORS A significant boundary both literally and figuratively is the contrast between light and dark. Literally, Disney's animated films frequently rely on the use of the archetypal metaphor of light and dark within the animation colors to delineate good and evil. Although Michael Osborn applies this metaphor to rhetorical discourse, its application to visual rhetoric is a logical extension, as noted in Chapter 2. Osborn comments on the power of archetypal metaphors to communicate morality: "Such metaphors express intense value judgments and may thus be expected to elicit significant value responses from an audience" ("Archetypal Metaphor" 118).

The contrast between light and dark is used in *Pocahontas* with more subtlety than in some of Disney's past films that rely more on pastels and shades of neutrals. Felperin observes, "The British scenes and characters are rendered in drab sepia colours so that the Native American setting, all bright and brutally blue skies, will seem all the nicer and friendlier." In wondering why these colors were chosen, Felperin concludes that the "merchandisers, who favour a more garish, child-luring range of hues, had to be appeased" (58). However, the contrasts also set off the moral distinctions between the two groups of people, enabling Disney to indicate the good group toward which it would have its audience be empathetic.[7]

For example, when John Smith and Pocahontas are together, the colors are clear blues—bright if it is daylight and a crisp bluish purple at night. When Ratcliffe sings about wanting more gold, the colors are dark, and the characters are digging in a much blacker night than the one Pocahontas and Smith share. When the scene involves the colonists as a group, the overall effect is quite dark, as opposed to the Indian scenes, which seem bathed in sunlight. When, however, both groups are considering war, there is an increase of shadow and of fires either in the Indians' tents or coming out of the colonists' guns. Colors are used to highlight emotions, but they also indicate where the directors want the audience's moral sympathies to lie.

More central to the plot of the film is the figurative use of light and dark as exemplified in several of the characters' conversion experiences. Conversion narratives are powerful rhetorical devices, communicating the darkness of ignorance that life had prior to seeing the light of the knowledge of a better way.[8] Robert James Branham argues in his analysis of the films *Eclipse of Reason* and *Silent Scream* that "for uncommitted viewers, the convert tale represents a strategy by which competing viewpoints and potential influences can be discredited" (424). Used unethically, conversion narratives can be extremely harmful because of their power to transform. As Golden, Berquist, and Coleman state, conversion rhetoric can modify dramatically "a listener's self-concept, attitudes, beliefs, values, and actions" (459). The light/dark imagery appeals to viewers by its archetypal nature, and it communicates dramatically.

Described as a "story of moral redemption" by Simon Schama, *Pocahontas*'s plot progresses only as various characters experience conversions (A21). By establishing the boundaries of heroes and villains and suggesting that some of the villains are really potential "good guys," the conversion is a necessary plot device to redeem these people. Thomas, Captain Smith, and the Virginia Company are shown to have redeemable qualities but are also allowed to establish their dark ignorance about the new land and its people. Once Pocahontas explains and sings of the error of his thinking, Smith sees the light of the Native Americans' better way. Thomas, too, sees that greed and violence brought the company to the verge of war and sees the light of peace symbolized by Pocahontas's saving Smith.

Similarly, Powhatan and Nakoma, though established as part of the heroic group, are also characterized as having points of ignorance: Powhatan in choosing Kocoum for Pocahontas and in not pursuing communication with the colonists; Nakoma in not trusting Pocahontas and telling Kocoum of her rendezvous with Smith. Yet, when Pocahontas's action reveals a better way, both characters repent and believe. Even Pocahontas's character reveals the tendency toward the darkness of irresponsibility as she flits where she will, when she will, even disobeying her father. She too is redeemed when she converts from irresponsibility to responsibility by choosing to stay with her people and encourage the peace process rather than following her love to England. (The theme from *The Lion King* of the need to grow up and take responsibility is reinforced here.) The conversion narrative contributes to the establishment of moral boundaries in that it clearly shows certain attitudes and actions as living in darkness—darkness dispelled by knowledge of the way life ought to be lived, in the light of the knowledge of others.

COMMUNICATION/MISUNDERSTANDING One of the pillars of moral order is communication that functions to uphold and facilitate the overall moral structure. Although Disney films traditionally involve the quest for self-discovery or happiness,[9] *Pocahontas* adds a secondary theme— the need for people to communicate.

The Native Americans and the colonists are cut off from each other, each having their own value system. Pocahontas proposes to her father that he talk with one of the colonists instead of assuming the necessity of war. They do not talk, and each side's own interests rule; they are cut off from one another. The Native Americans seek to protect their way of life and the land, while the colonists seek to master the environment and the Native Americans, all in service of their greedy interests. This is a key to Disney's moral vision in this film: communication is the answer to cultural differences.

But how that communication takes place is not clear, and this is where Disney's moral vision fails. The hard work of listening, relating interpersonally, self-disclosing, and so on is not represented as such. Instead, Disney adds the "magic." Language barriers are overcome mystically after the initial encounter between Pocahontas and John Smith. The Indians and the Virginia Company understand each other's words without ever having had to learn each other's language. That Disney chooses not to focus on what would have been an obvious difficulty suggests that it would rather emphasize that communication took place and not misunderstanding.

However, as Wuthnow observes, the very nature of language, including associated rituals and nonverbals, establishes barriers to communication (52). Pocahontas's initial contact with John Smith included the name exchange and "hello" rituals, in which each taught one culture's ritual to the other. But rather than misunderstanding, there seems to be no barrier to understanding. At this point, Pocahontas uses the Indian word *winggapo*. But then she is reminded of Grandmother Willow's advice to "listen with her heart" and finds no more need to use her language.

Pocahontas and John Smith do not speak the same language—a significant problem for most people, but not for them. At one point Nakoma asks, "How can *you* know him? . . . You don't even speak his language!" Pocahontas's response is "We speak with our hearts" (Ingoglia 67). At the same time, the message is that these two groups of people need to get together and communicate with each other. Pocahontas gets the grudging admission from her father that he might consider abandoning the warpath if one of the Englishmen would come and talk to him (Ingoglia 64).

If communication solves social problems, the romanticized treatment of the interactions between Pocahontas and Smith does little to guide the audience in understanding how to begin the communicative process. The message that using language facilitates communication is countered by the message that "listening with your heart" overcomes misunderstanding. Knowledge comes by responding to what is inside. Language barriers, rituals, and communicative problems will then disappear.

DEVIANCE/NORMALCY The next boundary includes discovering what is presented as deviant behaviors and attitudes and what is presented as normal. Wuthnow argues, "Symbolic boundaries are often maintained by litanies of deviant events that reveal normality by their very violations of it" (341). The interesting twist in locating these boundary markers is the plot's highlighting of traditionally accepted boundaries as inherently deviant and thus needing to be transformed.

Ratcliffe and the Virginia Company's stereotyping of Native Americans and of the new land is presented in an exaggerated, almost humorous form that indicates how outrageously deviant those attitudes are. The arrogance of Smith as he tells Pocahontas how they will civilize this land, the disrespect for anything unfamiliar, the greediness of Ratcliffe, the destruction of the land, the ignorance expressed in the song "Savages," the eagerness for war—all are presented as deviant attitudes and behaviors. They push the boundaries of what is right.

Normal morality is portrayed by the Native Americans. They live life in harmony with nature, not abusing the land but appreciating its gifts. They have a strong emphasis on community. The chief warrior, Kocoum, is honored for his deeds in their last battle, which was fought not for greed but to keep their people safe. Family is respected and cherished, as are friends and the spiritual world.

Nevertheless, both sides distrust and fear the unknown—each other. People who differ from each other in culture and/or physical appearance tend to withdraw or fight each other. As discussed below, however, Disney presents this "normal" boundary as something that ought to change.

Underlying these overt boundaries are attitudes and behaviors that are part of the "normal" but emerge as unacceptable. Nicola Beisel, in studying how boundaries are formed, "suggests that people use existing ideologies to try to transform social structures and moral boundaries" (Gans ix). Disney adds an ironic twist to identifying boundaries by doing this.

The heroine and hero are both deviants to their people. But in their deviance, Disney suggests, they are transforming the deviant boundary to the normalcy that ought to be. Pocahontas is acknowledged as a deviant—she follows her own path; she listens to her heart, not to her father. She chooses to love whom she will. She does not greet her father when the whole tribe does—she is off on the cliff following the wind, going where it takes her. When all are ordered to stay in the village, she disobeys to go and meet Smith. When the whole village is ready to go to war, she is willing to sacrifice her life for love and possibly peace.

Similarly, Smith is not a normal sailor. He is his own man. He does not have family to bid farewell to. He does not fear the terrifying weather on the voyage or the danger of jumping in the water to rescue Thomas. Nor does he fear Indians or Ratcliffe or death itself. When the entire company of men are ordered to dig for gold, Smith wanders off to explore. When others are hiding in a fort, he is out at night wandering the woods. When others are shooting at Indians, he is kissing one.

Both Smith and Pocahontas are deviants, but Disney elevates them to the central characters and lauds their behavior. Thus, it shows that what both the colonists and the Native Americans think is deviant behavior ought to be the norm and that what they think is normal ought to be considered deviant. We see a Disney-structured moral order emerge.

Reversing the perceived moral order is the task of the plot; the audience needs to see that what is perceived as normal is really deviant. That means that the "normal," or what is perceived as inevitable, behavior requires intentional deviance. Wuthnow suggests that intentional behavior contrasted to inevitabilities can sometimes cause the boundaries to blur: "If social circumstances change sufficiently to make any of these symbolic distinctions ambiguous, . . . then a sense of uncertainty or 'moral crisis' may come to be associated with the commitments at issue" (95).

Pocahontas experiences this crisis when she must determine whether or not to obey her father and marry Kocoum and later whether or not to stay in the village or go meet Smith. Her crisis culminates when she chooses to risk her life to save Smith's. Similarly, Smith experiences a blurring of moral boundaries when he listens to Pocahontas's words and converts to her way of thinking. He continues in this line when he disobeys Ratcliffe, and finally, his crisis culminates when he risks his life to save Powhatan's.

If Pocahontas and Smith are examples of deviance converted to normalcy, what might examples of normalcy revealed as deviance be? Powhatan's choosing Kocoum for Pocahontas's mate, the Virginia Company's obedience of Ratcliffe, Kakoma's telling Kocoum that Pocahontas was with Smith, Thomas's shooting of Kocoum, the Native Americans' willingness to go to war—all are examples of a part of a moral order that ultimately is reversed. As the song "Savages" helps build toward the climax of the film, the contrast between the motivations for war on both sides is obvious, allowing the audience to continue to empathize with the Native Americans. But ultimately, Pocahontas helps reveal that war is deviance and that the normal path ought to be peace.

Each group of people, though having been already associated with good and evil (the Native Americans and the colonists, respectively), reveals the social boundary that exists when they each sing the song "Savages." Whereas the colonists describe the Indians as "filthy little heathens" whose "whole disgusting race is like a curse," the Indians sing, "They're different from us, which means they can't be trusted." The song appears a second time, driving home the message that each group sees the other as "just a bunch of filthy, stinking savages!" But this second version also intersperses Pocahontas's singing to the "spirits of the earth and sky" to help her stop the killing of Smith. The emphasis on the song "Colors of the Wind" makes it obvious that *Pocahontas* is teaching the need to transform the traditionally accepted boundaries of race and to learn from each other.

TECHNOLOGY/NATURE Note that the very act of the colonists' digging is revealed as obviously deviant to the Native Americans, but it is the normal course of action for the colonists. Says John Smith to Pocahontas, "We're going to build them here [streets filled with carriages, bridges over the rivers, buildings as tall as trees]. We'll show the people of your village how to use this land properly. How to make the most of it" (43–44). That the colonists are so unaware of the beauty around them highlights their insensitivity to nature and their excessive need for technological development.

Associating technology with the villains, Disney emphasizes the contrasting attitudes toward environmental awareness. Ratcliffe insulates himself from his environment through the artificial constructions of the tent and fort. But his lifestyle epitomizes the vulgarity of the colonists when compared with the lifestyle of the Native Americans. His clothes are garishly out of place in the wilderness. His hair is well coifed, and he indulges his appetite while ordering his men to find him gold. He sees nothing of the spectacular scenery—a total contrast to Pocahontas, who is carried by the wind, meditates on a promontory high above the water, races the rapids, is protected by a hummingbird and a raccoon, and communes with a willow tree. The Native Americans sing of living life in balance while the colonists sing of finding gold. The latter employ explosives, digging and destroying, oblivious to their surroundings, and they use technology, in the form of guns, to kill. The boundaries here establish nature as beneficent and beautiful when respected and technology as intrusive and deadly when abused.

SACRED/SECULAR When the men of the Virginia Company invoke the name of God in their opening song, "The Virginia Company," that is the only "spiritual" reference from that group. Frances Mossiker observes that "the Puritans' moral purpose [was] loftier than the Virginians'. . . . The Virginia contingent consisted of soldiers of fortune, mercenaries, vagabonds, desperados, convicts, and debtors." Nevertheless, the company's royal charter does refer to the necessity of the missionary effort (5). By placing the reference to God in the song describing the company's goals, Disney allows the audience to read into the men a spiritual motivation if so desired. However, the reality of their spirituality is not otherwise visible. For although the men could mouth God's name, it is apparent that the role God played in their lives and their motivations is minuscule.

This is contrasted to the Native Americans' reverence of the land and the spiritual realm. They are concerned about being faithful to their traditions ("Steady as the Beating Drum"). Pocahontas has a personal relationship with the spirit of a tree—Grandmother Willow. The tree gave her mother advice and now counsels her. Smith is incredulous when he sees a face appear on the willow, but Pocahontas, the teacher in this film, helps him to listen and commune with the tree.[10] That Pocahontas not only is able to see the spiritual in a tree but also respects animals is implied in her friendship with Flit the hummingbird and Meeko the raccoon. The animals serve as the comic sidekicks but do not speak (perhaps Disney is responding to the criticism about anthropomorphism). Nevertheless, Pocahontas understands them, and they in return jealously protect her.

Disney's association of the spiritual with the heroes indicates that spirituality ought to be a part of the moral order. But the generalities of the Powhatan Indians' spirituality suggests animism and fits well with what today is called New Age spirituality. Traditional religions, with the limitations or taboos that most religions suggest, are all missing. The message is that spirituality may have a legitimate place in the moral order, but keep it broad and open to all.

CONCLUSION

Pocahontas is a successful film in terms of making money for the Disney Company. Sensitive to its critics, Disney sought to be politically correct by avoiding traditional stereotypes of Native Americans and women, but in the process it used a historical legend without being faithful to the facts as known and consequently presented an image of Pocahontas that still fit a stereotyped image of beauty.

By choosing to be creative with the historical account, Disney put its own ideological stamp on the story. To better understand the moral dimension of that stamp, we looked at the moral order in the film. Moral order, structured by communication, is best uncovered by examining the symbolic boundaries that are revealed by looking at characters, relationships, and cultural phenomena.

The polarities established by the boundaries indicate what Disney associates with good and evil or right and wrong. Disney films, with a target audience of children, have long relied upon these kinds of contrasts to communicate what have come to be accepted as morality plays. Just as the medieval church used morality plays to teach, so does Disney. The Disney moral order in *Pocahontas* allows for any of a number of moral lessons to be drawn, including the following:

1. Greediness and glory seeking are villainous attitudes.
2. Excess in eating is inappropriate.
3. Racism is wrong; stereotyping in general is wrong.
4. Being willing to listen and change one's mind is a good quality.
5. Good people respect the earth and live in harmony with it.
6. "Beautiful" means having a "perfect" figure, well-toned muscles, and long hair.
7. Similarly, "handsome" means having a strong body, well-toned muscles, and a sculpted face.

8. Males and females are never "just friends" but must have a romantic relationship.
9. Parents are not always right.
10. Closely related to number 9 is the need to follow one's own heart. The result may have negative consequences (as in Kocoum's being killed), but it may be necessary (because Pocahontas followed her heart, war was averted).
11. Blind obedience is wrong; obedience is good only when one agrees with the authority.
12. The darkness of ignorance can be changed to the light of knowledge; misguided people can be redeemed through education in the truth.
13. If men hold unenlightened views, it is women's job to educate them.
14. Communication is vital for people to get along.
15. Technology is destructive of the environment.
16. The earth is generous in its bounty to the people.
17. Spirituality can be a normal part of rational living.
18. The earth, animals, and humans are all related to each other and should be respectful of the spirits of each other.

Many of the boundaries Disney establishes are laudable, but not all; good lessons are mixed with bad. Concerns about racism, greed, courage, open-mindedness, and the destruction of the environment are prosocial messages. However, they are offset by an emphasis on superficial beauty, a need for romance as the basis of relationship, and the instruction to follow one's heart—which expresses an emotional individualism and a message that obedience to authority is fine as long as one agrees; otherwise, listening to one's own desires is best. Even the inclusion of spirituality as a positive dimension of life has the potential of being a negative message for many religious people who believe that there is only one way to salvation; Disney's message encourages a belief in animism, which runs contrary to traditional Jewish, Christian, and some other faiths.

Disney is not unaware of its powerful potential to affect children. The symbolic boundaries described here, representations of "communicative action" in Jürgen Habermas's words, are powerful rhetorical devices in the establishment and communication of a Disney moral order.

FOUR

The Hunchback of Notre Dame
COMICALLY FRAMING VIRTUE AND VICE

Archdeacon Frollo erupted in a "fiendish" laugh when Esmeralda's body swung spas-modically from the rope. Quasimodo, faithful defender of Frollo, "furiously rushed at the archdeacon and pushed him off the balustrade." Clinging to a waterspout, Frollo "glanced over the impassive carved figures of the tower, suspended, like himself, over the abyss but without fear for themselves or pity for him. Everything around him was of stone: the gaping monsters before his eyes, the pavement below him and, above his head, the weeping Quasimodo." . . . Quasimodo disappeared the day Esmeralda and Frollo died, but sometime later, in the vault where executed prisoners were placed, was found "two skeletons, one embracing the other." One was of a woman and the other had "a twisted spine, a head sunk down between its shoulders and one leg shorter than the other" and showed no signs of having died from anything but natural causes.   —Victor Hugo, *The Hunchback of Notre Dame*

He [Frollo] leaped onto a gargoyle that jutted over the square. In a whirl of black velvet, he whipped off his cape and flung it at Quasimodo. Caught by surprise, Qua-simodo lost his footing. As he slipped from the ledge, Esmeralda grabbed his hand. Quasimodo hung in midair. . . .

But then Frollo heard the crack of stone. The gargoyle was breaking beneath him. As it snapped free, Frollo, screaming, plunged to the square, far below. [Quasimodo falls too, but is caught part way down by Phoebus. Esmeralda and Phoe-bus emerge from the church hand-in-hand. Esmeralda reaches back to encourage

Quasimodo.] And that morning the city walls echoed with joyous cheers for Quasimodo—the hero of Notre Dame!

—Gina Ingoglia, *Disney's The Hunchback of Notre Dame*

The first quotation above concludes the tumultuous tragedy of *The
Hunchback of Notre Dame*. The second concludes *Disney's The Hunchback
of Notre Dame*. Disney's version defines the categories of good and evil
by embodying virtues and vices distinctly, in heroes and villains, respectively, all the while embracing a comic interpretive frame against or, in
this case, on top of the tragic frame of the original novel.

One might wonder why Disney, known for its didacticism, chose this
story for an animated film. The Disney Company explains: "Perhaps because Quasimodo is the ultimate underdog, trapped between Paris below
and heaven above. Indeed, everyone is an outcast in this tale. Even the
gargoyles. Somehow, Victor Hugo tells us, the human spirit endures. And
triumphs" (Walt, "Brief" 2). Rather presumptuous of Disney, it seems, to
claim Victor Hugo's approval of its radically altered version. But Disney
wanted to communicate an overt moral. Writer Tab Murphy, in explaining the process of adapting Hugo's novel for Disney, comments that the
most important thing "for Disney and for myself [is] finding a theme
that ran through the story that at [the] end of the movie would be able
to sort of explain all the characters: where they were at the beginning of
the story and how they changed at the end of the story" (Walt, "Writers"
1). According to screenwriter Irene Mecchi, the theme is "judge not the
outcast, for he may possess the greatest worth" (Walt, "Writers" 2).

Nevertheless, the communication of this identified theme is structured and emphasized in a dramatically different form from that of
the original novel. The tragic ending is gone, replaced by a different romance that leaves the involved parties optimistic about life. Disney, by
choosing to apply a comic frame over a tragic frame, creates a confused
morality.[1]

FILM BACKGROUND

The film is set in 15th-century Paris and centered around the great Notre
Dame Cathedral. The story begins with Clopin, king of the Gypsies, acting as the narrator of a puppet show and singing "The Bells of Notre
Dame." Use of this "play-within-a-play" technique, a common dramatic
device, enables the filmmakers to condense some of the story, telling us
the setting instead of showing it. It could be argued that, symbolically,

Clopin's puppet show is analogous to what Disney has done to Hugo's novel—reduced it to manipulated entertainment, à la "tragedy lite."

In a dark, emotional scene, the audience sees a Gypsy woman and her baby pursued on horseback by an evil and powerful-looking Judge Frollo, who inadvertently causes the woman's death on the steps of the cathedral. As he is about to drop the baby down a well, the church's archdeacon, in song, reminds Frollo that he is putting his soul in danger and that the cathedral of Notre Dame will see what he is doing. A terrified Frollo agrees that he will allow the child to live in the cathedral and will be responsible for him. As Clopin concludes this introduction in song, he introduces the major theme of the movie: "Who is the monster and who is the man?"

Suddenly the lighting and sound change dramatically. The bells are ringing on a beautiful day, and Quasimodo is helping a bird learn to leave its nest and fly from the tower. The plaintiveness of his words reveals his yearning to leave the cathedral to join the people gathering in the square below him for the Feast of Fools. He is encouraged by his three gargoyle friends, Victor, Laverne, and Hugo, to risk visiting the festival without his master Frollo's permission. They try several arguments, from the moralizing lesson of "Life's not a spectator sport. If watchin's all you're gonna do, then you're gonna watch your life go by without you" to "He'll never know you were gone" and "Better to beg forgiveness than to ask permission" (*Disney's Hunchback*).[2] "Quasi," as they call him, becomes determined to go, only to turn and encounter Frollo. As they eat and work on the alphabet, Frollo learns of Quasimodo's desire. Frollo explains why he cannot go, singing a perverse duet that reminds Quasi he is "deformed, ugly and a monster." Quasimodo's song of response after Frollo leaves, "Out There," communicates powerfully the longing he has for freedom, for companionship, and for community. His resolve to attend the festival is renewed.

Meanwhile, a new captain of the guard, Phoebus, is arriving in town. Leading his horse through the cobblestone streets, he observes Esmeralda and her goat, Djali, dancing. When guards begin to hassle her, he intervenes. Once at the Palace of Justice, Phoebus meets Frollo, who is busy torturing his former captain, and learns that his task is to root out and kill Gypsies.

The crazy song "Topsy Turvy" sets the scene for the Festival of Fools, an indeed topsy-turvy, Mardi Gras–like celebration that is in full swing and will culminate in the crowning of the ugliest fool. Quasimodo, surrounded by a cape, finds himself in the midst of the contest and ultimately selected by Esmeralda as the ugliest. When she realizes that his is not a mask, she is moved to pity, but the crowd is moved to violence. Quasimodo is tied to a turntable and pelted with rotten vegetables until finally Esmeralda approaches and wipes his face. Frollo orders her to stop, and she lectures him on his cruelty to Quasimodo and to her people, which only angers Frollo into ordering her arrest.

Esmeralda escapes into the cathedral where Phoebus, already smitten with her, encourages her to ask for sanctuary. In a tender prayer-song, "God Help the Outcasts," Esmeralda expresses a heart full of concern for others, which ultimately Quasimodo mistakes as a heart for him. Quasimodo shows Esmeralda his tower, his carvings, and his view. Esmeralda shows Quasimodo that his master may have taught him lies about himself and the Gypsies. Quasi helps her escape and returns to contemplate "heaven's light" in a gentle song by that name. Jarringly, the film contrasts Quasi's love with Frollo's lust in a darkly frightening song, "Hellfire." The film interweaves a ranting prayer to Maria with scenes of hooded spirits and Esmeralda dancing in the fire, revealing Frollo's confusing love/hate desires as the motivators for the coming scenes of hate.

The next scenes show Frollo hunting Gypsies, trying to bribe those he finds for information regarding Esmeralda and willingly murdering them when they are not cooperative. Finally, when Frollo orders Phoebus to set a peasant's house on fire with the family locked inside, Phoebus's conscience can take no more; he refuses. Frollo torches it anyway, and Phoebus rescues the family. As he tries to escape Frollo's wrath, he is shot by an arrow and falls into a river near where Esmeralda is hiding.

She rescues him and brings him to Quasimodo, whose gargoyle friends have just sung "A Guy Like You" to encourage him to consider Esmeralda his girlfriend. Esmeralda's appearance then is bittersweet, as Quasi's budding love is quashed by the presence of Phoebus. He sings of his realization that he will never know love, because of his ugliness.

Frollo suspects that the only way Esmeralda has escaped him is with Quasi's help, and so he lays a trap by suggesting that he knows where Esmeralda and the Gypsies are hiding and that he will attack at dawn. Quasi and Phoebus set aside their differences to go and warn them. They are immediately captured by Clopin and the Gypsies and ordered in song to the Court of Miracles, where they will be executed. Just as Esmeralda saves them, Frollo bursts in and arrests all.

Once again, we are confronted by a dark and frightening scene: Esmeralda is about to be burned at the stake in front of the cathedral, while Quasimodo looks down from the tower, where he is chained. Goaded by the gargoyles, he escapes to rescue Esmeralda and begin an apocalyptic-like battle full of fire and hail in the form of pieces of the cathedral. Ultimately, the Gypsies, led by Phoebus, escape to repel the guards while Frollo falls to his death. Esmeralda and Phoebus are reunited with Quasi's blessing, and Quasimodo is introduced to the cheering crowds.

As usual for Disney animated films, critics responded both positively and negatively to this film, with negative responses dominating. Mary Elson's strongly worded column argues that not only is the film "more for adults than children" but also that "this movie may be inappropriate for all ages" (1). As she suggests, most adults do not go to "G"-rated movies, which are traditionally marketed to the very young, and if they do go, they do not expect to be entertained with adult themes.

Journalist Linda Romine suggests, ". . . the Southern Baptists, who recently called for a boycott of Disney, may have a point. *The Hunchback of Notre Dame*, while not promoting so-called 'non-traditional' family values, is rife with more adult references than one might expect in a movie marketed to children" (15). Anne Thompson echoes the concern when she says the film "may be the darkest, most adult animated film Disney has ever made" (28). Even one of the actors, Jason Alexander, who was the voice of gargoyle Hugo, says, "I won't be taking my 4-year-old" (Thompson 28). The advertising for the film echoed the mixed message: "Children will adore it! Adults will flock back to see it!" (Elson 1). It seems that Disney wants to target everyone instead of primarily children.

But the result was a film with no clear audience. Janet Maslin of the *New York Times* describes the film as the "latest and most uncertain of Disney's animated efforts, with its manic mood swings and cloying, none-too-cuddly hero." And no matter how hard Disney tries, "There's just no way to delight children with a feel-good version of this story." It "tries so hard that it approaches the absurd" ("Dancing" C14). Paul Goldberger, also of the *New York Times*, writes even more harshly: "This is not animation turning its techniques on a great work of literature; it is grotesque, vulgar parody" (27). He argues further that what Disney has done is to take "a work of subtlety and complexity" and "render it laughingly simple, omitting every ambiguity, every shade of gray, every nuance" (26). Goldberger concludes that either Disney thinks it is too much for the audience or, more likely, these things [do not] translate into ticket sales, merchandise tie-ins, and all the other elements of mass-market entertainment success" (26).

Although the adult themes and critics' warnings to keep young children away certainly had a negative effect on box office success,[3] I believe there is more to the conflicting response of critics. *The Hunchback of Notre Dame* uses Victor Hugo's tragic novel as its foundation and the Disney genre of animated musical with comedy as overlay, yielding a mix of "attitudes," as theorist Kenneth Burke would say. Disney affirms that it tried to stay as close to the "spirit" of the novel as possible. Coproducer Roy Conli discusses Hugo's book: "The book is incredibly tortured and soul-shaking. But what we found was that we wanted to key into Victor Hugo's spirit. The support for the underdog, the common man striving for something better" (Walt, "Producers" 2). Therein lies the confusion. Does Disney's film fall in the tragic or the comic genre? This mixture results in a philosophical clash of values—the tragic vision with the comic vision. And each approach reflects a particular moral vision. Disney's choice to use both produces mixed results. Rather than blending into a new genre, the two genres work at odds as surely as oil and vinegar. When shaken well, they look like one substance, but when allowed to stand, the two begin to separate.

INTERPRETIVE FRAMES

The confusion of attitudes that the critics picked up on is best explained through theorist Kenneth Burke's work on interpretive frames as a dimension of motive analysis in symbolic communication. The interpretive frame establishes the direction of the narrative, as well as serving to reveal something of the motivation for the narrative.[4]

Disney's The Hunchback of Notre Dame differs markedly from Hugo's novel in that it falls within Burke's definition of a comic frame. Disney consciously chooses the comic frame for its animated musicals. This interpretive stance is life-affirming and moves its characters in an upward direction, which, along with the didactic tone, has characterized this film genre. The challenge for the creators of *The Hunchback* was to take a story that was written in the tragic frame and transform its direction. The result is a *Hunchback* with a life-affirming moral tale, as reasonably a happy ending as can be expected given a love triangle, and Hugo's characters transformed into "feel-good" caricatures—except of course for the villain, who is totally evil and deservedly killed off.

But too many dimensions of tragic framing are also included in the film, and the result is an uneasy confusion. Even with the upbeat ending, the tragic dimensions and the extreme evil displayed in Frollo establish conflicting emotions. Disney applies a comic frame overall, including banishing evil, represented almost solely in Frollo, from the story; resolving the romance between Esmeralda and Phoebus; and giving Quasimodo his wish to be "out there," accepted by other people. Nevertheless the tragic dimensions and characters of the original novel frequently emerge in this version, confusing the comic frame and leaving the viewer longing for the purging of tragedy or the transcendence of comedy but getting only hints of both.

According to Burke, the tragic frame is characterized by a "fatalistic turn" of the plot (*Attitudes* 42), a "transcendence downward" (*Attitudes* 106), and an "unhappy ending" (*Language* 398).[5] The character names tend to be "villain" and "hero" (*Attitudes* 4), yet all suffer a tragic fate. Typically, "tragedy deals *sympathetically* with crime" (*Attitudes* 39 n). Hugh Duncan also discusses tragedy as symbolic communication and suggests: "Tragedy purges through sacrifice of victims whose suffering and death serves as a vicarious atonement for our guilt" (*Language* 395). The downward turn of tragedy depends on the intervention of fate, leaving the characters no recourse. Tragic figures inspire pity if not empathy.

We see the tragic at work in Victor Hugo's *Hunchback of Notre Dame*. Meant to be a social criticism condemning the church and authorities for the lack of social justice, this novel tells the tale of numerous characters whose bleak lives may experience a few moments of kindness but who ultimately die tragic deaths. Disney's version, however, ends with the bells ringing and the people smilingly accepting Quasimodo. The heroes are triumphant, and the villain has lost; Disney has given the plot an upward transcendence. Or has it?

Disney's version is both tragic and comic. Disney keeps the tragedy of Quasimodo present. He remains disfigured, and he doesn't get the girl he loves. We feel pity for him even though he is at last able to go out among the people. Frollo clearly acts as a villain, someone characteristically found in tragedies. He is "better than ordinary people" in his piety and in the fact that he is the authority figure in the film. But pride is still a real problem for him (in addition to his feelings for Esmeralda). Plot motivation is driven not by Quasi's desire to "find himself," as in other Disney films, but by Frollo's dark desire for Esmeralda.

Parts of the film address crime, in Burke's words, "sympathetically," as if the offense were ours. Phoebus disobeys the authority of Frollo and suffers the consequences, but his offense—acting on conscience—is something an audience could easily project on themselves. Quasimodo also disobeys Frollo, both in going to the festival and in hiding Phoebus and helping Esmeralda. That too arouses audience sympathy. The story seems to offer little hope to the characters.

Finally, this plot development "purges through the sacrifice of victims" in that Quasimodo remains a victim of unrequited love. His happiness is sacrificed so that we, the audience, will be more comfortable seeing Esmeralda with someone handsome. Quasi functions as a tragic victim from this perspective, but he also demonstrates the comic side of purging in that his lost love positions him as a victim with whom we suffer. Fulfilling both tragic and comic dimensions yields disturbing mixtures of feelings about the characters.

Disney overlays the tragic dimensions with many other dimensions of the comic frame to give the plot the upward transcendent turn.[6] These comic dimensions are seen in a cast of characters who are, in ways, considered "worse than ordinary people" (Burke, *Language* 398). All are outcasts, suggests screenwriter Tab Murphy: "Quasi is an outcast because of his looks, Phoebus comes to town to do his duty and becomes a fugitive, Esmeralda is an outcast by virtue of being a Gypsy. The Gargoyles were supposedly carved and discarded by the stone masons because they were imperfect. Even Frollo, through his zealotry, makes himself an outcast" (*Disney's Hunchback: Press Kit* 31).

Burke advocates the comic frame as the best attitude toward life because of its attitude of acceptance. The comic frame has "transcendence upwards" (*Attitudes* 106); characters that tend to have an exaggerated characteristic (*Attitudes* 400) and are described as "tricked" and "intelligent" rather than villains and heroes (*Attitudes* 5); and finally, "a plot that builds toward a 'happy' ending" (*Language* 398). Although Burke may use the term *comic,* that does not necessarily mean the same thing as *humor;* rather he sees art forms as "'strategies' for living" (*Attitudes* 43). As a strategy, the focus of the comic is on living life here and now.

In terms of characteristics, the comic vision turns the direction of the tragic attitude in incongruous ways: "Like tragedy, comedy warns against the dangers of pride, but its emphasis shifts from *crime* to *stupidity.*" Comedy tends to picture "people not as *vicious,* but as *mistaken*" (*Attitudes* 40), and just as tragedy purges, so too, according to Duncan, does comedy. The difference, however, is [that] "comedy purges through victims who assume our degradation and suffering so we can confront it together in rational discourse" (395). Thus Burke argues: "The comic frame should enable people to *be observers of themselves, while acting.* Its ultimate would not be *passiveness,* but *maximum consciousness.* One would 'transcend' himself by noting his own foibles" (*Attitudes* 171). With a comic vision, the foolishness of humanity is laid bare and the potential for intelligent choice arises.

While both Phoebus and Quasimodo have rebelled against the authority, the "criminality" of that rebellion is tempered by the underlying question of why they did not do so earlier, a stupidity implication. Nevertheless, the crimes of Frollo's inhumanity to Quasimodo and insane attacks upon the Gypsies remain crimes and not stupid mistakes. He is vicious, motivated by a prideful love/hate complexity. It is that complexity that keeps Frollo in the tragic frame. But as he gives way to the hate, he moves to a comic caricature of evil, thus enabling Disney to have him die without sympathy. Frollo is both tragic and comic pulling us at once toward recognizing our own evil in him and enabling us to dismiss it as a stupidity far from who we are. Phoebus and Quasi are transformed by the comic frame from being lawbreakers to simply being mistaken. Ultimately the audience feels purged through Quasimodo's suffering and, to a lesser extent, that of Esmeralda and Phoebus.

A second dimension of this story that makes the comic overlay a difficult fit is when Esmeralda first meets Quasi and assumes he has a mask on. That encounter says something about how ugly Quasimodo appears and just how unrealistic Disney's comic frame is. When even the heroine of the story sees the ugliness before she sees the person, the possibility for Quasi to live among the people "happily ever after" is not there, despite the ending that suggests otherwise. Also the cruelty Quasimodo experiences at the Festival of Fools continues for too long for the audience to have its memory wiped out by a transcendent turn. The crowd subjects Quasi to remarks about how "hideous" he is and then crowns him king because of his ugliness. Quasi's sensitivity and kindness, as the film established earlier, would make him well aware that he is being cheered not for himself but rather for his ugliness. When he is tied to the pillory wheel and pelted with tomatoes, it seems that the cruelty will never end. Finally, Esmeralda stops it, but that element of "transcendence" is not enough to overcome the tragedy of these prior scenes.

Washington Times critic Gary Arnold reinforces the comic-tragic framing described above: "The Disney animation team finally juggles too many irreconcilable aesthetic contradictions while trying to coax a happy-face musical-comedy-tearjerker out of Victor Hugo's imposing, sorrowful classic. Some of the would-be inspirational flourishes here would work better in a spoof" (M20). That Disney chose to work with a tragedy and impose its own genre restraints over Hugo's novel instructs us in identifying some of the internal tensions within the film. Table 4.1

TABLE 4.1. Characteristics of Tragic and Comic Attitude Frames

	Attitude Frame		
	Tragic	*Comic*	*Disney (in Hunchback)*
Plot	Unhappy ending	Happy ending	Comic
Characters are . . .	Villains and heroes	Tricked and intelligent	Both
Characters' fate	Tragic	Happy	Comic
Dangers of pride are . . .	Crime	Stupidity	Both
People are . . .	Vicious	Mistaken	Both
Strategy for living has . . .	Cosmic vision	Here-and-now focus	Comic
Purges through . . .	Victims who take on our guilt	Victims with whom we suffer	Both
Vision has . . .	Downward transcendence	Upward transcendence	Comic

summarizes characteristics of tragic and comic framing, showing what is at work in Disney's film.

That the plot of Hugo's story was "Disneyfied" raises concerns with regard to morality: how appropriate is the content for children? Recognizing that there is difficult content, codirector Kirk Wise observes: "We knew it would be a challenge to stay true to the material while still giving it the requisite amount of fantasy and fun most people would expect from a Disney animated feature. We were not going to end it the way the book ended, with everybody dead" (Thompson 30). But journalist Goldberger is frustrated by that:

> The issue is not animation per se, or entertainment; it is faithfulness to the original material, which requires a willingness to accept the fact that everything is not entertainment. [The story] is not supposed to be fun, or cute, or lovable. It is difficult and painful and ugly, which is why it has never been considered a story for children. (27)

Nevertheless, Disney uses Hugo's story, confusing the comic with the tragic, changing some characters and plot movement to be more palatable, yet leaving in other dimensions that young children may not understand or may be frightened of, all the while losing sight of just who its audience is.

Disney frames its version of *The Hunchback* comically. This interpretive frame overlaid on a tragic plot results in enough confusion to affect the reception of the film. More important is that the comic frame places certain expectations on how morality is communicated. Virtue triumphs, and vice is destroyed. Good always wins and is rewarded. Disney needs to make very clear what the good or the virtuous is, as well as to make clear vice or evil. These sharp distinctions characterize Disney's didacticism but also trace their roots to an ancient school of ethics.

VIRTUE ETHICS

Character ethics, also known as virtue ethics, is an approach to systematizing ethics that traces its roots at least to Aristotle but has recently reemerged in current discussions of morality.[7] Aristotle developed the concept of virtue in *Nichomachean Ethics*. He distinguished between intellectual virtues, which arise from teaching, and moral virtues, which are "formed by habit" (33). Thus, repeated moral action is the emphasis. According to Aristotle, virtuous acts are those done by a person with the following characteristics: "First of all, he must know what he is doing; secondly, he must choose to act the way he does, and he must choose it for its own sake; and in the third place, the act must spring from a firm and unchangeable character" (39). To determine which acts are virtuous, Aristotle argued for the mean between extremes (thus the description of Aristotle's ethical approach as the "Golden Mean"). For example, if one were in danger, to act virtuously would mean not to be foolhardy nor to be cowardly but rather to act courageously. Aristotle's concept of virtue has influenced many thinkers throughout history.

In order to identify virtue, Tom Beauchamp advises looking for "the morally commendable" (150). Because of Disney's didactic approach to storytelling, there is almost no question of how to define that term. Morally commendable characters emerge as the heroes of the story. Along the way, visual cues are given as to who they are in the use of light and color. For example, producer Don Hahn explains: "The art direction helps us to visually reinforce such contrasting themes as dark and light, good versus evil, physical versus spiritual beauty and sounds and silence" (*Disney's Hunchback: Press Kit* 38). Music is interwoven to both further story and character as well as to establish the mood and feel of the scene. All the elements are carefully labored over in order to produce a seamless film with a unified story that works together to communicate the moral theme.

Virtue and vice, hero and villain. When one looks at morality through this lens, one focuses on character traits and habits. Philosopher William K. Frankena defines virtues thusly:

> Virtues are dispositions or traits that are not wholly innate; they must all be acquired, at least in part, by teaching and practice, or, perhaps, by grace. They are also traits of "character," rather than traits of "personality" like charm or shyness, and they all involve a tendency to do certain kinds of action in certain kinds of situations, not just to think or feel in certain ways. They are not just abilities or skills. (63)

Virtues, then, are both learned behaviors as well as character definers.

One way to define virtue ethics is to examine what it is not. The traditional approaches to ethics have tended to fall into either deontological theories, which focus on duty or motivation, or teleological theories, which focus on the ends of the action. These positions vary widely over the nature of ethics and the requirements of morality, but they tend to emphasize act over agent. As Beauchamp notes, there is a commonality in their conception: "Ethics provides general guides to action in the form of principles and rules" (149). Whereas both discuss duty judgments over right and wrong or good and bad action, the focus of virtue ethics differs in that its primary concern is judgment about character, so for Beauchamp a moral virtue is "a fixed disposition, habit, or trait to do what is morally commendable" (150); it is rooted in the person and not the act. Thus, we must look at the individual characters in *The Hunchback* in order to understand more clearly what Disney identifies as virtue and vice.

Quasimodo

One of the heroes of Disney's story is Quasimodo, a physically deformed person who longs to be an accepted part of everyday city life. In his first appearance, he is shown vigorously ringing the bells, followed by a quick cut to the open tower. There Quasi, standing in the beautiful morning light, overlooking the city of Paris, tenderly encourages a bird to take its first flight. In a conversation with the gargoyles it becomes apparent that Quasi longs to go to the festival rather than be the passive observer. Yet he never expresses bitterness toward Frollo or questions why Frollo keeps him in the tower, forbidding him from ever leaving; Quasimodo's gentle spirit, trusting nature, good will, and loyalty are already established.

Quasi decides to take his friends' advice and disobey Frollo. Note that this device of using other characters to suggest the disobedience works well to help an audience rationalize what might be considered a character lapse (the act of disobeying). Quasimodo also demonstrates great self-control when he is treated poorly at the festival. With his strength he could have reacted violently, but he chose not to. In front of Frollo after his horrible experience at the festival, Quasi is contrite and humble. Following Esmeralda's kindness in treating him well and not as a monster, Quasi gratefully and willingly risks his life to help her to freedom. He again displays loyalty when Phoebus comes looking for her, for he is willing to fight to keep the guards away. Innocently and trustingly, he believes his gargoyle friends when they tell him that Esmeralda is his girl. When he discovers that she really loves Phoebus, he does not get angry but risks Frollo's wrath as he hides and cares for Phoebus—another selfless act.

Phoebus tries to make him feel guilty for not going to warn Esmeralda of Frollo's imminent arrival, but Quasi is torn, knowing he ought to obey Frollo. When obedience and loyalty conflict, Quasi chooses loyalty to a good character rather than obedience to a bad one. His commitment is tested again when Frollo binds him in chains to the tower to watch as Frollo burns Esmeralda at the stake. For once, his friends' encouragement (he still believes and trusts them) sends him in a helpful direction. He rescues Esmeralda, again risking his life, and discovers that Frollo has hidden the truth about his mother from him and that Frollo is about to kill him. Still, Quasi seeks no revenge; rather he picks up Esmeralda to carry her to safety, and in the final scene, he gives his blessing to the romance between Esmeralda and Phoebus by joining their hands together.

Quasimodo is too good to be true. He is described in the *Press Kit* as "symbolically viewed as being an angel in a devil's body trapped between the two worlds" of "heaven above, [and] the gritty streets of urban Paris viewed as Hell" (29). As such, Quasi demonstrates a virtuous character with consistent traits of trust, faithfulness, loyalty, humility, forgiveness, and self-sacrificing compassion. He is a person of integrity and worthy of being a role model for a virtuous individual.

Esmeralda

Producer Don Hahn says that Esmeralda "is all about freedom and life"; consequently, Disney chose Demi Moore as the vocal actress because she "is this life force of a person who brings that energy to the part" (Walt, "Producers" 1). Tony Fucile, supervising animator, highlights her "spontaneity," "goofy side," and "quirky sense of humor" (*Disney's Hunchback: Press Kit* 36). Tonkin describes Esmeralda as another Disney babe: "She perfects the cussed, can-do spirit of today's animated heroine. Lustrous Esmeralda has it all: ethnic minority status, A-plus for assertiveness, a flair for unarmed combat—and a pet goat, Djali" (40).

Esmeralda's first appearance in the film shows her to be full of that spirit. She is dancing for money, but when accosted by the guards, she proves an able fighter. Next she runs into Quasi at the festival and assumes that he is wearing a mask, indicating that his is the best example of ugliness she has seen yet. However, her initial disgust at the appearance of Quasi is overcome when she bravely wipes his face after he is pilloried and then stands up to Frollo to plead for justice for Quasi and for her people. Esmeralda demonstrates enthusiasm for life and bravery, concern for justice, and a willingness to stand up and fight in the face of injustice. Her concern for others is emphasized when she sings her prayer for the outcast of society. That scene is followed by a tender moment with Quasi in which she convinces him that he is talented for being able to carve all his figurines, that he is no monster, and that Gypsies are not evil.

In another demonstration of bravery and compassion, Esmeralda risks her life to save Phoebus from drowning in the river, and when her Gypsy companions want to execute Phoebus and Quasi in the Court of Miracles, she speaks up to save them. In the final scene, she again shows her compassion in that even though she has Phoebus, she does not forget about Quasi but draws him out of the church. Her warm acceptance encourages the crowd to accept him as well. Esmeralda is a spirited, brave, and compassionate woman.

Phoebus

Constructing a Disneyfied Phoebus required significant change from the original novel, in which he was a womanizer and was unwilling to take a stand when Esmeralda was punished unjustly. As screenwriter Tab Murphy reflects: "We decided to make Phoebus more heroic and central to the story" (*Disney's Hunchback: Press Kit* 7–8). Animating supervisor Russ Edmonds describes Phoebus as "a very human character and even though he takes his share of lumps throughout the film, he always makes a joke about it," and—whether or not this says much about his character or more about Walt Disney—Phoebus "is the first Disney hero to have facial hair" (*Disney's Hunchback: Press Kit* 36–37).

Phoebus first appears entering the city with his horse, Achilles. He is cavalier, observant, and not afraid of a fight. Even though he is a high-ranking member of the guard, he shows no loyalty to them in his first encounter; rather, he is immediately attracted to Esmeralda and aids her escape by having his horse sit on the guards. Next, he reports to Frollo and learns that he has been called to help root out the Gypsies from the city. He makes no objection. At the festival, however, he demonstrates compassion when he requests permission to free Quasimodo from the pillory, but when he is denied, he does nothing. Thus far, Phoebus is established as an individual who will follow what he chooses, yet is hesitant to directly disobey Frollo—an interesting counterpart to Quasi, who does disobey Frollo.

A short while later, Phoebus sees Esmeralda sneak into church and follows her there. When Frollo orders her arrested, Phoebus encourages her to claim sanctuary. Later, when he comes looking for Esmeralda again and encounters Quasi, he shows kindness to Quasi by complimenting him on what a good friend he is to Esmeralda. But his concern for Esmeralda is not something he quickly acts on. With Frollo, he begins the doleful process of hunting all Gypsies, arresting them, and destroying their property. Only when faced with the task of murder does he finally stand up to Frollo, and then he not only refuses but also risks his life to save the Gypsy family.

Phoebus's character is ambiguous and unsteady. He is willing to obey some of Frollo's evil orders, but only some. He seems able to think for himself and to act according to conscience, but his conscience is slow to work. When he does act, too often it neatly coincides with what is best for his self-interest. He goads Quasi into helping him find Esmeralda when he knows Quasi could get in big trouble and that Esmeralda loves only him. Finally, in the last scene, he chooses his allegiance. Freeing himself and other captured Gypsies from the cages, he urges: "Citizens of Paris! Frollo has persecuted our people, ransacked our city! Now he has declared war on Notre Dame herself! Will we allow it?" He leads the assault on the soldiers, catches Quasi when he falls from the tower, and ultimately receives Esmeralda's heart as his reward.

Phoebus is given the role of the romantic hero but demonstrates a vacillating character in which self-interest often rules over courage to stand up against the evil orders. That he does finally take a stand redeems him for hero potential, but he has shown that his character is not as virtuous as Quasimodo's.

Frollo

The opening song/narrative describes Frollo as one who "longed to purge the world of vice and sin. . . . And he saw corruption everywhere except within." Frollo's first appearance is in a dark scene where he ruthlessly hunts the Gypsies, causing Quasi's mother to die. He pronounces Quasimodo "a monster" who ought to be sent back to hell, all on the basis of one quick look. When ordered not to kill the baby, he finally acquiesces on the basis that "even this foul creature may yet prove one day to be of use to me." Thus, with this short introduction to Frollo, we understand he is a character full of vice—he is hypocritical, judges people based solely on looks, is willing to murder, and is a person who uses people.

The next time he appears is when he comes to visit Quasi before going to the festival. He reminds Quasimodo that he, Frollo, deserves thankful obedience from Quasi for saving his life after his "heartless mother abandoned" him and that Quasi is "deformed," "ugly," and a "monster." The very next time we see him, Frollo is having the former captain of the guard whipped and is encouraging the guard to make it painful. Meanwhile, he explains to Phoebus that the task is "to save the weak-minded from being so easily misled." When we see Frollo at the festival, he is once again in the role of cruel master. He forbids first Phoebus, then Esmeralda, from freeing Quasi in order that Quasimodo will learn a lesson about disobedience.

Frollo demonstrates his disrespect for the church a second time when he orders Esmeralda's arrest while she is inside the cathedral, breaching ancient laws of sanctuary. As he comes closer to threaten her, it becomes obvious that he is full of lust as he caresses her neck and smells her hair.

Frollo's supervising animator, Kathy Zielinski, describes the character as "mean, elegantly sinister and fascinating." He is a character "who is so complex and has such dimension . . . so cold and controlling that he doesn't have to move a lot" (*Disney's Hunchback: Press Kit* 36). That Frollo is capable of such hatefulness and at the same time is obsessed with desire for Esmeralda establishes the complexity. He sees himself as such a righteous man, yet he struggles with lust. Evil so consumes him that he is willing to murder innocent people, including the captain who had been loyal to him, to find Esmeralda.

Frollo eventually recognizes that Quasi must have helped Esmeralda escape and lays a trap for him. He captures the Gypsies, Quasi, Phoebus, and Esmeralda and prepares to burn her at the stake. His obsession with her knows no end, for even as he is about to set her on fire, he offers her freedom if she will choose him. Once Quasi rescues her and brings her to the tower, Frollo is relentless in his pursuit. His true motives toward Quasi are revealed as he is about to murder him.

Frollo is a character full of vice. He is a hypocrite, a racist, a murderer, cruel, lustful, sly, and manipulative. He is easy to dislike and difficult to identify with—the kind of villain that Disney needs to communicate that these characteristics truly are vices and should have no place in a moral society.

The Gargoyles—Victor, Hugo, and Laverne

Dave Pruiksma observes, "[The gargoyles] serve two very important roles in the film. One is comedic; the other is emotional. As emotional sounding boards for Quasi, they help to illustrate his inner thoughts" (*Press Kit* 37). Their first appearance in the film emphasizes the comedic, grade-school humor with lines like "Go scare a nun!" and "Pour the wine and cut the cheese" (while the gestures indicate what kind of cheese is to be cut). They quickly move into giving him the advice and encouragement to go to the festival, to disobey Frollo. If they are acting as Quasi's alter ego, they are establishing a desire to disobey—as long as one is not caught.

They also encourage Quasi to hope for love with Esmeralda, which again seems to be an unneeded cruelty. They tell him that "she'll be back," "she likes you," "we always said you were the cute one," "you're irresistible," and "she wants you." Finally, when Quasi has been chained to the tower, they give him useful advice: "You gotta break these chains," and ". . . we're only made of stone. We thought you were made of something stronger." As examples of vice and virtue, the gargoyles are not given much opportunity to develop their characters. Because they demonstrate their love for Quasi, their advice is received as misguided and not malicious. Their complete unconditional acceptance of Quasi is a virtue that enables their comedic presence to transcend the tragedy of the situation.

Clopin and the Gypsies

Described as "very flamboyant and physical" and "a nice bridge between realism and the cartoon world," with "proportions [that] are odd,"
Clopin acts as the story narrator and moralizer (*Disney's Hunchback: Press
Kit* 35). The first characters we meet in the story are Clopin as storyteller
and the Gypsies, who are trying to get safe passage into the city. Painted
as underdogs from the first, they are also established sympathetically as
family people, e.g., it is Quasi and his mother and father that Frollo ap-
prehends. But other than brief appearances, Clopin and the rest of the
Gypsies lack developed characters. In the novel, they were much more
central, but here Clopin is pictured as a clown and given the job of story
narrator—perhaps to counter the sinister elements that emerge when he
is ready to kill Quasi and Phoebus without even giving them a chance to
speak. Disney seems to be saying: Focus on the good qualities of this
Gypsy people; there is no reason to be prejudiced against them. Thus,
Clopin is a flat character who acts more as an object, a story device, than
as a person.

The Cathedral of Notre Dame

Disney invested much time and research into the actual cathedral in Paris
in order to translate its feel, lighting, and sound into the film. Disney observes that the cathedral would take on the role of a character in the film,
as it did in Hugo's novel. Codirector Kirk Wise comments about the character of the cathedral in the film:

> It reacts differently to whoever is in its proximity. It welcomes friends
> and punishes its enemies. It glares reproachfully at Frollo and wel-
> comes and nurtures Quasimodo. When Esmeralda enters the church,
> the light through the stained glass seems to envelop and encourage
> her. These various characterizations are reflected in the art direction
> through color and lighting. (*Disney's Hunchback: Press Kit* 33)

After visiting the site and listening to an organ concert, the directors
were also convinced of the need to include pipe organ music as part of
the film's soundtrack. The mysteries of the silences and sounds, the light
and the dark, and the cold and the warm presence of the cathedral communicate character, but the character is that of a building and not of God.

Another significant dimension of how the cathedral communicates is the bells; they act as the cathedral's voice. Quasi has personalized them with names. They help defeat the attack against the cathedral by contributing the hot, molten metal that had been prepared for their repair. But more important, they ring to tell the story of Quasimodo and Frollo and to make clear the moral of "who is the monster and who is the man." In the opening and closing narrative songs, Clopin sings about how the bells structure the day. The bells mark the rhythm of the city people's lives and remind them that "the eyes" of the cathedral are always on them. In so doing, the bells publicly argue for moral behavior, and the one who originates the sound, the bell ringer, is Quasimodo. Is Disney trying to associate Quasi with the moral authority of the church?

The idea that the cathedral—and more broadly, the church or religion—is characterized needs to be explored in terms of virtue and vice. Regarding religion in film generally, Margaret Miles observes that "the media often reduces it to flawed institutions, discredited myths, and morally flawed practitioners. But this understanding excludes too much; it precludes exploring the way religious loyalties function in human lives and communities" (13). Here in *Disney's The Hunchback of Notre Dame,* Disney has changed Frollo's title from Hugo's "archdeacon" to "Minister of Justice" in an attempt to head off any criticism from religious people (Thompson; *Disney's Hunchback: Press Kit* 30). But Disney kept the self-righteous language of Frollo, his references to religious concepts such as blasphemy and eternal damnation, and his piety as evidenced in his evening prayer, in which he struggles with his own demons. Even his last words sound scriptural: "And He shall smite the wicked and plunge them into the fiery pit!"[8] In almost all respects except the title, he is presented as a religious leader. The association of the church with this kind of evil leadership implies a church that is ineffective if not hypocritical and full of vice—the very thing Hugo was criticizing in the original novel.

Religion, represented by the cathedral, the archdeacon, and Frollo's piety appears as an impotent, irrelevant caricature. The darkness of the cathedral; the darkness of Frollo, who seems to be the mouthpiece of a twisted religion; the ineffectiveness of the church to combat the persecution of the Gypsies—all contribute to the feeling that religion offers little light or direction for people. Yes, ultimately the church's intervention prevents Quasi's death and later prevents Esmeralda's arrest. Yes, the light softens when Esmeralda is there, but the overall effect of the film is that the city is dominated by this hulking, dark presence that seems unable or unwilling to stand against the evil Frollo and fight for justice for marginalized people.

Significantly, when Esmeralda sings a beautiful prayer asking God to help the downtrodden, the outcast—her people—it is a prayer to an unknown (unknowable) God who may or may not exist. The song is reverent, and the setting so holy, but in the background various peasants are singing greedy requests for wealth, fame, and glory. The song represents God as a whimsical Santa Claus without the joy. The archdeacon, although dressed in white to conventionally signal that this person is on the good side, is overweight (a signal to the spectator that he has a serious character flaw of excess), rather weak-spirited, a bit of a bumbler, and ineffective in making much of a social impact. The church may provide sanctuary, but it certainly is not a proactive part of the everyday lives of people other than to mark the time with the bells and to be an architectural reminder of religion.

By relegating the church, and more specifically God, to irrelevancy, Disney refuses to admit a serious role for religion. Marx's view of religion as "the opium of the people" might well apply to Disney's attitude: it is OK if people want religion in their lives, but it should not impinge on the everydayness of living. In terms of virtue ethics, then, the church is neither virtuous nor completely full of vice.

CONCLUSION

Disney's The Hunchback of Notre Dame, the 34th animated Disney film, is based on the story originally told by Victor Hugo. His novel was a tragic critique of the injustice and spiritual decay of the city of Paris in the 15th century. Although Disney's story originated in the novel, the Disney version takes a decidedly different turn. Rather than being a tragedy, Disney's version has a happy ending. Rather than presenting an indictment of church leaders, Disney pushes the church to irrelevance. Rather than having Esmeralda hanged, Phoebus marrying for money, and Quasimodo pushing Frollo to his death and then tragically committing suicide in the tombs, wrapped around Esmeralda's body, Disney gives the story the upward transcendent twist of the comic frame. Frollo accidentally falls to his deserved death, Esmeralda and Phoebus find love with each other, and Quasimodo is heralded as the town hero (but doesn't get the girl).

By imposing this comic vision onto the tragically framed story, Disney created an uneasy dissonance. Perhaps this helps explain why the film was not the box office success of its predecessors. That Disney believed it could take a tragedy and transform it with a comic frame is instructive not only aesthetically but also morally. The task required the manipulation of originally tragic characters to fit the Disney genre, which involves the telling of a moral tale.

The construction of character means clearly identifying (in Disney style) the good and the bad characters and revealing their respective virtues or vices, a philosophy of moral living known as virtue ethics. In this film, those characters teach a number of lessons about good and evil. Quasimodo, Esmeralda, and Phoebus are held up as examples of virtues that include humility, obedience to authority, kindness, gentleness, compassion, trust, loyalty, slowness to anger, lack of a vengeful spirit, bravery or courage, and a willingness to be self-sacrificing. Frollo provides an example of vices that include hypocrisy, murder, anger, racism, cruelty, lust, manipulativeness, and a vengeful spirit.

The overt messages of the film are strong: "It is what's inside that matters," but the subtext does not always support this idea. It is that conflict between the overt and the subtle that makes for a confusing and morally ineffective film; the subtext obfuscates the main theme by making it more complex and, in some instances, working against it. For example, the message that Quasi has character where it counts—inside—is countered by the message that people are afraid of him and cheer when he is pilloried and subjected to cruel tauntings and being pelted with rotten vegetables. The film thus illustrates, right or wrong, that looks do matter—at least initially. The character of Phoebus is morally ambiguous; his reluctance to stand against Frollo immediately makes him less strong as a role model who fights injustice. The focus on Frollo's internal battle with lust is a message that at best children do not understand and at worst confuses them.

Although some of these points may seem minor, that they are present in the film and are at odds with its overt messages yields a film with less communicative power than a more consistently framed film would have. Disney's comic frame overlay on a tragic story requires definitive virtue and vice but falls short on communicating a consistent understanding of morality.

FIVE

Hercules

A CELEBRITY-HERO

What comes to mind when you hear the name Charlton Heston?—
Moses, the Ten Commandments, or possibly chariot races? A man of
strength and integrity? Charlton Heston is usually associated with some
of the great mythic roles he has played. That mythic association, Disney
hopes, will occur as Heston begins to tell the story of Disney's *Hercules*.
But Heston's onerous voice is interrupted by a hip Greek "gospel" chorus
of muses. They usurp the role of storyteller, advancing the plot and
providing transitions in the story line, all the while emphasizing that
their story is a more fun "Gospel truth" than Heston's. Discerning which
"truths" and moral lessons Disney teaches in this film through the use
of identification in particular narrative strategies is the task at hand. But
first we will look at what the story is about and what Disney intends to
teach.

FILM BACKGROUND

Plot Summary

We meet Hercules on Mount Olympus as the beloved son of Zeus and
Hera. A plot of Hades, god of the Underworld, to take over the world and
rule in place of its gods causes Hercules to lose his immortality (but not
his strength) and strands him on earth. Always the unaccepted outsider,

Hercules is informed by his earthly parents that he isn't really their son. The quest to find himself begins, and Hercules meets with Zeus in the temple. There he learns of his lineage and finds his mission: he must become a hero on earth in order to have his immortality restored.

Determined to "go the distance,"[1] Hercules (or Herc) enlists Philoctetes (Phil), a half-goat, half-man satyr, to be his trainer. On one of his first tests, Hercules must fight a huge centaur who is threatening a damsel in distress, Megara (Meg). Unknown to Herc, Meg is working for Hades. Earlier, she sold her soul to him in exchange for the life of her boyfriend, who then abandoned her. It becomes obvious that Herc and Meg are attracted to each other, but Phil moves Herc on to Thebes, the "Big Olive," in search of hero opportunities. Meanwhile, Hades, furious that Hercules is still alive to possibly ruin his plot, sets Meg and his sidekicks, Pain and Panic, to work, creating a situation for a hero. Hercules thinks he is rescuing two trapped boys (Pain and Panic metamorphosed) but in reality releases the dreaded Hydra. Ultimately, Hercules wins this battle (to Meg's relief and Hades' horror) and fights many more, turning him from "zero to hero," as the muses sing.

Now, as a celebrity-hero, he has his own merchandising mania, with products from sandals and cups to his own store and even a "Buns of Bronze" workout tape, but when Herc asks Zeus if now he can come home, Zeus says he's not yet a *true* hero. Disappointed, Herc returns to his celebrity duties, and Meg steps in to take him away from the business and have some fun. But Hades isn't finished yet. He realizes he needs to throw another "curve"—Meg—at Hercules and so reminds her of her obligations. Phil overhears the conversation and tries to convince Herc that Meg is no good, but he won't listen. Suddenly Hades appears before Herc, holding Meg hostage.

Herc agrees to give up his strength for 24 hours in exchange for Meg's freedom and safety. As Herc loses his strength, Hades reveals that Meg works for him. Hades proceeds to free the Titans and urges them to destroy Zeus, an action that begins an apocalyptic battle. Cyclops attacks Thebes and finds Herc, all too willing to sacrifice himself. Meg, desperately fearing for him, enlists Pegasus to go get Phil. When they return, a battered, weak Herc still manages to outsmart the Cyclops and send him into the sea. But just then, one of the columns falls over onto Meg. Herc can't move it, until suddenly his strength returns. Hades has broken his promise that Meg wouldn't get hurt. Meg, in a weak breath, urges Herc to save Mount Olympus.

After a successful battle, Herc returns to find that Meg has died. Furious, he follows her into the Underworld and again makes a deal with Hades that if he dives into the River of the Dead and rescues her, Hades can have Hercules instead. Herc, almost a skeleton, emerges from the vortex of souls but then turns radiant. He has become a god and has discovered, as his father says, that "a true hero isn't measured by the size of his strength but by the strength of his heart." Meg and Herc visit Olympus, where Herc is welcomed home, but instead he chooses to stay on earth with Meg.

The story has all the mythic elements of a hero on an adventure who feels compelled to take a journey of self-discovery and ultimately returns enlightened. It also has the requisite Disney romance, comedic sidekicks, animation in the hyperrealist style,[2] and upbeat music. Yet once again, critical response to the film is mixed.[3]

Although some critics enjoyed the film,[4] many negative reactions highlighted its departure from the original myth. For example, Lee Hall calls *Hercules* "a tease and a cheat: a tease because the title promises an opportunity to know one of the most popular legendary heroes of the ancient world; a cheat because this pastel version desecrates the substance and spirit of mythology itself" (11). Hall argues, "Mythology has always exposed to us our deepest secrets, most insistent passions, darkest fears and most splendid hopes. . . . *Hercules* insults us and violates the roots of our intellectual and spiritual heritage" (11).[5] Traditional mythology is valued by many who believe that it has lessons to teach.

Another criticism focuses specifically on the lessons taught. Rita Kempley notes, "Chock-full of celeb cameos, puns and contemporary camp, the movie is annoyingly hip. It wants to belong even more desperately than its title character." Charles Taylor bemoans *Hercules'* lack of real mythology and says that, unlike the Greek myths, "it doesn't give them any sense of wonder or daring or tragedy, even on a corrupted pop level." Instead, it's turned Hercules into "a little self-empowerment lesson" ("Myth-Conceived"). Matt Stamper, in criticizing Disney for stripping away the power of the myth of Hercules, argues, "The Disney version keeps a mixed-up version of the paganism—he is represented as an almost messianic son of a god—but the morality is softened into light entertainment" ("Film"). Messages about belonging and self-discovery are routine to Disney's formula, but they do alter original story lines. People going to see a Disney rendering of ancient myth are disappointed, but that doesn't mean that the Disney film doesn't teach, for it does.

Intentional Identification

Perhaps the best place to begin to ask what lessons *Hercules* teaches is with Disney itself. What did the company intend, or in Paul Wells's words, what was its "preferred" meaning (89)? According to Tom Schumacher, executive vice president of Walt Disney Feature Animation, *Hercules* is specifically designed to teach important lessons: "It's about the idea of strength, of who you are and what character is. It also deals with the notion of what celebrity is, what pop culture is, what it means to be popular" (*Disney's Hercules: Press Kit* 15). Teaching these ideas means getting the audience to identify with the characters: "At the same time, the emotional core is there too in Hercules' relationship with Meg and Phil, that will really get audiences involved with the characters" (15). One of the directors, John Musker, liked the concept of Hercules because "he was the common man's hero" (16).

This idea of creating identification between the characters and the audience is a powerful means of persuasion. Disney is very intentional in its attempts to get the audience to buy into its theme message, which is why it is so important to interrogate that message more closely. Critic Kenneth Burke observes, "there are . . . ways in which we *spontaneously, intuitively,* even *unconsciously* persuade ourselves. In forming ideas of our personal identity, we spontaneously identify ourselves with family, action, political or cultural cause, church, and so on" (*Language* 301).

In a postmodern world, competing visions of morality exist. Disney steps into the fray to advocate certain moral lessons and does so by creating characters who experience universal emotions and angst, characters with whom children will identify. And kids do identify with characters. For example, one study by Cynthia Hoffner of children and their "wishful identification" with television characters found that most children have same-sex characters as their favorites and that, for girls, characters that are funny and smart are predictors for parasocial interaction. For boys, characters that are not only smart but also strong and good-looking are predictors for identification (389–402).

Positive and negative identifications are both at work in the film. On the positive side, the explicit messages are generally accepted as good moral lessons. The need for having a caring, giving character or heart is stressed. On the negative side, children may be identifying with the implicit messages, which are often the areas of critical disagreement.

Jürgen Habermas distinguishes between concepts of the good life, or what he calls "evaluative questions," and the more rational principles of justice, which he terms "moral questions" ("Discourse" 300). Although ultimately morality must be concerned with justice, he observes, "within the horizon of the lifeworld, practical judgments derive both their concreteness and their power to motivate action from their inner connection to unquestioningly accepted ideas of the good life, in short, from their connection to ethical life and its institutions" (300). This connection between values and morals in the narrative strategies is what I will explore in Disney's *Hercules* by noting how Disney creates identification through the characters' actions, the visual imagery, the music, and the use of symbolism and how Disney's version of myth supports the social order that teaches life's lessons.

IDENTIFICATION THROUGH NARRATIVE STRATEGIES

The rhetorical tool of identification seeks to build common ground between the story—both plot and characters—and the audience. Disney expects children to look for characters they can identify with and hopes to imbue those characters with enough good traits to equip the children with similar positive tendencies. Communicating dimensions of right and wrong to an audience is a function of rhetoric. As Burke asserts, "there is nothing . . . *essentially* outside the traditional concerns of rhetoric" (*Rhetoric* 64). In film, this rhetoric occurs in visual, musical, and language form. When these forms are combined, the force of this rhetoric can be very powerful and is accomplished in great part through identification.[6] To discover how identification is at work, we will look at some of the ways the story is told, or what Wells calls the "narrative strategies" (68 ff.). One strategy is in how the animators develop characters through their actions. Asking what the main characters need to do or want in the story is what Wells calls the "super-objective," or the goal toward which the central characters are working (106).

Characters' Actions

The super-objective for Hercules is to become a hero in order to rejoin the gods. His motivation is that he doesn't want to feel so alone; he wants to belong. That taps into a universal need, one that the audience can identify with and be sympathetic to. Hercules' quest to become a hero, to find his "true self," is a longing innate in humans. The growing-up process is a process of discovering who one is or wants to be. But it soon becomes evident that Hercules has a secondary objective, almost as important as becoming a hero—that of attaining and keeping Meg's love. Initially he is motivated by the first goal, a self-serving one. Later, romance motivates him—also a self-serving objective.

Joseph Campbell describes the goal of the mythic hero in a different way from Disney's: "'The ultimate aim of the quest must be neither release nor ecstasy for oneself, but the wisdom and the power to serve others.' One of the many distinctions between the celebrity and the hero, Campbell said, is that one lives only for self while the other acts to redeem society" (Flowers xv). Hercules may do heroic acts, saving Thebes and ultimately saving Meg, but he acts out of self-interest and not altruistically. In the first instance, he is trying to prove his heroism so that he might be able to return to the gods, and in the second case, he is motivated by romantic love that fulfills his own needs. Hercules feels the obligations of his heroism even when marching to what looks like certain death to fight the Titans with his mortal strength. Yet that self-sacrificial attitude was initiated by his self-destructive wish; he was despondent over his discovery of Meg's treachery and no longer cared about his life. What is missing from Disney's understanding of the hero is what Campbell mentions—motivation that reveals that the hero is acting for others first, rather than acting for self first.

The female lead, Megara, is given no super-objective. We first meet her as a tough, sexy, seemingly self-sufficient woman battling a monster. Hades, however, soon appears and reveals that she works for him. Her actions through most of the story are motivated by her obligations to Hades. She does what she is told even when her words suggest that she wants to see Hercules win. When she is finally given her freedom, her one exercise of will is to sacrifice herself to save Hercules. When he asks why, her response is, "I guess people do crazy things when they're in love." As a role model for identification, Meg offers little to inspire self-actualization other than romantic love. It motivated her initially to sell her soul to Hades and then to save Hercules' life. Yes, this romantic love prompted her to be selfless, which is a terrific lesson, but it also was her only reason for action. There is no need for self-discovery or service to others for this female. She lives to get and serve her man.

If taken as examples of right living, both Herc and Meg overtly demonstrate a positive lesson of self-sacrifice. Loving each other is risky, but they accept the risk. Yet, when we look more closely, we see that self-sacrifice evident only when there's "something in it for me."[7] That "something" is romantic love that emanates from an understanding of reality that sees romance as the driving force of life. Without the romantic element, life's journey lacks meaning and fulfillment. Putting the heart first in everything creates a one-dimensional understanding of life. As a motivation for right behavior, it tends toward emotivism, which finds the meaning in morality to be an expression of attitude or emotion designed to influence feelings.[8] Superficiality in morality is the result.

Herc's main sidekick, Philoctetes, or Phil, is a character who is "rough around the edges." Shown as a lecherous Peeping Tom when Herc first encounters him, it quickly becomes obvious that he has been a failure who is putting on a good front. Chasing the nymphs but not catching them, he says, "Nymphs. They just can't keep their hands off me." He says it in a way that suggests he is putting up a good front in the face of failure. He reveals his dream—of training a hero who is so good that his stars are placed in the sky. Then people will look up and say, "That's Phil's boy!" Disney rewards his dream of personal success in the end of the film with just such a scenario. That wanting recognition is an acceptable goal or value in life is the message Disney reinforces.

Imagery

Not only does identification take place in the characters' actions, but it is also encouraged in the renderings of the images themselves. Burke reminds us that "*images* can have the force of attitudes" (*Grammar* 243). The style of animation, the colors, and the resulting images all reflect carefully crafted choices.

Even though the animators created mythical creatures of fancy and imagination in addition to people, *Hercules* is true to the Disney style of hyperrealism. The plot is logical, the characters' actions are motivated, and the humans' movement is somewhat realistic (Wells 23, 35). The tie-ins to reality yield better entrée for identification. What messages, then, do the images of the lead characters send? What are those images' relation to and departure from reality?

Part of the process of Disney's animation involves choosing a color palette. The colors are designed to reflect both the logical and the emotional content of the scenes and to act as a storyteller themselves. The colors suggest the attitudes of the characters and provide subtext to the words through general association or broadly understood stereotypes—e.g., black is bad and white is good. This coding is a common technique in animation. The artistic director of *Hercules*, Tom Cardone, affirms this role of color: "This film is quite varied in terms of environment and emotion and we tried to discover ways of showing that through the color"

(*Disney's Hercules: Press Kit* 23). For example, Mount Olympus was painted in blues, pinks, and lavender, colors that are often associated with the ethereal, whereas Thebes was drab like its nickname, the "Big Olive." Hades is dark, with grays and blacks, and the scene where Herc and Meg almost kiss is in deep blues and purples that suggest a romantic evening. The color coding acts as a kind of filmic shorthand for the animators. At the same time, it reinforces the stereotype of black as evil, the myth of the romantic setting, and so on.

While backgrounds and colors contribute to the overall message, the more obvious messages come through the central characters with whom Disney wants its audience to identify. The images of Hercules that best create sympathy are those of when he is a teenager and older. As a teen-ager, Hercules is a gangly, awkward kid with big feet and hands. He is not movie-star beautiful, but he is struggling to be accepted. Kids iden-tify with this stage, and it provides the hook that grabs their sympa-thies. Soon, however, Hercules has grown into a gorgeous, muscular, "Hunkules," as the muses sing, with a winning smile and expressive eyes. Becoming, in Burke's words, "consubstantial with" Hercules early in the film may help the audience better learn the overt message of the nature of a true hero, but another message is also sent (*Rhetoric* 20–22). Heroes are good-looking, muscular young men with smiles that will make the girls crazy. Looks matter is the subtext. Burke speaks of "spontaneous" identification with "implicit or concealed" messages (Burke, *Language* 301). The audience may or may not be aware of those messages, for identification is something an audience can do unconsciously as well as consciously.

That looks matter is also the message that Meg and the muses send even more overtly. Outward beauty is vital to the story line. Meg first captures Hercules' interest with her physical appearance. Phil refers to her as "sweet cheeks." Hercules is stunned by her. As she leaves Herc, she sways her hips suggestively. Her figure is an unrealistically thin hour-glass, with cleavage showing. Meg resembles a vamp who knows that she is attractive and uses it. Now, Disney may have intended to set this up so that Hercules is the character to identify with,[9] but the girls in the audi-ence will learn from Meg too. They will observe what the hero of the film is attracted by and how the female lead uses her sexuality to attract him.

When an audience watches a film, they participate in the transcen-dent experience of identifying with someone outside themselves. Identi-fication "invites participation" (*Rhetoric* 58). For Burke, the repetition can function rhetorically: "We must think of rhetoric not in terms of some one particular address, but as a general *body of identifications* that owe their convincingness much more to trivial repetition and dull daily reinforcement than to exceptional rhetorical skill" (*Rhetoric* 26). Disney repeatedly sends the message that outward appearance is what is attractive to the opposite sex. And because the driving motivation of this film is to get the girl or guy, the significance of that message is heightened.

For a children's film, Disney places too much of an emphasis on sexuality. The muses are another example of using sex to sell. As storytellers, the muses make it clear from the beginning that they are attracted to Hercules as a good-looking man first of all and not as a good person first. The priority is physical appearance. That priority is true for the muses as well. They are all dressed in slinky, tight-fitting dresses with slits high up the thighs. Every step they take on their tiny feet reveals an entire leg. Their movements suggest that appearing to be "sexy" is what counts, even in their minor roles. Four of the five have extremely small waists and are well endowed, two with cleavage showing. One of the muses is overweight, but she is stereotyped as "fat and happy," the comic figure. The message she sends is that she is still sexy (look at her clothes and movements), *and* she likes to have fun. The moral message sent? Even though they are the musicians, and a "Gospel" choir at that, their manner of movement and dress portrays them as sexual beings first and foremost. This use of sex in a children's film is disturbing.

Another set of images needs mention—the not-so-subtle self-parody on Disney merchandising. At first glance it may seem to show what a good sport Disney is, able to laugh at itself. Even Phil sings that Herc needs a "good merchandiser" before he has agreed to train him. The images of McDonald's Happy Meal drinks, air-Herc sandals, action figures, and the "Hercules (read Disney) Store" are more of an advertisement than a parody, their own product placement. It guarantees that children will get the message to consume. As soon as parents leave the movie, they will be bombarded with more messages about these products, and what began as parody becomes simply a preview of Disney reality. Profit making through commercialization is still Disney's foremost value, and this film's images reinforce that.

Music

Not only are the characters' actions and images carriers of Disney pedagogy but also the music. Disney animated films rely heavily on music as background, transition, emotive vehicle, and carrier of theme. The lyrics in particular are an important carrier of rhetoric, but I do acknowledge that there are also rhetorical dimensions of music itself.[10]

Mark Booth focuses on lyrics in his study "The Art of Words in Song." He acknowledges that "lyrics are of course subject to the pressure of their accompaniment all the time," but he also believes that the lyrics represent "an art of words for music, of language that expects to live with music" (242). He compares songs to oral poetry in that they often contain formulas or the redundancies that draw from audience identification: "The experience of a new song must be the imagining anew of some simplification of life that is more or less in our possession already" (246). Disney's use of songs is an important vehicle for communicating its films' themes. By interweaving the theme or themes with some of the audience's experiences or existing beliefs, the message is embedded at a deeper level. Booth notes, "Our songs embody always snippets of the myths we hold. . . . By myth here is meant myth as giver of identity, as template for self" (248). The potential for Disney to influence or shape moral identity not only through the narrative but also through the songs is tremendous.

The film pays homage to the seven Greek muses by including them as a five-woman gospel choir that sings "The Gospel Truth." Gospel music is high-energy and full of contagious enthusiasm. However, gospel music also refers to the Gospels, or the "good news" of the first four books of the Bible's New Testament. What Disney does with the Gospel content not only cheapens gospel music to nothing more than style but also extirpates it from its religious roots. What remains are empty allusions to "Gospel truth" that in reality have no connection to the New Testament Gospels. That's the power, however, of identification. The music taps into something that has associations or connotations with the religious. The audience then can make the connections consciously or unconsciously between Hercules' storytellers and religious music without having any of the negative religious baggage that the words might suggest, but allowing for the positive associations that the spiritual might have.

Some songs refer to the theme of popularity and heroism. The executive vice president of Walt Disney Feature Animation, Tom Schumacher, says this film "deals with the notion of what celebrity is, what pop culture is, what it means to be popular" (*Press Kit* 15). Popularity, or belonging and acceptance, is an exigent issue for all people but particularly for the young. The muses summarize the background to the plot and provide transitions in their three renditions of "The Gospel Truth," but they don't address popularity at this point. But when Hercules sings "Go the Distance," he expresses his longing for cheering crowds to give him a "hero's welcome." Phil's song, "One Last Hope" begins to set Hercules straight on what it means to be a hero. Phil tells him: "It's a work of heart. . . . [It] comes down to what's in you." But Phil also sends another message when he tells Herc that he needs a "good merchandiser."

This is the problem. Disney keeps waffling on the message it sends. Disney says that it wants to teach the lesson that a true hero is defined by the strength of his heart, but it also wants to teach the audience to value materialism: more stuff is good. After all, Disney needs to sell more to keep its profit margin acceptable for its stockholders. So the big production song "Zero to Hero" expresses the superficial values of the importance of being popular on the "opinion polls," having good looks ("the girls went wild" and "folks lined up just to watch him flex," and "a major hunk"), and being rich and famous with "cash to burn." Incidentally, he's a nice guy too. In other words, Hercules wasn't worth anything until he became popular, admired, and rich; "he was a no one, a zero." The images reinforce the words that define what this heroism means. A few scenes of Hercules fighting monsters are interspersed with pictures of autograph seekers, money raining down on Herc, Herc putting his handprints on the sidewalk, a Grecian Express card with his name on it, a statue and plays in his honor, his merchandise, and a wall mosaic of him.

The plot seeks to compensate for this negative definition of heroism by having Zeus refuse to accept it. But the music is so much fun and so high-energy that it makes it attractive in contrast to Zeus, who is presented as an abstract bag of wind. Which message will kids be attracted to? What part of the video are they likely to replay? The fun music. Just as in *The Lion King*'s "Hakuna Matata," it's easy to decontextualize "Zero to Hero" and let it stand on its own apart from the plot that contradicts the song's message. The alternative value of having a strong, giving heart, the supposed moral of this story, is sentimental mush when Disney places it in the context of romance. Meg's only song, "I Won't Say (I'm in Love)," reinforces the message that Herc's heroism is attractive. She has fallen in love with him. And what attracted her but his looks, his muscles, his success, and his kindness? One wonders if he stood a chance by just being kind.

The final song, "A Star Is Born," reminds the audience that they too can be heroes if they look to their own hearts; they too can be crowd pleasers. Again, the mixed understanding of heroism is evident. This sounds more like the description of a celebrity who is seeking the limelight and not the hero who may have to stand alone.

Symbolism

Not only does identification work through the narrative strategies of actions, images, and music, but it is at work through elements of symbolism. The narrative becomes more complex when studied from this perspective. Symbols may be consciously employed or they may be unintentionally used, thus bearing, in Wells's words, "meaning over and beyond the artist's overt intention." Wells explains, "In other words, an animated film may be interpreted through its symbolism, whether the symbols have been used deliberately to facilitate meaning or not" (83). It is at this level that one can argue for multiple meanings in a text, what Wells calls the "attendant" meanings, or the implicit messages that are at work symbolically.

By drawing from Greek mythology, Disney also draws on the symbolism of that mythology, allowing the film to set forth possible alternative or additional messages. Superficially, Disney's *Hercules* is a carefully researched, meticulously planned hodgepodge of Greek myths sanitized according to Disney's formula in order to achieve its preferred message of youth self-discovery and romantic achievement. To accomplish that, the directors had no problem departing from the original legend. Codirector John Musker said, "'We, Ron Clements and I, knew we would probably only make one Greek movie. We borrowed elements and made it sort of a stew of mythology'" (Tucker 38). Despite the mix, myth is still a significant part of this film. And mythological stories work in part symbolically, making sense of the world and humanity's place in it.

Hercules draws on these myths. but its "stew" mixes names and stories. For example, the mythic Hera, wife of Zeus, was no loving mother. She sent snakes into the cradle of Hercules (sometimes called Heracles) to kill him ("Heracles"). The mythic Hera was angry at her husband for his adulterous ways; Heracles was the result of the union of Zeus and a mortal married woman, Alcmene. However, in Disney's *Hercules,* Alcmene and her husband, Amphitryon, find Hercules and adopt him. This Disney version cleans up the mythological version, in which Zeus has an affair with Alcmene while Amphitryon is away. Other examples of changes Disney made in its version of the myths are in Hercules' love interest and in his exploits. The mythological Hercules does marry

Megara but eventually kills her in a mad fit (Hamilton 162). The original myth had Hercules doing penance for the act in his 12 labors, which included fights with various monsters, quests, and stories in which Hercules supplants local heroes (Pinsent 93–101).

That Disney was willing to change the myths of Hercules raises the question of why it chose what to include and what to exclude. Certainly, fitting the Disney formula was a serious part of its rationale. What happens, however, is that the new version sanitized or erased many of the moral lessons that those myths did teach. Joseph Campbell argues, "Myths tell us how to confront and bear and interpret suffering, but they do not say that in life there can or should be no suffering" (Flowers 160). But that's exactly what *Hercules* implies. Disney creates a picture of life with minimal suffering and with tragedies that are always remedied by the end of the film. Because its goals for its films are to get children to identify with the characters (in order to want more—more films and more material goods to remind them of their identification), we need to be concerned about children getting the message that suffering is not a part of life.

Perri Klass, a pediatrician, is disturbed by those people who would sanitize life: "If children's entertainment is purged of the powerful, we risk homogenization, predictability and boredom, and we deprive children of any real understanding of the cathartic and emotional potentials of narrative" (1). She believes that literature enables children to learn powerful lessons, which may be dramatic but are not harmful.

Yes, it could be argued that the murder of Hercules' wife and children probably wouldn't make a good children's film, so Disney takes creative license and changes the story. But that's what Disney does. In order to continually release new films, it needs creative content, and its content must follow the Disney formula for success, which means shaping the story as it sees fit.

Campbell suggests that myths serve at least four functions for society, including the mystical that highlights the mystery of life, the cosmological that explains the nature of the universe, the sociological that gives support for the social order, and the pedagogical that teaches humans how to live (Flowers 31). We see in Disney's version a new myth created that reveals a Disney perspective on our social order and serves as a teacher, particularly to the young.

Because of its pedagogical power, we look not only at the preferred message, in this case the story that incorporates Greek myths, but also at the attendant messages. Those attendant messages can be deduced metaphorically. Using this lens, we see other possible readings of the text, including allusions to biblical stories.

The story of Samson has several parallels to that of Disney's *Hercules* (1 Samuel 13–16). Samson was sent by God to be a part of a "normal" family but was endowed with extraordinary strength. He performed mighty acts of bravery that set him apart from his people. He fell in love with Delilah, a woman who sold her soul so to speak to the Philistines. She was willing to betray Samson. The result was that Samson lost his strength and was captured. Samson pleaded with God for one last measure of strength and in a final effort managed to bring the house of his enemies down, killing three thousand people and himself. Although Hercules didn't end this way, he was betrayed by a woman, lost his strength, and managed to make a last effort that enabled him to defeat the Cyclops and ultimately send Hades back to the Underworld.

Other biblical symbolism could be construed from the *Hercules* narrative as well. Hercules could be seen as a symbolic savior. Just as Christ, who was both human and divine, could be the only one to save the world (Romans 8:3–4), Hercules, a god-man appears to be the only hope for the people in this story—the only one who stands between the world and Hades' domination of it. The allusion continues when Hercules (like Christ) must descend to the Underworld to rescue Meg. But this is where the parallels end. Hercules' goal is to save his love, whereas Christ's goal was to save the world by conquering death. Once again we see how Disney's use of potentially symbolic stories strips them of their meaning and organizing power by turning the story into a romance-driven plot.

The similarities to biblical stories do deepen the potential for unconscious identification for those audience members familiar with the Bible. Linking the religious to the Disney narrative renders meaning that has potential persuasive power or rhetorical identification. But instead of teaching the lessons of life embedded in the original stories, Disney teaches a sanitized world composed of people seeking their own satisfaction in romantic love.

Other uses of symbolism in the film work to link the narrative to contemporary society. The character Hermes, voiced by Paul Shaffer, is also drawn to resemble him—sunglasses and all. Shaffer, sidekick and band leader on David Letterman's television show, exists in a way to herald Letterman. Letterman's work on late-night television has made him a cultural icon. By representing the mythic Hermes, creator of the lyre, fertility god, and herald of Zeus ("Hermes"), as someone associated with today's entertainment culture, the story takes on a satirical edge with potential for critique.

Seeing animated film as a site for cultural criticism suggests that the film constructs cultural values; yet the flip side is true too. The film reflects and begins to critique cultural values—when it serves the overall corporate strategy. A good example of this is the stereotyped city of Thebes, metaphorically referred to as the "Big Olive." It's portrayed as a dangerous place, full of creeps, crazies, and crime. One man steps up, opens his cape, and says: "Do ya wanna buy a sundial?" Another dressed only in a barrel pronounces, "The end is coming." Phil warns Herc not to make eye contact with anyone. This "Big Olive" is a bleak place without a hero, but Herc is here to rescue it. What picture does that leave of today's "Big Apple," New York City? Is Disney suggesting that it needs a hero?[11]

Hercules' references to the entertainment culture are both metaphorical and overt. Meg is the knowing "dame" of film noir. That reference incorporates, then, a forewarning that this woman could be dangerous and knows more than it may first appear. Obviously, few children would understand the symbolism, but Disney aims a subtext of its film at adults as well. By including allusions and humor that only adults would understand, Disney provides a certain level of pleasure that encourages adults to see the film with their kids.

Many references to the culture of celebrity are overt, as was mentioned above, but there are also symbolic references. When Hades is consulting the Fates, he is playing chess with *Hercules'* "action figures." Pain and Panic show up wearing "air-Herc" sandals and drinking out of a Hercules cup—the kind that came with McDonald's Happy Meals. Associating the film's promotional merchandising with the plot itself is blatant self-promotion that seeks to draw on symbolic power. Disney's preferred message is that a true hero is not necessarily someone who is a celebrity but someone who follows his heart. What a missed opportunity for critique substituted with a vacuous bit of sentimentality!

CONCLUSION

We need critiques of celebrity culture, but Disney's *Hercules* offers no alternative values to replace celebrity critique except sentimentality and stereotypes of men as strong and violent and women as thin, beautiful, and sexy. By looking at how the process of identification is at work through the characters' actions, the visual images, the music, and the symbolism, we've identified a conflicted moral agenda. *Hercules* sends double messages rooted in a mixture of ancient myth and contemporary cultural values. Those messages ultimately support the cult of celebrity-ism and self-serving promotions.

Because Disney seeks to establish identification between the characters and the audience, it is imperative that the audience recognize the values being taught as both positive and negative. This knowledge can empower parents to decode the film with their children in such a way that they can still find pleasure in the entertainment but have the ability to counter or reinforce the values as they see fit, becoming their own Charlton Heston–like narrator of their cultural lives.

SIX

Mulan

EAST MEETS WEST

Smashing stereotypes and crossing cultures, *Mulan* breaks out of the Disney mold for recent animated films. Abandoning most of the formula for the romantic animated musical, Disney uses a well-known legend in China, the story of Mulan, which originates about 1,500 years ago as a poem (Seno). The focus of this story is not girl (or boy) needs a boy (or girl) to find true happiness. Although Disney manages to include the romance in the end, the focus is on a story about a loving daughter and loyal subject who is willing to sacrifice herself for her father and for her country. One unique dimension of this film is that the female heroine is a self-empowered agent for change rather than a romantically motivated character.

However, in telling this Chinese legend, Disney has created a version that is a "chop-suey" mix of Eastern and Western cultures (Seno), sending mixed messages about what constitutes right and wrong behavior.[1] That does not negate the universality of some values, as Richard Corliss notes. He believes this to be a powerful film that digs into deeper values than the usual Disney fare: "family love and duty, personal honor and group commitment, obedience and ingenuity" ("Ode").

Nevertheless, it is the anachronisms of the mix between Eastern and Western, traditional and contemporary, male and female, along with fast-talking Eddie Murphy as sidekick, miniature dragon Mushu, and a good-luck cricket who doesn't speak at all, that allows Disney to claim this story as its own. Disney puts its stamp of ownership on this Chinese legend by juxtaposing these elements, allowing them to create both irony and humor, but at the same time confusing Eastern perspectives (both ancient and contemporary) on group behavior, communication, and values with Western perspectives. *Mulan* is filled with contrasts that build toward the climax of unearthing an authentic self. By examining these contrasts, we are able to discern the tension in the values espoused.

FILM BACKGROUND

In general, *Mulan* was very well received domestically. It took in well over $120 million at the box office domestically and $182 million internationally (Internet Movie Database). Critics praised *Mulan,* referring to it as "gorgeous-looking" (Keogh), "unassuming" (Murray), and "subtle" (Shreve). Roger Ebert observes that "the outcome manages somehow to be true simultaneously to feminist dogma and romantic convention" (27). Balancing that tension enables Disney to build support for the film.

The Disney Company itself praised the film for its responsible appeal to universal needs. Peter Schneider, president of Walt Disney Feature Animation, explains that what the company liked about Mulan was that it was a story "about a young lady coming of age; of trying to find herself." He continues, "I think a lot of our exploration as human beings is finding who we are and where we belong. And what we can do for ourselves and for our country" (*Mulan Press Kit* 14). Similarly, codirector Tony Bancroft observes, "What I like about Mulan is not that she changes herself but it's really that she changes society and their way of seeing her. That's what allows her to be accepted in the end. She ends up being accepted for who she is which is a pretty universal want for a lot of different people" (*Mulan Press Kit* 15). Finding one's self is a central theme of many Disney animated films.

Nevertheless, as is almost always the case, some critics expressed disappointment with *Mulan.* Janet Maslin of the *New York Times* called *Mulan* "inert and formulaic" and full of Disney stereotypes. She also criticized its lack of detail in the animation, its cross-dressing, and its violence (*"Mulan"*). Reviewer Jill McGreal speaks more directly to the issue of values: "We are saturated by a web of manipulative storytelling as the Disney machine steamrollers over local customs and cultures, imposing internationally translatable values (so effective at the box office)." Furthermore, she argues, "the opportunity for children to learn about cultural difference and history is rejected in favour of low-level, unchallenging entertainment" (48). The remarks seem contradictory. If the focus is on values that cut across cultures, why should Disney abandon that in favor of showing values of only one culture? But the question demonstrates the uneasy juxtaposition of contrasts in this film.

Jennifer Gin Lee echoes the love-hate tension toward *Mulan*. She is torn between loving Mulan for breaking stereotypes and hating it for infusing "Western idioms, personalities, and values," asserting that "Disney has shaped Mulan into an American, an Asian-American but an American no less." She laments, "Disney has taken away something uniquely Chinese and reinvented her in American form" ("*Mulan*"). That, however, was not the intention of Disney. Producer Pam Coates says, "We felt an obligation to correctly portray the images and the customs that we observed [in China]" (*Mulan Press Kit* 14). Nevertheless, tension arises when Disney infuses the production with dimensions of the Western culture that it is a part of, even as it attempts to be faithful to the Eastern story.

In the preceding chapters, I've looked at how Disney teaches morality in its films by using a number of different lenses, including myth, archetype, and ritual; symbolic boundaries of good and evil; the comic framing of tragedy, which necessitates emphasis on virtue and vice; and the narrative strategies used to teach morals, such as character action, visual imagery, and music.

Mulan morality could be examined fruitfully from a number of these concepts, but the moral lessons are molded within the framework of two cultures. To better understand how *Mulan* is a film constructed of contrasts and how it stands at the crossroads of different cultures, I'll examine some of the distinctions of Eastern and Western cultures, distinctions that, when blended in one film, create contrasts. These contrasts in turn shape some of the moral lessons taught in this film.

INTERCULTURALISM

Because *Mulan* is a film produced in the United States but is based on a Chinese legend, the potential for misunderstanding and misrepresentation is great, especially since Disney's attempts to reach the largest audience possible, including the international audience, mean that it tries to include something for everyone. Consequently, Disney needed to clearly establish the Chinese cultural values in order to respect the original material, but it also needed to communicate contemporary Western values in order that a Western audience would accept the film.[2] Significant dimensions of interculturalism that Disney ought to have considered include the Chinese collectivist mind-set, the high communication context style, and cultural values.

Individualism-Collectivism

One of the most common cultural distinctions made between the East and the West is that of the poles of individualism and collectivism. The Western cultures are said to be driven by a sense of individualism, whereas Eastern cultures are oriented toward a collective view of life. According to Geert Hofstede, "Because they are tied to value systems shared by the majority, issues of collectivism versus individualism carry strong moral overtones. Americans see their own culture as very individualistic" (150). That contrasts to the traditional Chinese, in whom "a very different moral stance is found" (151).[3] That the film *Mulan* is a story about a Chinese legendary heroine but is made by an American company raises questions of how the individualism-collectivism (I-C) values intersect.

Even as we look at these generalizations, it is important to remember that these are generalizations. As Russian language theorist M. Bakhtin notes, at any given time within a culture there are both "centripetal" and "centrifugal" forces at work—forces that unify and forces that work against homogenization (270–275). Although an I-C construct can open up understanding, it is only a rough guide. Similarly, William Gudykunst et al. commented on both the reality of the I-C distinction and the possibility for individual agency to contradict the generalization. Nevertheless, a generalization is helpful to get an overall orientation toward individualism and collectivism (see Table 6.1).

Individualist cultures are characterized by an emphasis on concern for the self before the group, on independence, and on individuality. In contrast, collectivist cultures put the group's welfare before the individual's, are more interdependent, and are concerned about others' perceptions. This means the collectivist culture avoids any behavior that would hurt others or cause embarrassment resulting in "losing face" (Hofstede 149–152). Quoting Ho, Hofstede defines "losing face" as "when the individual, either through his action or that of people closely related to him, fails to meet essential requirements placed upon him by virtue of the social position he occupies" (151). The individualism-collectivism orientation will surely then affect the characters' attitudes and behaviors in *Mulan*.

In the film, Mulan herself demonstrates an ongoing tension between collectivist and individualist values. The initial story conflict is created

TABLE 6.1. Individualism-Collectivism

Individualism	Collectivism
Self-concerned	Group-concerned
Independent	Interdependent
Motivated by individuality	Motivated by "saving face"

because she wishes to bring honor to her family, but she is such an individual that her efforts fail. She dishonors her mother and shows a callous disregard for her mother's desires to help her, by being late to the beauty preparations for the appearance before the matchmaker. When at last she is ready, she again is late to join the other girls. She loses face before the onlookers and other candidates when she speaks out of turn. The scene with the matchmaker (which is more Japanese than Chinese) demonstrates that Western values dominate Mulan. She is very much an independent-minded individual who finds it difficult to conform to the group. She acts on her own initiative to write a cheat sheet on her arm and fails the test to pour tea gracefully, act demurely, and not speak. Mulan is her own person—an individual who stands out from the usual candidates to be matched and doesn't seem to "lose face" when she fails.

Although her motives for going to war in her father's place initially seem pure and selfless, she later confesses that perhaps she did it more for herself than her father; she wanted to prove she could do something right. The emphasis on individual achievement over interdependence and putting the group first, before the self, is apparent. At the army camp, it's obvious that she longs to fit in, but the message comes through that she never will. The irony is that of course this is true—she is a woman. Nevertheless, the reality is that she doesn't fit in because she chooses to follow her own desires first and not that of the collective. Her lack of strength and inadequate skills show that she is not a helpful addition to the group; rather, she may actually endanger them.

Once again, rather than losing face for her weakness, she persists through the difficult training. The result is acceptance by the other recruits and grudging respect from Captain Shang. The message sent by the narrative is one of believing in one's self. We are impressed with her perseverance in the face of difficulty and with her lack of losing face despite failing to carry her load. She is one who believes in herself. That's a message that corresponds to Western emphases on self-help and self-esteem, but it contrasts to an Eastern mind-set of being other-focused and concerned about not losing face.

Vertical and Horizontal Collectivism

Much has been written about the collectivist-individualist continuum as a way of distinguishing between Eastern and Western cultures.[4] Within the Chinese culture, however, there are differing ways of understanding the collectivist values. Xing Lu cites the distinction between "vertical collectivism" and "horizontal collectivism" as an example.

> The vertical model defines the relationship between individual and group . . . [as] characterized by superior-subordinate relationship, individual dependency on the group, and individual's willingness to sacrifice self to the group. The horizontal collectivism is defined as a self-peer . . . relationship characterized by accommodation and interdependency for the sake of group affiliation and solidarity. (92)

In either distinction, however, concern for the group and others is central to one's orientation.

Social relations for the characters in *Mulan* display both of these dimensions, particularly when the army is under duress. Mulan is part of the vertical hierarchy in that she (as Ping) was subordinate to Shang, was willing to sacrifice herself to the Huns in order to shoot the rocket, and ultimately depended on the group to save Shang, the horse, and herself from certain death. At the same time, she accommodated to the group in trying to join the song "A Girl Worth Fighting For," and she demonstrated solidarity with them when she returned to warn them despite her loss of face. Mulan then got them to work together to dress as concubines and fight for the emperor.

Yi/Li Values

Lu makes another distinction within the collectivism construct that enlightens our understanding of the moral values that Chinese respect, by highlighting differences within the Chinese culture between two competing philosophical systems. These systems demonstrate two different collectivist cultural values coexisting, but with one having a negative connotation. He identifies these values as *yi* and *li,* with *yi* distinguished by "morality, benevolence, righteousness, and faithfulness" and *li* characterized by the values of "benefit, utilitarianism, and profit" (93). *Yi* is demonstrated in commitment to one's friends (Chu and Ju 172). Lu notes that although *li* is similar to American individualism, the two have different philosophical bases and therefore differ.

> American individualism is based on the valuative principles and abstract ideals of freedom, sacredness and autonomy of the individual in the Western tradition. Chinese value of *li*, on the other hand, is derived from a pragmatic philosophical tradition that aims at seeking mutual gain or self-interest for concrete material benefits. (105)

In addition, although individualism has been accepted as a rational, moral term with a positive connotation, *li* has historically been more negative (although that is changing) and more concerned with utilitarian gain (Lu 105). The values of *li* are more similar to Western capitalist values, but the overall negative connotation has kept them from being a driving motivator.

Mulan is a historical story set in a time when *li* would have a very negative connotation. Even the Chinese audience of today would be hesitant to embrace the idea of *li* as a positive lesson for their children. The first time we see Mulan, she is ingeniously getting her dog to do her chores, demonstrating her utilitarian mind set along the lines of *li*. Despite the problems of *li*, Mulan expresses that negative aspect of collectivism when she admits to seeking the adventure of soldiering to demonstrate that she could do something right. She was seeking a mutual gain—for her father and for herself that would bring the benefits of honor. She operates on a utilitarian principle of bringing the greatest good for the greatest number—something the Eastern idea of collectivism denigrates. Rather, it seeks to put the group first, whether or not that brings a concrete "good"; the morality lies in depending on the group and seeking their interests before self. The distinction may seem subtle, but it is significant in that one's own "good" doesn't figure into the Eastern equation the way it does in the Western mind-set.

High/Low Communication Context

A final necessary dimension of intercultural communication to consider is that of communication styles. Identifying communication styles is not clearly a question of either-or. Individual personality directly affects

TABLE 6.2. High/Low Communication Context

High Context	Low Context
Indirectness	Directness
Implicitness	Explicitness
Nonverbal expressiveness	Verbal expressiveness
Passive, "fitting in" style	Assertive, initiative-taking style

Source: Gao and Ting-Toomey, *Communicating Effectively With the Chinese*, 3–4.

style, as does the context. Nevertheless, Gudykunst et al. have found that collectivist cultures tend to use more high-context messages—i.e., "implicit and indirect messages"—that are best understood within the context of the culture, whereas individualistic cultures tend to employ a more direct, assertive communication style, with the meaning found in the message that is sent (511). For a summary of these two communication styles, see Table 6.2. Although there are always people who don't fit the generalization, the generalization does help us in making contrasts between the different styles of communication.

Mulan's father is a good example of the Chinese high-context style. When Mulan comes to tell him what happened at the matchmaker's, he tries to comfort her—not in a direct, American style but in a high-context style. He points out a blossom on the tree and says, "This blossom's late. But I'll bet that when it blooms, it will be the most beautiful of all."[5] The emperor also demonstrates the high-context style when speaking to Shang as Mulan rides away: "The flower that blooms in adversity is the most rare and beautiful of all." Shang looks confused, so the emperor then tries the low-context style: "You don't meet a girl like that every dynasty." The contrast in styles creates humor and demonstrates the potential for misunderstanding.

The high/low context of communication also yields insight into some of Mulan's behavior when Mulan first enters the male environment of camp. The Chinese dependency on context means that nonverbal communication is of high importance to accurate communication. Added to this dimension is the complication of being a female in a man's world. Whether or not one subscribes to the feminist approach to gendered communication, which ascribes language differences to issues of power and powerlessness, or to the popularized cross-cultural model, which suggests that communication between the genders is more a question of nature, nurture, and knowledge,[6] differences between men's and women's communication styles are assumed. Mulan would naturally want to adapt her nonverbals to the male setting, particularly since certain behaviors have been expected of Chinese women. Chu and Ju, in studying the changes in Chinese society, note the following: "Women were expected to use a pattern of language that showed their humble nature. Their manners were controlled in such a way as to reveal their inferior status" (238). That is a traditional value that is declining today[7] but was certainly a part of the culture that Mulan lived in. Mulan recognized the need to change her nonverbal behavior, but changing it got her into a great deal of trouble when first encountering the men, in great part because she listened to the poor advice of Mushu.

Chinese Values

Many of the differences in cultures discussed above have their roots in the traditional Confucian values. Chu and Ju note the dominant influence that Confucianism had on Chinese culture: "As a code of ethics regulating day-to-day behavior and a body of rituals for ancestor worship that formed a link with the world of the unknown, Confucianism served for centuries those social and psychological needs that were generally fulfilled by religion" (252).

Pan et al. identify core values, noting that that doesn't mean the values are stagnant. In fact the more communication there is between cultures, the more those cultures influence one another and the more changes in core values occur.[8] Nevertheless, "traditional" values, though somewhat stereotyped, can still be identified.

Chinese cultural values are distinguishable from Westernized values in part because of the influence of Confucianism, as mentioned. Central to Confucianism are three dominant and interrelated values based on the idea of "linear hierarchy," which governs "family structure, political structure, and the supernatural world" (Pan et al. 21). These three values include "filial piety," which dictates a strict obedience of the son to the father. That value is related to the second value, subject/emperor relations, in which "complete devotion and self-sacrifice" are demanded of the subject. Finally, the hierarchy applies to male/female relationships in which male superiority is assumed and the woman has definite roles of submission, chastity, devotion, and duty to her husband and her husband's family (Pan et al. 21–22). The traditional values that emerged from this philosophical system are identified in Figure 6.1.

Many of these traditional family values are declining in Chinese society not just because of modernization (Pan et al. 68); rather, this de-

FIGURE 6.1. Traditional Chinese Values

Traditions and Heritages
    Long historical heritage
    Respect for traditions
    Loyalty and devotion to the state
Family Relations
    Benevolent father and filial son
    Glory to ancestors
    House full of sons and grandsons
Social Relations
    Way of the Golden Mean
    Generosity and virtues
    Tolerance, propriety, and deference
    Harmony is precious
    Submission to authority
    Pleasing superiors
    Discretion for self-preservation
Roles of Women
    Chastity
    Three obediences and four virtues
    Differentiation between men and women
Work Ethic and Social Status
    Diligence and frugality
    Farmers high and merchants low

Source: Chu and Ju. "Five Categories of Traditional Chinese Values." *The Great Wall in Ruins: Communication and Cultural Change in China,* 244.

cline is attributed more to China's history than to outside influence. The Cultural Revolution instigated changes that at times diametrically opposed traditional values. That vestiges of Confucianism remain indicates how deep-seated the values once were, but their decline indicates how effective Communist propaganda was (Pan et al. 234).

These values would have been strongly held in Mulan's time. An emphasis on traditions, family relations, social relations, the role of women, and conceptions of the work ethic dominated the cultural landscape. Mulan would have been expected to honor the emperor, the historical state, and her ancestors; to do everything in her power to marry and produce sons; to seek a life of moderation; to practice tolerance when experiencing injustice, propriety in respecting the hierarchy of nature, and deference, which usually meant, in part, being quiet and demure; to promote harmony; to obey those in authority; to actively avoid situations that might get her in trouble; to be chaste; to obey her father, husband,

and son (if her husband were to die), as well as to practice a woman's morality, language, manners, and work; to respect the superiority of men; to be hardworking and frugal; and to respect the hierarchical structure of society.

Having these values identified helps explain the ancestor worship, the family's excitement over Mulan's appearance before the matchmaker, and the father's determination to fulfill his honor by serving the emperor. The attitude of the men in the army toward women and Shang's deep sense of betrayal when he discovered that Ping was really Mulan are also easy to trace to this value structure.

Mulan is also consistent in its portrayal of women's low status in the general society. The song lyrics especially communicate the society's perspective on a woman's place and role. When Mulan is preparing to go before the matchmaker, the women all sing about what men want in women, including an emphasis on work, looks, demeanor, and ancestors. Shang sings about making these recruits, these "daughters" (derogatory), into real men, and later the army sings about a "girl worth fighting for," revealing the various dreams of what a woman should be. Mulan tries to suggest a different vision of a girl "who always speaks her mind"; the men quickly reject it as ridiculous.

Traditional values in Chinese society are declining but have shaped that culture's current values. For example, although the expectations for women have changed, the Chinese are still generally more restrictive in their views of male/female relationships (Pan et al. 214). Susanne Günther, in speaking to Chinese linguists, found many presumed differences in women's and men's communication styles:

> Women swear and curse less than men. . . . Women are supposed to be quiet when men speak. . . . It is a woman's job to listen to men. If she does not listen but speaks up, her speaking is often ignored. . . . Generally, women are more careful of what they say and are more polite when they speak. . . . A "dominant woman" has a very negative image in China. . . . The ideal Chinese woman should be shy, timid and reserved. (169)

In addition, there are behavioral expectations for a woman that include not laughing or talking loudly and not sticking out in a group. If she violates these expectations, she will be thought to have a "bad character" (170).

TABLE 6.3. Contrasting Values

Chinese Values	American Values
Intense kinship responsibilities, to male's family and ancestors	Responsibilities to immediate family, weak responsibilities to extended family
Women's roles rigidly defined	Women individualistically oriented
Seeks harmony with nature, passively	Seeks to master nature, actively
Emphasizes inner experience and feelings	Emphasizes outer experience and materiality
Worldview values stability and harmony	Worldview values progress and competition
Oriented toward tradition and past	Oriented toward rationalism and future
Emphasizes vertical interpersonal relationships; hierarchy	Emphasizes horizontal interpersonal relationships; equality
Respects duty to family (extended definition) and state	Respects individual personality
Values fitting in	Values self-actualization, initiative
"We" identity, meet needs of the group	"I" identity, meet own needs
High-context communication (indirectness, implicitness, and nonverbal expressions)	Low-context communication (directness, explicitness, and verbal expressions)

Sources: Pan et al., *To See Ourselves: Comparing Traditional Chinese and American Cultural Values;* Gao and Ting-Toomey, *Communicating Effectively With the Chinese.*

Mulan's aggressive pursuit of her goals contrasts with acceptable behavior. When Disney adds Western behavior, in addition to the Chinese styles, Mulan's attractiveness for the Chinese decreases. Pan et al. and Gao and Ting-Toomey have identified some generalizations about the contrast between Chinese and American values (see Table 6.3). These values meet in *Mulan* sometimes in harmony and sometimes at odds with one another.

As the lead character and the heroine, Mulan embodies the anachronistic mix of Eastern and Western values, with the Western side being dominant. As Pan et al. note, there is a growing trend in China today toward similarities in values. Nevertheless, Mulan weighs in on affirming contemporary values (be they known as Western or modern) and stands against traditional Eastern values. That may have been disconcerting for the Chinese audience.

Westernizing an Eastern legend negatively affected the international box office. Disney hoped to market the final product not only in the West but also to the huge Chinese market. When the approval was finally received to release the film in China, Disney expected magical results in terms of audience size. The actual box office result, however, was disappointing (Peng). Although timing of the distribution affected the box office, so did the contrasting values. *South China Morning Post* articles interviewed viewers who responded negatively. One mother said, "Chinese believe culture should be more reserved, but many of the scenes appear to be Western-style" ("Mulan Wins"). Another person from Hunan said, "the heroine's 'complexion, disposition and manner of behaviour' were different from the Mulan of Chinese folk stories and poems" ("Mulan Debut").

The legend of Hua Mulan is a treasured one in China and one of the most well known. Those going to see a version of the story expected a representation of Mulan that showed her as "hard-working, intelligent, filial and noble-minded," according to Cheng Quiang, a researcher of Chinese folk literature. Other characteristics that make the legendary Mulan great are her heroic spirit, bravery, courage, social responsibility, willingness to make personal sacrifices for her family and nation, and humility (Linyong).

The Disney version includes many of these values but infuses a Western interpretation of them. Mulan is hardworking—when it suits her purpose. She enlists the dog's help for chores rather than getting up early enough to complete them herself. Her filial responsibility is great, but later in the film she admits that maybe she did it not for her father but for herself instead. That individuality is the driving motivation for Disney's Mulan, and that is a contrast for the Chinese. There is a definite mix of cultures in this film.

The differences in Western and Eastern cultures are significant despite the decline in beliefs in traditional values for the Chinese. These cultural differences contribute to differing mind-sets, attitudes, expectations for appropriate behavior, and perspectives on what is acceptable. Disney said it wished to respect the Chinese culture in this film, and it took great care in researching dimensions of the historical time, including the music, clothing, food, and setting. Nevertheless, the tensions between the two cultures are evident. Given the differences in values discussed above, let's examine how these tensions play out in the moral messages in *Mulan*.

MORAL TENSIONS

Central to the Disney narrative style is creating a heroine (or hero) with which children can identify. And as we have seen earlier, identification is a powerful means of persuasion. Finding universal values is key to Disney's ability to see a film to an international market.[9] Communication across cultures is best achieved by seeking the broadest spectrum of values. Nevertheless, the challenges of working between two cultures results in having to make choices—choices that sometimes allow one culture to dominate the values of the other culture. How the female is defined, the contrasts between the Eastern and Western values as seen in attitudes toward truth telling, individualism, and the concept of *yin-yang* in *Mulan* demonstrate the tensions.

Defining the Female

Contrary to traditional Chinese expectations for women and to past Disney films, *Mulan* presents a heroine who is intelligent and self-empowered, not driven by a need for romance. Yes, she encounters an attractive man in Captain Shang and admires his physique and his leadership, but her actions are not propelled by a desire to capture his romantic interest. Because this story is such a well-known and respected one in China, Disney is able to use the theme of female empowerment and have the idea be acceptable to both an Eastern and Western mindset (although we shall see how there is still a tension even in how that empowerment is presented).

   If Mulan's motivation is not finding a man, what is it? Here is where the tension in values is embodied. Mulan is motivated to action in part by her desire to bring honor to and protect her family and to honor and protect her country—values cherished by the Chinese. But she also admits to being motivated more by the desire to find out who she really is. Self-discovery is the motivating theme.

That Mulan is able to buck the usual Disney formula of romance is attributed to the film's "lack of studio status": "Everyone on the [creative] team came from the lower rungs of Disney's hierarchy." It was even produced in Florida, where a feature animation had never been done. This group was charged with combining an old short called "China Doll" with children's book author Robert San Souci's ideas based on the Chinese poem "The Song of Fa Mulan." After attempting to use an attitude-filled, romance-seeking Mulan, the creative team felt it was wrong, threw it out, and began with the mandate that "though Mulan has a crush, love wouldn't blossom until after the closing credits" (Brown and Shapiro). There was a conscious, concerted effort to keep romance and overtly sexual bodies out of the story.

Nevertheless, the message is still tucked in for the romantic at heart through the character of the grandmother. Grandmother Fa is the comic relief who acts before she thinks. It's apparent that she is more indulgent of Mulan. She seems particularly focused on Mulan's success, which to her means getting a man. Before going to the matchmaker, she risks her life to test the luck of a cricket, which she then presents as a gift to Mulan. She encourages Mulan to eavesdrop on the emperor's message to the men of the town. And she is concerned that Mulan catch a handsome man. Her comment at the end, a suggestion shouted out at Shang that he "stay forever," reflects a Western assertiveness that stands in contrast to how women were supposed to communicate—quietly and respectfully. It also communicates the expectation for romance that Disney audience's have come to expect.

Another area where Mulan demonstrates her Westernization is in her willingness to touch. The Chinese culture is a "noncontact" culture: ". . . open displays of intense feelings or emotions in social interactions are to be avoided, as such displays are deemed uncivilized. Also frowned upon are touching behaviors or physical closeness in social contacts among adults" (Chen 349). When Mulan, as Ping, expresses her sympathy over the death of Shang's father, he places his hand on her shoulder in a gesture of "thanks." Later, when she is being honored by the emperor, she throws her arms around him in an embrace. That behavior in the Chinese culture would be frowned upon in the first case and not tolerated in the second. The reaction of the males around Mulan was first one of incredulity, but then acceptance as if to say "she's an unconventional female."

Overall, *Mulan* offers wonderful lessons to girls that encourage healthy growth. In today's culture, in which family relationships are often fractured, Mulan has a loving and supportive family, despite her failings to bring them honor as a bride. She demonstrates many admirable qualities: ingenuity, courage, self-discipline, and persistence. She shows the audience that a girl can do more than her stereotype and still be a girl, and that she doesn't have to do and look like everyone else to be loved and accepted; rather, it is important to believe in herself and be willing to work for her goals. What a terrific heroine! And what a demonstration of universalizable values—for the most part. Because this Chinese legend was about an unconventional female, many of the plot elements that could be categorized as Western were simply related to the actual unconventional character. At the same time, certain elements of Mulan's interactions and basic character reflect a more Western orientation.

Truth Telling

It's too bad that the plot was constructed in such a way that Mulan is willing to cheat to accomplish her goals. The story opens with Mulan needing to do her chores, so she enlists the family dog by attaching a bone on the end of a stick as well as the bag of chicken feed with a hole in it. Ingenious, yes, and perhaps a harmless way of getting out of her chores. However, the next instance is not as cute. When she goes to meet the matchmaker, she has her own special "cheat sheet" written on her arm. The matchmaker even suspects that she is cheating, but the matchmaker can't find the evidence. The evidence comes off on her hand when she grabs Mulan, and then it covers the matchmaker's face in an unbecoming goatee. The audience, rather than seeing negative consequences of cheating, sees the negative consequences as the result of a misbehaving cricket.

Yet, overall, even this is seen as part of the developing character of a young girl as she learns the need to be honest, particularly with herself. For much of this story, Mulan lives a life of deception—deceiving the matchmaker, deceiving her parents by sneaking out, deceiving the army and Captain Shang. After her secret is revealed and the army has left her alone in the mountains, she confesses to Mushu that perhaps she even deceived herself in all of this: "I thought I came here to save my father, but maybe what I really wanted was to prove I could do things right." There is moral development in Mulan's story, just as Disney consciously chose to put it there.

According to Thomas Schumacher, executive vice president of Walt Disney Feature Animation,

> The fundamental element of *Mulan* that was most exciting to us was to tell a story of a young woman who makes a decision to save her father's life. In order to do that, she must tell a profound lie, but only when she is acting as herself—not made up as a bride-to-be, not in armor pretending to be a man—does she truly succeed in becoming a hero and save the Emperor's life. . . . There is a very clear underlying message about honesty and truth and how your greatest empowerment comes from being your true self. (*Mulan Press Kit* 14)

But that message of honesty does not come through clearly. What are the consequences of Mulan's telling all of these lies? Nothing. At first it looks like she may have lost the trust of Shang and the other men, but they trust her again after the Huns do appear in the city. The underlying message is not that a person should be honest; rather, it is that one should be creative in one's communication, including lying whenever it is necessary to achieve one's goals. That may be widely accepted in the United States, but it is not a prosocial lesson.

Individualism

The message to creatively use communication for one's own purposes, even to the point of lying, leads to the ultimate Westernization—one of the morals of the story. Although the Chinese cherish the story of Mulan, the things they value in it are not all the same as those that Disney has set forth as important. The Chinese culture holds duty to others in high regard, be it to family, to the social hierarchy, to authority, or to the group. Westerners are more goal-driven and value individuality. Disney's Mulan is motivated ultimately more by the goal of self-discovery than the duty of service to family and emperor. Perhaps the strongest message in the film, the moral to the story, is the familiar Disney refrain—to follow your heart. Because the standard ingredient in the Disney narrative is a young person on a quest to find himself or herself, this is not a surprising message.

In *Mulan* this problem is established early on when Mulan sings, "I see that if I were truly to be myself, I'd break my family's heart." She doesn't recognize herself as a bride-to-be and wonders when her reflection will be an honest one. The final song, "Be True to Your Heart," carries one of the film's "central themes" (*Mulan Press Kit* 21). Echoing the philosopher's voice of "To thine own self be true," this theme appears to be a sound one. But look closer. The song says, "Your heart can tell you no lies" and "Your heart knows what's good for you." This goes against the Chinese emphasis on the collective. It is a self-interested, individualistic, and emotional way to live and demonstrates the cultural, moral tensions that Mulan embodies. That it may be a reflection of American values is possible, but that it is not a prosocial value is problematic.

Westernized *Yin-Yang*

Mushu, the tiny dragon sidekick, is a contrast in character to Mulan. He is irreverent and disrespectful, is a nonstop talker, lies whenever it is convenient, doesn't hesitate to use sexual innuendo, and demonstrates few, if any, interpersonal skills. His behavior is so ridiculous that it is funny. His desire to hold a position of respect with the ancestors motivates his dedication to Mulan's cause. His persistence in the face of overwhelming odds helps Mushu teach a good lesson about not giving up.

His jokes and running commentary, if seriously examined, however, would teach some lessons about American cultural values. For example, Mushu suggests several different personae as he tries to impress Mulan, including the swagger of a street talker ("a sucker loses"), an irreverent tent evangelist, a worldly wisecracker who suggests lifestyles that most of the children in the audience wouldn't understand ("Your great-grandmother had to be a cross-dresser. Miss man decided to take her little drag show on the road"), and a seductress ("I am the powerful, the pleasurable," while gesturing a seductive female body). Concepts still valued in China like reverence for ancestors, respect for others, and modesty are turned into convenient jokes for Mushu, demonstrating that the American sense of humor holds those values in little esteem.

Mushu's misperceptions and ready wisecracks offer a kind of Western *yang* to the Eastern *yin* of Mulan. Chen identifies the concept of polar opposites, or *yin* and *yang*, as central to Chinese thinking. These opposites are complementary. Finding the balance between the two creates harmony or unity.

Although this dichotomy is familiar to Americans, observes Chen, "The differences lie in where the emphasis is placed: on the halves for the North Americans, and on the whole for the Chinese" (348). The contrast of a streetwise, smart-mouthed miniature dragon to the reserved Chinese culture is a polar opposite, but in a Westernized version of the *yin-yang*. The emphasis is on the individuals of Mulan and Mushu, not on their making a complete whole. Chen comments, "It is widely acknowledged that the Western way is predominantly a perspectival approach to everything/anything, with linear/causal thinking and a strong sense of ego/individual, whereas the Eastern way is the opposite in virtually every respect" (346). *Mulan* presents a conflicted version of Chinese culture, one that attempts to acknowledge the collectivist mind-set but in reality sets it within a Western idea of individualism.

CONCLUSION

The "chop-suey" of values embodied in *Mulan* offers a delightful but mixed taste of cultures. Bound together in a Disney sauce composed of some of the standard recipe ingredients such as heroine on a quest of self-discovery, humorous sidekicks, handsome man, threatening evil character, and happy ending, but flavored with new spices like another culture's setting and a female not motivated by romance, this film is a fresh dish on the Disney menu. The intercultural dimension of *Mulan* shapes the story through the individualism/collectivism poles, the high/low communication context, and the Chinese value system and results in a story composed of contrasts and moral tensions.

Mulan is a fascinating mixture of American interpretation of Chinese legend. Attempting to be responsible and faithful to the Chinese culture, the film embraces positively some of the priorities of Chinese cultural values. Nevertheless, *Mulan* is still produced by a company seeking to appeal to the broadest possible audience. Thus, in constructing its narrative, it ultimately prioritizes the values that can be universally accepted. This move, which from one perspective is morally legitimate, nevertheless has inherent prejudices against particularizing a culture, in this case the Chinese. In addition, it infuses Western values into both plot and character, thus biasing the story toward the Western mind-set. In other words, the attempt to respect Chinese culture ultimately undermines the film by emphasizing a different priority of values, different from the culture in which the story takes place.

SEVEN

A Disney Worldview

MIXED MORAL MESSAGES

To the audiences of the 1920s, Disney was entertainment. To the audiences of the 1960s, Disney was an icon. To the audiences of the 1990s, Disney is myth.
—Betsy Hearne, "Disney Revisited, Or, Jiminy Cricket, It's Musty Down Here!" *Horn Book,* 1997

The Disney animated films have evolved over time, adapting to cultural changes. However, as Hearne observes, the place of Disney films in culture has also changed, so that now Disney is revered as an honored storyteller. Disney animated films, and these five in particular, are a central part of mainstream culture, dominating the box office in animation with 18 of the 20 top-grossing animated films (see Table 7.1) and reaping Oscar awards, critical acclaim, and condemnation. That Disney acts as a moral teacher is not disputed, nor is Disney unaware of its powerful potential to affect children. Kilpatrick cites Linda Woolverton, who was the screenwriter for *Beauty and the Beast* and *The Lion King:* "When you take on a Disney animated feature, you know you're going to be affecting entire generations of human minds" (37).

The problem for many critics comes in how those minds are being affected or in what children are learning about right and wrong. Disney picks and chooses what it will use from myths, legends, history, and other people's stories. It "Disneyfies" each plot to fit its formula for commercial success and its perspective on reality. In these films, certain moral lessons are chosen over others, according to Disney's value structure.

TABLE 7.1. TOP ANIMATED FILMS

Film	Rank	Year	Box Office
The Lion King	1	1994	$313 million
Pocahontas	10	1995	$142 million
Mulan	12	1998	$121 million
Disney's The Hunchback of Notre Dame	17	1996	$100 million
Hercules	18	1997	$97 million

Source: Internet Movie Database, Box Office archives (http://www.imdb.com), as of February 24, 2000.

A DISNEY WORLDVIEW

Definition of Worldview

If, as Margaret Miles proposes, films are viewed as answers to the question of how we should live, then film is an inherently value-laden medium that argues rhetorically for a particular moral vision (8–9). Although that argument may be implicit rather than explicit in a given film, and the moral vision may be conflicted, films do communicate arguments for a moral life or an immoral one. Miles notes, "the pulse of a society, its interests and longings, its fears and anxieties, can be taken by examining its repetitive self-representations" (xv). Given that Disney has, in these five animated films, made arguments for moral living, the question now is, What sort of worldview do these arguments construct? Is there a picture emerging of a Disney worldview, a Disney lens?

Clifford Geertz refers to the moral dimension of society as its "ethos" and defines *worldview* as a people's "picture of the way things in sheer actuality are, their concept of nature, of self, of society." He adds, "It contains their most comprehensive ideas of order" (127). A worldview provides the lens in Burke's "equipment for living"; it is part of the "terministic screen" used in one's "frame of interpretation" (*Permanence* 7; *Attitudes* 92–93). As I noted in Chapter 1, Brian Walsh and Richard Middleton's definition is particularly clear: "A world view . . . provides a model *of the world* which guides its adherents *in the world*" (32). Albert Wolters elaborates: "A worldview, even when it is half unconscious and unarticulated, functions like a compass or a road map" (4). Or in Jürgen Habermas's words, "worldviews lay down the framework of fundamental concepts within which we interpret everything that appears in the world in a specific way as something" (*Theory* 58). A worldview is the means by which experience and belief are merged and organized and by which values are prioritized. But is it really possible to construct a worldview, given the potential for varied interpretations?

The answer to that question is a conditional "yes," in that I acknowledge the potential for polyvalent readings, but because I am seeking to unearth a Disney-originated worldview, the polysemous nature of textual interpretation is not a central issue. Nevertheless, I wish to concede that polysemy (i.e., polyvalence) is a valid dimension of textual interpretation,[1] and thus I move to a brief discussion of it here.

Polysematic Readings

Although Disney works within a traditional genre form (the animated musical) and uses fairy-tale conventions to clearly delineate good and evil, all the while trying to be politically sensitive,[2] we have seen that various critics react to these moral tales positively *and* negatively. The overt message may be positive, but other readings of the films are still possible. David Bordwell maintains that although limiting the polysemous nature of the text is possible, "the filmmaker cannot control all the semantic fields, schemata, and heuristics which the perceiver may bring to bear on the film." He adds, "The spectator can thus use the film for other purposes than the maker anticipated" (*Making Meaning* 270). Disney itself is aware of the polysemy of its texts. Referring to *The Hunchback*, producer Don Hahn says, "Our theory is that our films can exist on several different levels. We have the sexual obsession and we have the subtexts, but they will go right over the heads of children" (Vincent, "Will" E3).

Polysematic readings of these Disney films are prevalent. Even when one looks for presuppositions in common issues between films or common to all the films—i.e., the worldview dimension—the identification and interpretation of presuppositional material provide opportunity for disagreement. Nevertheless, a critic's work entails opening up the text to interpretation; therefore, I argue for a particular understanding of a Disney worldview that is debatable but also is grounded in text. Given the postmodern mind-set, with its proclivity for open texts,[3] worldview discussions are often dismissed or considered irrelevant; one worldview is as good as another. However, Disney's pervasiveness, which empowers it as a cultural storyteller, enables it to proffer its worldview as truth. When it is one of the few voices speaking openly about morality, albeit in animated narrative form, children experience it as a "dominant ideology" that exercises "hegemonic" power over their understanding of morality.

Disney films are open to multiple interpretations, but from the polyvalent perspective, in that certain overt messages are inescapable. When one examines the variety of critical responses, it is still possible to discover the underlying worldview that informs the overt messages and yet allows room for the diversity of responses. The divergent criticisms often highlight conflicts residing within Disney's worldview or illuminate the particular dimension of worldview being proffered by Disney as an aspect of worldview with which the critics take issue.

UNDERSTANDING A DISNEY WORLDVIEW The individual Disney films act as chapters in the Disney book on what the world looks like or ought to look like. Matt Roth bemoans what he sees as the increasing dominance of culture by the Disney conglomerate and suggests that we can see what the world will look like by looking at Disney animated films: "We do have one reliable oracle of the future: Disney's own propaganda. Thinly veiled in its animated full-length features are Disney's own ambitions, reactionary views of the world and blueprints for social change" (40). In other words, the animated films reveal a Disney worldview.

In order to uncover the Disney worldview, we need to interrogate the films. The following questions, questions of the fundamental nature of cultural life, enable the process:[4] What does it mean to be human? What is the structure of society? And how does one know? Answers to these questions, when taken together, begin to reveal a Disney worldview, a broad picture or map of Disney's understanding of the territory of reality. In other words, these questions constitute the components, or the "control beliefs," of Disney's basic assumptions and presuppositions about the nature of human existence.[5]

WHAT DOES IT MEAN TO BE HUMAN—MALE AND FEMALE? Disney answers the question of what it means to be human differently for women and for men. The place of romance in human existence is central to the definition of a female in four of the five films discussed in this book but is only a part of a male's life.

In *The Lion King,* Nala finds her fulfillment in becoming Simba's wife and the mother of his child. Nala, physically stronger than Simba, certainly his equal in intelligence, runs away from the Pride Lands because she "couldn't take it anymore" (Ingoglia, *Lion King* 71). But it is only Simba who is able to stand up to Scar and who has a purpose in life other than to be someone's spouse. Simba's mother, Sarabi, is shown only as an insignificant (so the movie implies) wife and mother. She plays no role in teaching Simba any of life's lessons. Her role as head of the lionesses—the ones who hunt and provide the food for the pride—is mentioned only in passing. When she is finally shown in that role, it is in subservience to Scar and in a weakened condition. The role of a female in *The Lion King* is primarily that which is associated with love, either romantic or motherly. Certainly, that is a valuable role, but it presents women as one-dimensional.

Initially, Pocahontas appears to be the most radical of Disney's heroines, exercising true agency in the development of the narrative, a feminist role model. She acts as ambassador to the colonists and as peacemaker. She has dreams that are bigger than marrying someone her father chooses for her. She wonders what is "just around the riverbend," hoping to find the object of her dreams. She is a contemporary woman who knows what she wants and voices those wants, acting on her convictions even if it means opposing the patriarchal tradition. But wait. Pocahontas, like every other Disney heroine, finds that her dream is located in a man; she wants romantic love. That is what fulfills her and empowers her to stand up to her father. Her convictions lead her to fling herself over Smith to save him from death, not because it might start a war or because the Indians simply do not understand the Virginia Company's intentions, but because he is her "path," the direction of her life. She does it because, as she says, "I won't [stand back]! I love him" (Ingoglia, *Pocahontas* 85).

That the film ends with Pocahontas rejecting the opportunity to travel with Smith back to England does not negate the fact that her happiness is located in romantic love. By staying, she fulfills her duty to her people, but she sacrifices her happiness found in Smith so that he can have a chance to live—as Thomas points out (Ingoglia, *Pocahontas* 94–95).[6] Although he is going to return to England, she assures him, "You will never leave me. No matter what happens, I'll always be with you. *Forever*" (Ingoglia, *Pocahontas* 95). That this is almost a spiritual marriage, at least on Pocahontas's part, is symbolized by her mother's necklace. The necklace was given to her by her father as a symbol of her upcoming marriage to Kocoum. As Kocoum fell dying, he ripped it off her neck, breaking it. At the end of the film, it is returned to her by the animals—repaired—representing Pocahontas's commitment to Smith and nature's approval. Although she seems to be choosing a life of service to her people over the fulfillment of romantic love, the implication remains that it is a sacrifice; she will stay to be a peacemaker and help her people, but she will not find ultimate happiness in it. Her happiness will be in her commitment to Smith in her heart, where he will always be with her. Pocahontas is a feminist heroine, but she is also a romantic at heart.

Esmeralda in *The Hunchback of Notre Dame* is in a much worse state than Pocahontas. She has no talent, like Quasimodo's carving ability, except to dance—to flaunt her body. She tells him: "If I had your talent, you wouldn't find me dancing in the streets for coins" (Ingoglia, *Hunchback* 43). She has no purpose in life until she falls in love with Phoebus. Then she lives to save him, to help care for him, and ultimately to join her future to his. Similarly *Hercules'* Meg sacrifices herself twice for love: the first time she agrees to give her soul to Hades to redeem her former boyfriend; the second time she gives her life to save Hercules from being crushed by a pillar.

Mulan offers the only alternative to this view by presenting a heroine who is motivated by the search for self-understanding and by desires to bring honor to her family and protect her emperor. She achieves her goals and is rewarded by having Shang pursue her. She gets her man too! (Disney's later return to the formula of "female needs male" in *Tarzan* and in *Dinosaur* suggests that *Mulan* was an aberration in the Disney films of the 1990s, rather than one that set a new direction for Disney.) Romantic love is the fulfillment of a female's life in the Disney worldview.

For the male hero, the romance is a part of his quest but is not central to it. Simba needs to grow up, come to terms with his guilt, and accept the responsibility of being king of the Pride Lands. Smith is seeking new adventures when he meets Pocahontas, not romance. Although he falls in love with her and learns from her, he does not insist on marrying her or staying in Virginia, and he makes no promises about returning to her. Smith's purpose for existence is not to find a woman.

The Hunchback of Notre Dame is more complex in that there are two important male characters. Phoebus is smitten with Esmeralda, but he also has a job to do. When he loses his job, he is focused on Esmeralda, but a new role emerges for him, as leader of those opposed to the injustice of Frollo. Quasimodo, too, is in love with Esmeralda, but his dream is big enough that it is not solely defined by romantic love. He just wants to be "out there" among the people.

Hercules' dream is to be a hero so that he can once again join the gods. Along the way he falls in love with Meg, and, as perhaps the most liberal Disney hero, he gives up life as a god to live with Meg, but only after he has found the answer to his quest—that he already is a true hero. Shang in *Mulan* is more of a one-dimensional character. His job is to make men of the recruits and then to protect his emperor. Along the way he comes to respect and ultimately to desire Mulan, but he does so only after doing his duty.

Both males and females judge each other in light of cultural expectations—expectations defined by Disney—but the definition of a heroic male is much broader than is that of a female. A heroic man is encouraged in his journey to find himself—be it in a role (as Simba did), in an adventure (as Smith did), in self-knowledge (as Phoebus did), in the pursuit of a dream (as Quasimodo did, almost unknowingly, and as Hercules did), or in doing his duty (as Shang did)—but not to find himself solely through a love interest. Yes, romance is an important part of living for men, but only a part of living—not the reason for existing. Even Hercules, who ultimately chooses romance over what he thought was his goal—becoming a god—finds his dream in becoming a hero.

The model of a woman to emulate, in Disney's worldview, is one who lives to get her man. She may adopt some of the contemporary feminist attitudes, including being more vocal, being physically strong, and being self-sufficient, but she only finds fulfillment in romantic love. If she has a dream, it is to get her man. Disney sends two mixed messages here about who we ought to be as females or males: (1) finding oneself *through* love is the heart's desire for a woman, but finding oneself *and* love is the heart's desire for a man; and (2) females can be strong and self-sufficient, but females are only truly happy when they have a man.

Another dimension of Disney's lesson on the nature of male and female is the importance of good looks. The female central characters have perfectly developed bodies, well-sculpted features, and beautiful hair. Nonverbal reactions from the men (e.g., Smith raises his eyebrows and smiles delightedly when he sees Pocahontas; or Phoebus smiles and stares openly at Esmeralda; or Hercules stops in midflight to Phoebus because of Meg) indicate that physical beauty in a female is centrally important. Likewise, the girls fall in love only with the characters who are good-looking and perform heroic acts. Quasimodo never stood a chance with Esmeralda romantically—he was too ugly. A related lesson on the importance of beauty—especially for the female—comes from the muses in Hercules. They are portrayed as extremely sexy women. The one muse who is overweight is given the stereotypical role of the comic. She may be fat, but she's happy and funny. A conflicting moral message emerges: what is inside is what is important, versus physical beauty is important.

The lessons Disney teaches to girls, then, about the centrality of romance and the necessity of good looks ought to raise serious concerns, for Keisha Hoerrner, citing previous research, states, "girls develop a preference for same-sex models and are more likely to imitate stereotyped behavior displayed by those models" (226). Girls' self-images are shaped by these messages.[7] Boys, too are affected either in self-image or in expectations from girls. When popular culture reinforces the centrality of romance and the importance of looks, breaking out of this mold becomes extremely difficult.

To be human, according to Disney, is defined by gender. To be female means to be focused on romantic love and the necessity of good looks. To be male is to pursue one's dreams and become an active part of society. Romance and looks are important to the male, but so is defining himself apart from the romantic relationship.

WHAT IS THE STRUCTURE OF SOCIETY? These animated Disney films all demonstrate an affinity for hierarchical social structure headed by males. Being part of the social structure is easier for males than for females in the Disney world of patriarchal authority. There is a preference for the status quo, for the passive mass ruled by the hierarchical authorities—male authorities—even if the reality on which the story is based is matriarchal. For example, Sarabi, Simba's mother, exercises no agency in *The Lion King,* and though she is the mate of the king, she has no authority in ruling the Pride Lands. When Mufasa is killed and Simba leaves, it is the male Scar who takes the reins of power. In *Pocahontas,* the Indian society is ruled hierarchically by a monarchical figure. The Virginia Company, likewise, is commanded by a male figure who represents the monarchy in England. *Disney's The Hunchback of Notre Dame* presents a society that is dominated by a male authority figure, Judge Frollo, who in turn represents the king. Likewise, in the world of *Hercules,* Zeus rules, while his wife, Hera, exercises little if any leadership. (In pre-Hellenic times, Hera had a cult following that rivaled that of Zeus.) We see a conflicting message in that Disney has an affinity for male authority and for social hierarchy even while it affirms female capabilities.[8]

Perhaps Disney is aware of its patriarchal emphasis and acknowledges it as an ongoing tension by having characters disobey that authority. Four of these five plots require the hero or heroine to disobey the father or father figure: Simba disobeys his father; Pocahontas disobeys her father; Quasimodo disobeys his father-figure. Even Hercules breaks away from both his earthly parents and, eventually, his heavenly ones. Mulan goes against her father's wishes by enlisting in the army—as a man.

A quick look at a few more recent Disney films indicates a trend:

Tarzan disobeys his ape "father"; Jasmine disobeys her father in *Aladdin;* Beauty disobeys her father in exchanging her life for her father's in *Beauty and the Beast;* Ariel disobeys her father by going to see humans in *The Little Mermaid.* Why the pattern? What is Disney communicating to kids? One answer is that Disney teaches that children actually know best. At least in *The Lion King,* Simba's disobedience got him into trouble and led to consequences—his father's death. However, when the heroes or heroines in the films disobey, that action sets the direction of the narrative toward a resolution that favors the heroes or heroines. Although Disney emphasizes patriarchy, it also presents a conflicting message: family values such as obedience are important, but the trend here indicates that one ought to disobey authority as needed—with need determined by the child.

When we look at why these characters disobey, we see another conflicting message: be responsible, but follow your heart. The implicit assumption is that the individual human heart knows what is right and good and has the ability to follow that. In learning responsibility, the characters arrive at the end of their quest only by following their hearts. Simba, Pocahontas, Quasimodo, Hercules, and Mulan all find strength by looking inward and ultimately following what they knew—intuitively, from their hearts—to be true. That then became the responsible thing to do.

Another aspect of social structure is how Disney addresses diversity in society. Historically, Disney has not represented racial diversity in a positive light. *The Lion King* was particularly criticized for its potential negative racial stereotypes. Disney is hearing the complaints and seems to be struggling to be less patriarchal and more representative of diversity, as seen in two of the films discussed here: *Pocahontas* and *Disney's The Hunchback of Notre Dame.* Pocahontas presents the image of a Native American woman who is strong, smart, and not racially stereotyped. Similarly, Esmeralda represents Gypsies in a more positive light. Disney is affected by its culture just as it affects its culture, but its underlying worldview contains patriarchal, racist, and hierarchical dimensions.

Sociologist Henry Giroux, however, is frustrated over Disney's hegemony in culture and sees negative patterns of racism: "The strategies of entertaining escapism, historical forgetting, and repressive pedagogy in Disney's books, records, theme parks, movies, and TV programs produce a series of identifications that relentlessly define America as white and middle class" ("Memory" 47). The tensions in Mulan between Eastern and Western ways illustrate Disney's cultural hegemony.

Although portraying Scar and the hyenas in *The Lion King* as having a dark mane or dark coats may seem to be innocuous symbolic coding, the alternative reading is not far-fetched; associations of darkness with evil may be archetypal, but they are also offensive to African-Americans. By voicing complaints to Disney, the company's sensitivities are raised. Nevertheless, a mixed message again emerges: do not stereotype, versus black is evil.

In addition to sending conflicting messages about valuing all races, Disney implies in *Pocahontas* that certain personality types are not valued. Pocahontas rejects Kocoum as "so serious." Similarly, in *Hercules,* the one muse who is not stereotypically beautiful is the one muse who is the comic. It seems that only fun-loving or extremely beautiful people are valued. The mixed message is that all people are valued, but really only lively, fun people are valued.

Finally, Disney implies that communication is the key to overcoming cultural differences within a society, but it is a conflicted solution. Communication may be the key to overcoming problems, but the magic of the heart is what really overcomes. *The Lion King* implies that if Simba had been open about his actions and communicated his desires to his father, he never would have been so easily duped by Scar. Communication would also have prevented his exile and his burden of guilt. However, only when he finally follows his heart back to the Pride Lands is a solution to the problem (of Scar) realized.

Communication is also suggested as the solution to the problem in *Pocahontas*. Whether the problem is differing value systems, lack of knowledge, or a preference for war, the solution advocated is communication. But that is only possible through a magical overcoming of language barriers by listening to one's heart.

Less overtly evident, perhaps, but still applicable is *The Hunchback's* emphasis on communication as a solution to society's problems. The problem of injustice is Frollo, and the solution is, ultimately, his death. But to arrive at that solution, the main characters have to follow their hearts. Similarly, Hercules needs to follow his heart to true happiness, rather than discuss alternatives with his parents or with Meg. Thus the mixed message remains: communication is the key to overcoming problems, versus the magic of the heart overcomes problems.

HOW DOES ONE KNOW? Disney makes it very clear that truth is what culture comes to know on an individual basis. Individualism is at the heart of moral decisions in the films, and when emotion and individual experience are emphasized, the result is a knowledge based in subjectivity over rationality and community.

The heroes of the five films share the common goal of obtaining some kind of self-knowledge. To achieve this, Simba is encouraged to look inside himself and be who he is meant to be. That is what motivates him to go back to the Pride Lands. Pocahontas is told to listen with her heart to understand what action she should take. Quasimodo is encouraged to follow his desire to go to the festival even though he would be disobeying. Esmeralda helps him know who he is and who Gypsies are through how he feels about her. Hercules is encouraged to look inside his heart to find out what makes a true hero. Mulan admits that she went to war more to find herself than to save her father.

I do not deny the importance of human emotion and the complexity with which it contributes to moral action, but throughout these films, the majority of rhetorical appeals apply to the emotions and lack rational grounding. Tempering the emotional call to action by justifying it rationally avoids the relativism of pure emotional response. Situating decisions within a communal context strengthens the moral decision, and appealing to transcendent principles or grounding those decisions in duty or in first principles minimizes individualistic relativism.[9] Although Disney implies that there are some things that are true or accepted as truth within a culture (e.g., how we ought to value other people, or the importance of diversity), contrarily it also teaches that, ultimately, truth is only what the individual believes is right for that individual.[10]

This mixed message works conveniently for Disney in how it handles history. For example, Disney was insensitive to its Native American consultant as well as to other Native American criticism that Disney was destroying historical legend in *Pocahontas*. Disney also ignored the complaints of Victor Hugo's family regarding its rewrite of *The Hunchback of Notre Dame*, altered Greek myth in *Hercules*, much to the indignation of the Greeks (Carassavas), and put a Western spin on a treasured Eastern legend. These examples indicate that Disney has not acquired a great deal of cultural sensitivity or respect for historical accuracy. Once again, a conflicting moral message occurs: show historical truth, but really tell only what will sell.

The Disney animated films of *The Lion King, Pocahontas, The Hunchback of Notre Dame, Hercules,* and *Mulan* reveal a Disney perspective on the nature of humanness, on the structure of society, and on knowing. The moral messages taught by these films are characterized by inconsistency. For a summary of these mixed messages, see Table 7.2.

TABLE 7.2. DISNEY'S MIXED MORAL MESSAGES

What does it mean to be human—male and female?

Finding oneself through love is the heart's desire—for a woman	Finding oneself and love is the heart's desire—for a man
Females can be strong and self-sufficient	Females are truly happy only when they have a man
What is inside is what is important	Physical beauty is important

What is the structure of society?

Females can be leaders	Male leadership ought to be the norm
Family values are important	Disobey authority as needed
Responsibility is valued	Follow your heart
Stereotyping is wrong	Black means evil
All people are valued	Only lively, fun people are valued
Communication is key to overcoming problems	The magic of the heart overcomes problems

How does one know?

Truth is important and culturally known	Truth is what the individual knows
Historical truth is valued	Tell only what will sell

When examined as a whole, do these messages contribute to a more consistent worldview? The answer to that is found in the cultural context of postmodernism. A Disney worldview emerges not as a single, unified worldview but as a combination of views. To put a label on Disney worldview, we can say that it alternates between a constructivist postmodern position, while at the same time holding many tenets of modernism.

Disney's Worldview as Postmodern

Disney demonstrates characteristics of the postmodern mind while at the same time fighting some of the postmodern tendencies. Fredric Jameson argues that "postmodernism replicates or reproduces—reinforces—the logic of consumer capitalism" (205). Although Disney may desire to use history accurately, its dominant goal is to promote consumption of its products. Ultimately, the postmodern emphasis wins out.

In a summary of the postmodern mind, Gene Veith characterizes postmodernism as assuming "that there is no objective truth, that moral values are relative, and that reality is socially constructed by a host of diverse communities. . . . Religion is seen as a preference, a choice" (193). And "morality, like religion, is a matter of desire" (194). This understanding of postmodernism doesn't apply to Disney well. Truth does exist in Disney's worldview as objectified good and evil defined in narrative and rooted in virtue ethics. Disney advocates moral values, thus countering postmodernism. Nevertheless, Disney does support the position that religion is simply a choice.

Another characteristic of postmodernism, according to Veith, is its emphasis on "play and chance" over purpose and design (43). Perhaps that is why the recent Disney films (from *The Little Mermaid* on) have made humor a more significant part of the narratives. The role of "sidekick" as buffoon is seen in the characters of Pumbaa, Timon, Meeko, Flit, Percy, Victor, Hugo, Laverne, Phil, and Mushu. The need for comic relief grows in a "comically framed" worldview, to use Burke's meaning, when an audience expects more overt dimensions of play in addition to the pleasure of a happy ending.

Other characteristics of the postmodern include emphasis on the tribal over local communities; eclectic culture; and the development of a "multicultural awareness" (143). The tendency, says Veith, is growing stylistic awareness of cultural diversity, but that awareness is superficial and avoids the ethical structure embedded in different cultures. *Pocahontas, The Hunchback of Notre Dame,* and *Mulan* all reflect Disney's growing awareness of multiculturalism and its embrace of a more politically correct stance regarding racial diversity and the empowerment of women. It wants to market its films worldwide.

Yet the tensions remain in the films, as evidenced in the criticisms of racism, the sexist depiction of the female body, the focus on romance, the increasingly adult themes and jokes, and the use of history and literature in the pursuit of profits. These criticisms may seem surprising, given that Disney is a conglomerate that claims a corner on the family values market. Is Disney a force that is both fighting and embracing the postmodern (a stance that in itself is postmodern)?

Finally, postmodernism, as described by Veith, has a "loss of an overarching cultural identity" (144). One wonders if Disney attempts to counter that loss by providing a "Disney identity"? Or perhaps, because of frequent criticism for wanting to return in time to an earlier America (e.g., see Zipes 40), Disney is seeking a return to a time when society was more homogeneous while at the same time it tries to appeal to a post-modern audience.

The better answer, I think, to the question of Disney's relationship to the postmodern worldview comes from a description of postmodernism by Carl F. H. Henry, who suggests that there are two tracks in the post-modern worldview—the "hard core deconstructive" and the "soft core constructive":

> The destructivists, by their elimination of God, purpose, truth and meaning, the self, and of a real world, seek to demolish any and every worldview. . . . Absolute relativism prevails; objective truth is intolerable and nonexistent. . . . In short, destructive postmodernism eliminates not only God but also freedom, purposive agency, the self, realism, truth, good and evil, and historical meaning. It holds that there are no shared values. . . . [I]nterpretation is king. (38–39)

Describing Disney as having a destructive postmodern worldview is impossible, given this definition. Disney values individual freedom too much and builds its profit on advocating a world in which good and evil exist. Henry describes the alternative constructivist path as follows:

> The constructivists elaborate a postmodern worldview that correlates scientific, moral, aesthetic, and religious concerns with a corresponding world supportive of ecological, pacifist, and feminist emancipatory proposals. . . . Constructive postmodernism emphasizes that even where shared truths or values are theoretically or verbally denied, a shared content nonetheless in practice remains quite common, and that "common sense notions" provide humanity with an escape from unrelieved relativism. . . . [It] includes among such notions the conviction that one has personal freedom, that the distinction between better and/or worse is necessary. (38–39)

Henry's definition of constructivist postmodernism could be describing Disney and its tendencies toward assuming a politically correct position while assuming certain moral "truths" or lessons it can teach. But at the same time Disney maintains remnants of a romantic mind-set.

Disney's films reflect the tensions inherent in conflicting worldviews by revealing growing concerns for the environment, for a society built on peace, and for women who are empowered to act on their own behalf. However, building from a tradition that was rooted in the Aristotelian ethical system with the goal of happiness, but operating in a culture that is increasingly postmodern in outlook, Disney seeks to satisfy both traditional and contemporary values. For example, while the conglomerate's history as an institution is strongly patriarchal, white, and middle class, its recent films are speaking to a postmodern culture that no longer is unified by those values.

This conflict in worldviews is being thrashed out before our eyes in these animated films. Disney continues to believe in the utopian vision grounded in romantic ideals, but the happy-ever-after romantic endings do not always make sense in a postmodern view in which females are empowered to act on their own behalf. The result, as seen in *Pocahontas* and *The Hunchback of Notre Dame,* is an ending that implies that the main characters might live happily ever after but, by having removed the romantic satisfaction, will not be completely satisfied. The conflict thus emerges between valuing romance as the only motivator for women who live for their men and valuing women's empowerment per se as a worthy goal.

That Disney is unwilling to maintain an older worldview that facilitates the propagation of racism, for example, is to its credit. Its desire to be a positive social force and its struggles to come to an understanding of what that means as it defines good and evil are laudable. Disney is at least partly a constructive force in society. And yet, many aspects of its worldview lead to the conclusion that it is a destructive force because of the relativizing of truth by its emphasis on "emotiveness." Henry's description of the constructive postmodern worldview works well to describe Disney, then, with its increasingly stronger, feminist heroines, ecological protection, and desires for societal peace accomplished by having a strong sense of the nature of virtuous behavior.

At the same time, Disney believes in tolerance for differing views of truth, for differing expressions of spirituality. This position may be stated in this way: religion can be an important part of life—whichever religion one chooses. There is no one right way to believe. The important thing is that one follows one's heart by doing whatever he or she feels is right. Tolerance, Veith argues, is "perhaps the only absolute moral value insisted upon by postmodernists" (154). Right and wrong are socially constructed concepts worked out in the public sphere, which is composed of dimensions like Disney animated films. Veith expresses concern over this situation: "With no absolute canons of objective truth, the rational is replaced by the aesthetic. We believe in what we *like*" (176). This perspective dovetails nicely with Disney's emphasis on following one's heart.

Nevertheless, Disney continues to contend with remnants of a worldview that stereotypes the role of women in society and their dreams of self-fulfillment as located in romantic love solely, and that idealizes patriarchal authority and assumes the superiority of the white race. Disney's worldview is a conflicted constructivist postmodern view. Inconsistencies may exist, but for the postmodernist, that situation is irrelevant and endemic. And with the absolute value of tolerance, Disney can appeal to the widest possible audience. In a society, however, in which foundational thinking is no longer valued, in which anyone claiming to know truth as a transcendent reality is marginalized as fanatical or foolish, there still exists a need for community. This need may be met by Disney's omnipotence as an institution, as a creator of dreams, and as an authority on morality.

IMPLICATIONS OF THE DISNEY WORLDVIEW FOR CULTURE

Given the significant presence of Disney in culture, as well as its active worldview (even if it is a conflicted worldview), Disney may be becoming a competitor of religion and a hegemonic power that not only dominates interpretations of narratives but also creates the narratives while it acts as moral educator.

Disney as Religion's Competitor

As society grows increasingly skeptical of organized religion, Disney steps in to fill a moral need in culture. Geertz discusses ethos, worldview, and religion as interconnected. Defining *ethos* as the "moral" or "evaluative" aspects of a culture (126) and *worldview* as the "cognitive" aspects, he sees religion as the glue that "mutually confirm[s]" the two: "This demonstration of a meaningful relation between the values a people holds and the general order of existence within which it finds itself is an essential element in all religions, however those values or that order be conceived" (127). This book has examined Disney both from the moral perspective and from the more cognitive understanding of worldview. The dimension that lies between the two is religion.

Arguing that Disney is becoming a competitor to religion for moral authority may be seen to be an extreme position, but the presence of Disney as a moral force in society, primarily through its animated films, is significant. As Disney increasingly educates on moral behavior and commands such a large following as to be a billion-dollar conglomerate, Geertz's words arrest our attention. He defines religion "in part" as "an attempt (of an implicit and directly felt rather than explicit and consciously thought-about sort) to conserve the fund of general meanings in terms of which each individual interprets his experience and organizes his conduct" (127). Religion, then, aids in the organization of the terms of meaning, terms that people use to measure their conduct against. Disney films, too, help organize meanings and act as tools for defining and encouraging morality.

Geertz also notes that religion uses symbols to preserve meanings:

> Meanings can only be "stored" in symbols: a cross, a crescent, or a feathered serpent. Such religious symbols, dramatized in rituals or related in myths, are felt somehow to sum up, for those for whom they are resonant, what is known about the way the world is, the quality of the emotional life it supports, and the way one ought to behave while in it. (127)

Disney preserves meaning in the use of symbols within its animated films. As already noted, myths, archetypes, rituals, and symbolic boundaries are all active in these films. The power of symbols, argues Geertz, is that they bring together the moral dimension with the intellectual worldview. It is impossible to have "an autonomous value system independent of any metaphysical referent" (127). Morality and religion are closely related.

In other words, an argument that Disney is simply structuring a moral view in its films apart from a philosophy about how to live is not tenable. Whether or not Disney has become a "religion" unto itself is not strictly the point here, although it has been argued.[11] Peter Verburg makes this observation when he writes: "Disney has been described as the perfect pop religion for modern society, one that cossets its adherents in a feel-good cradle-to-grave philosophy." Later Verburg paraphrases the Bible: "families today can live and move and have their being in Disney" (1). Similarly, Boyd Tonkin argues that just as religion has become increasingly irrelevant today, Disney is filling a need:

> Their art also prompts the idea that Disney's movies function as the Gothic cathedrals of our age. Almost anonymous, they are laboured over by an army of skilled drudges (628 people worked on *The Hunch-*

back), packed to the rafters with vertiginous visual effects, filled with memorable music and designed to illustrate a few simple tales about good and evil, love and hate. . . . They're likewise planned by cunning and voracious men of power. (*Disney's Hunchback Press Kit* 40)

Tonkin recognizes the tension between the growing place of Disney as a religious force and Disney's ongoing function as a business for profit.

One implication, then, of a Disney worldview is that it has the potential to become a significant organizer of meaning, competing with, if not supplanting, traditional religion. Disney communicates its good news that it can organize meaning through its animated films, and it reinforces that message in its emphasis on consumptive values.

That the films are animated adds an interesting dimension to the implication that Disney's worldview has the force of religious beliefs in its emphasis on consumption. Animation is abstraction from reality. Imitation of the animation is easily accomplished in consumer goods; the consumer impulse is built into the animated films and taught to children at an early age. Giroux notes: "Disney's pretense to innocence is shattered under the weight of a promotional culture predicated on the virtues of fun, innocence, and, most importantly, consumption" ("Memory" 47). Product tie-ins, the proliferation of film-character sponsorship of everything from clothes and eating utensils to luggage is a constant reminder that the Disney experience entails the elimination of evil and the triumph of good. Disney is selling its worldview. The promise of a world where evil is conquered, and where happy-ever-after is possible through Disney, is an escapist utopia that can be bought and experienced, if only for a couple of hours (while watching the films), or longer if you own the exact replica of your favorite character in some form or another.

Ultimately, Disney is first and foremost a business seeking to make money for its shareholders. Michael Eisner, in his 1996 "Letter from the Chairman," writes that "our only criteria for our products should be excellence and fiscal viability" (4–5). Contributing to a better society is certainly part of Disney's definition of excellence, but when these values come up against each other, the bottom line reigns supreme. For the hard-core Disney fans who not only have to see the films but also compulsively need to own the videos, T-shirts, toys, and other Disney-related products, Disney has made a significant imprint on their identity and on the way they interpret the world. As William Powers writes, "children grow into adults, who are fond of Disney because it shaped the way they think about the world" (G1). The films provide children with some of their first narratives with which to compare other stories, perhaps throughout their lives, for their measure of fidelity to "how the world really is." There is cause for concern, however, when one begins to examine the variety of moral messages being taught in Disney's animated films. While some are wonderful, others are not.

Disney's powerful presence as an agency of profit provides fuel for the argument that Disney has the potential to compete with religion, although it must be bought and believed, rather than simply believed. Disney functions as a source of symbols that shapes not only people's morality but also their broader outlook on life, their worldview. Michael Real contends, "Disney *instructs through morality plays that structure personal values and ideology*" (*Mass-Mediated* 81). Disney sells a worldview, and that worldview has the force of religion for many people.

Disney Domination

Expressing deep concerns about Disney's powerful presence in popular culture, Henry Giroux argues that the animated films are only the tip of the iceberg: "The boundaries between entertainment, education, and commercialization collapse through the sheer omnipotence of Disney's reach into diverse spheres of everyday life" ("When" 79). Similarly, Verburg expresses his concern for the potential reach of a Disney worldview: "When a conglomerate like Disney dominates such a vast stretch of popular culture, it can define and even dictate basic assumptions about everyday life and social relationships" (4). Disney's centrality in culture, its dominance of the children's film market, and its constructivist postmodern worldview contribute to the understanding of it as a major force of influence in culture, a hegemonic agency.

Hegemony theory is frequently applied in cultural studies and critiques.[12] John Storey observes in *What Is Cultural Studies?* that hegemony is a concept that has expanded from Antonio Gramsci's original meaning, which emphasized its use in "explor[ing] relations of power articulated in terms of class." Today the term has broadened "to include, for example, gender, race, meaning and pleasure" (10). Despite the diverse applications of the concept, it still relates to the interplay between culture and cultural beings, between "agency" and "structure," and continues to be a "dialectical play between resistance and incorporation" (11). Although, as Condit observes, hegemony is frequently used as a substitute for "dominant ideology" ("Hegemony" 205), I use the term here because of its ability to communicate not only a sense of a dominant worldview but also the willing participation of an audience in that worldview.

Hegemony, for my purposes, will be understood to mean the exercise of a dominant influence over culture by an agent, both in terms of its economic power and, more significantly, in terms of its ideological or worldview dominance. The exercise of this power is possible only with the consent of the people who encounter the agent of power. That people will cooperate in acting as subjects of domination may seem surprising. Here Aldous Huxley's *Brave New World* continues to ring with a prophetic voice when he suggests that a culture could love to be dominated by manufactured pleasure.

The Disney conglomeration exercises a dominant influence in our culture, providing entertainment, economic participation, and utopian experiences. At the same time, people willingly allow Disney's hegemony by actively attending its films and purchasing its products.

Disney's films in particular manufacture a postmodern worldview that invites diverse participation, with broad toleration for disagreement. The content of the worldview is aesthetically packaged in excellent animation and music and is accessible for the youngest members of society. Much of what is communicated is prosocial by any measure, contributing to the establishment of a moral society. However, certain assumptions about women, society, and truth are controversial but, paradoxically, are also part of their worldview. The mix of the good and bad is processed by children who are in the beginning stages of moral growth, and consequently, the hegemony that Disney exercises has powerful implications for future generations.

Raymond Williams writes about the potential for hegemony to occur in the socialization process:

> Any process of socialization of course includes things that all human beings have to learn, but any specific process ties this necessary learning to a selected range of meanings, values, and practices which, in the very closeness of their association with necessary learning, constitute the real foundations of the hegemonic. (117)

The "foundations" of Disney as a hegemonic agency lie in the children. The socialization process works especially on the young. As William Damon argues in *The Moral Child,* scientific evidence identifies how children develop morality as a result of early experiences:

Morality grows readily out of the child's early social experiences with parents and peers. It is through common activities like sharing and helping, as well as through universal emotional reactions like outrage, fear, and shame, that children acquire many of their deep-seated values and standards of behavior. Adult influence, too, plays a crucial role; but it is a role that is necessarily limited as well as mediated through the child's other life experiences. (xiv)

That Disney has the cultural presence and resources to dominate the messages children receive raises concerns. Yes, Disney communicates some wonderful messages about morality, including leaving room for spiritual realities, the clear delineation of good and evil, numerous examples that help define those categories, and the importance of open communication—all messages that will teach important lessons.

At the same time, Disney communicates messages about the dominating role of romance in women's lives, about the importance of physical appearance, about the preferred structure of society as patriarchal and hierarchical, about coming to knowledge through feelings, about when to respect authority, and about the need to purchase Disney products. Disney, in acting as a moral educator is socializing people, particularly children, into a Disney worldview with its particular virtues and vices.[13]

By looking at the rhetorical dimensions of Disney morality in five of its films, it has been possible to unearth a Disney worldview. Disney's voice as a competitor to religion and as a hegemonic cultural force is revealed in its animated films. The significant role that Disney plays in culture is affirmed by Michael Eisner's words in his letter to shareholders as he explains the corporation's actions in acquiring a new president, a new chief financial officer, and Capital Cities/ABC: "Cosmically speaking, we successfully engineered three stellar events that will affect the future alignment of Disney's planets" (Walt, "Letter," 1995). The emphasis on Disney as worldwide "engineer" and as center of the universe suggests a desire to dominate culture—a characteristic of a hegemonic agency.

CONCLUSION

A Disney worldview addresses the nature of humanness, the structure of society, and the process of knowing as being conflicted. It sends mixed moral messages, ultimately revealing a worldview that is also in conflict. We might call it a constructivist postmodern view with an emphasis on consumerism. Given Disney's powerful presence in society, the implications of its worldview suggest that the company has the potential to act as a competitor to religions' place in culture and as a hegemonic force.

The conglomeration that is Disney has a pervasive, some might even say invasive, presence in the late 20th to 21st centuries' culture, both American and, increasingly, international. At a time when questions of morality have taken center stage in the public sphere of discussion, Disney continues to market itself as the purveyor of family values. For example, in a response to the Southern Baptists who called for a boycott of all Disney products,[14] Disney referred to itself as "the world's largest producer of wholesome family entertainment" (Verburg 2). Disney wants to be associated with prosocial values. The animated films it produces are especially good vehicles for conveying morality, in that they employ a variety of rhetorical techniques that carry moral messages. As this study noted, Disney makes a conscious effort to send a positive message or theme with each of its films. *The Lion King* cogently communicates that, for Simba to find himself, he had to accept responsibility. *Pocahontas* powerfully presents a case for equality of different people and different races, as well as for environmentalism. *The Hunchback of Notre Dame* argues for the humanity of all people, including the outcast and the marginalized. *Hercules* encourages self-sacrifice as the defining quality of heroism. *Mulan* exemplifies qualities of duty, honor, and courage—in a woman. These are prosocial messages—values that help nurture children into mature, caring adults who are able to form principled communities, and morals that create a more just society. At the same time, these films communicate many inappropriate social values.

Discovering both the positive and the negative moral messages within the films is best accomplished by a close examination of the text from a rhetorical standpoint. While different theoretical tools might fruitfully be applied, an overall rhetorical questioning of the messages identified in the context of worldview questions yields a bigger picture. I have argued that with its constructivist, postmodern worldview, Disney has little difficulty with incongruous morality. The Disney worldview encourages tolerance of a variety of beliefs, as well as being influenced by the surrounding culture. Movements in culture toward more emancipatory understandings of women's roles and toward more just perspectives on diversity are portrayed in the films. At the same time, Disney features remnants of a modernist mind-set. All of this is driven by bottom-line considerations. The result, as evidenced in the films, is inconsistencies in moral messages.

Dismissing Disney films critically as hegemonic agents of self-interested, consumeristic values that communicate patriarchal, racist, hierarchical, and antiauthority visions of morality misses powerful dimensions of prosocial morality and aesthetically delightful animated art. Nevertheless, embracing Disney as harmless children's entertainment that teaches family values yields the influence and ability to teach one's own worldview. Given Disney's power as both a competitor to religion's moral voice and a hegemonic agency, the audience for its films needs to be critically aware that it is the recipient of a worldview that may be communicating more than "just family values."

CHAPTER 1. DISNEY, FILM, AND MORALITY: A BEGINNING

1. I refer to *Disney* throughout this research. I use the term to refer to more than just a person or a trademark. In particular, I personify the Walt Disney Company and the people who work for it, including directors, writers, animators, and musicians, as well as the broader cultural presence the company has in terms of its theme parks, products, and other facets of the conglomeration. This research assumes, as David Bordwell discusses, the "ideological, even mythological status" of the Walt Disney Company, which grew out of the person Walt Disney. But in order to discuss morality or ideology, I must also assume some constancy in the different films. Bordwell refers to this understanding of authorship as a means of "unearthing" stylistic, thematic, or technical commonalities ("Bounds" 78). Hence, when I refer to *Disney,* I am referring to the mythological presence of a conglomeration that stamps many different works with the same signature.

2. Disney's influence on culture is wide-ranging. Its very name has been turned into a noun, *Disneyfication,* which refers to a high degree of control and commodification that has signified Disney enterprises.

3. The focus of this research is primarily on morality as perceived from a United States perspective. Nevertheless, the Walt Disney Company's influence extends throughout the world. For examples, see the essays on cultural imperialism in Smoodin's *Disney Discourse* or Dorfman and Mattelart's *How to Read Donald Duck: Imperialist Ideology in the Disney Comic.*

4. Disney's pervasiveness grew in 1995 when it acquired Capital Cities/ABC for $19 billion. According to *Business Week,* following that merger, the Disney Company controlled 85,000 employees; 3 production studios; 11 net-

work TV stations; 228 TV affiliates; 21 radio stations; ESPN, Lifetime, A&E, and Disney cable channels; newspapers in 13 states; and 2 magazine publication houses ("ABC"). In five years the number of its employees grew to 120,000, and it increased the diversity in its holdings, including the development of an Internet Group (*Hoover's*).

Combined with its various business interests, Disney's reach into almost every part of our society is amazing. Its theme parks and resorts define family vacations. It has its own store, which has established itself nationally. Its films, music, books, and merchandising have invaded almost every home with children in it. A 1996 agreement with McDonald's ensures that for at least 10 years children will associate the pleasure of fast food with Disney (Elliott). It has even developed its own idyllic community, Celebration, designed to include housing for 20,000 people (Walt, "Fourth Fiscal Quarter").

Disney continues looking for new marketing opportunities. In the summer of 2001, it made an agreement with Kellogg's to sponsor a mini-website to promote *Atlantis: The Lost Empire* (Owens). In January 2001 it signed a deal with Deluxe Corporation that allows the corporation to print checks with Disney characters ("Deluxe Inks"). In its ongoing search for more markets, Disney plans a 2002 debut for a new cable station, Playhouse Disney, aimed at preschoolers. The name will also be used to start a new line of merchandise (Hiestand).

5. In addition to its financial success, one might also look to the Internet as a clue to Disney's popular appeal. A general search for *Disney* reveals hundreds of sites. Fans proliferate, forming the Disney Lover's Web Ring, which links almost 80 sites, and the "Friends of Disney Alliance," which links 820 sites, as well as creating a Disney search engine for 918 sites (Disneyseek.com).

6. Various people at Disney over its history have made significant contributions to the worldview it expresses. First Walt Disney and now Michael Eisner formalize that in official statements like the *Annual Report* of letters to shareholders. But that worldview is also constructed by a host of others in the execution of the projects. Consequently, I am not arguing that there is a "conspiracy" or coordinated effort to include all the messages I identify; rather, I call what I see in the text without attributing the messages to a person or plot.

7. Beginning with *The Lion King*, released in 1994, Disney has released at least one new animated film each year and has plans to continue this trend well into the new millennium (Walt, "Letter," *1996*). Investor pressure for greater returns has Disney cutting back its animation department, but the company still has immediate plans for releases through 2006 ("Disney Plans").

8. The film does resemble a cartoon series by Japanese animator Osamu Tezuka, *Kimba the White Lion*, but Disney insists that the idea for *Lion King* was its own and not based on Tezuka's work (Koenig 231–232; Schweizer and Schweizer 163–179).

9. See, for example, the "Special Issue on Rhetorical Criticism," *Western Journal of Speech Communication* 54 (1990). Michael Leff and Andrew Sachs, representing the critics who believe they need to focus on the text as the site of their criticism, square off against Michael McGee ("Text") and others who believe that criticism must also include the context in order to illuminate the representative textual fragments that actually constitute the rhetoric, and so the debate over rhetorical criticism, or critical rhetoric, continues. In this same special issue, John Campbell responds to Leff and McGee, arguing for a compromise position.

10. Recent years have seen a resurgence of rhetoricians who justify a historical-critical approach to research as opposed to those who see research as valid only on the basis that it tests or applies a theory. A list of related works by these scholars would include Thomas W. Benson, "The Study of American Rhetoric"; Stephen E. Lucas, "The Renaissance of American Public Address: Text and Context in Rhetorical Criticism"; David Zarefsky, "The State of the Art in Public Address Scholarship"; and the collection of authors in *Doing Rhetorical History: Concepts and Cases*, ed. Kathleen Turner.

CHAPTER 2. *THE LION KING:* MORAL EDUCATOR THROUGH MYTH, ARCHETYPE, AND RITUAL

1. Not all critics would agree. Richard Alleva states that "the songs . . . are miles below the level established by the last three Disney features." But he does cite the voice work as strong and says that "some of Disney's best animation ever appears in this movie" ("The Beasts" 18). Janet Maslin echoes the frustration with the music, and the delight with the animation, and she believes this is "the wittiest group of voices Disney has yet assembled" ("The Hero" C11).

2. Hofmeister states that *"Aladdin* is Disney's second-biggest grossing film" [next to *The Lion King*], with $217 million in box office sales (37).

3. Some examples include Roberta Trites's article criticizing the sexism in *The Little Mermaid* and a similar feminist criticism by Susan White. Richard Schickel in *The Disney Version* criticizes the racism in many early Disney films, and Alex Wainer examines the stereotypes in *Dumbo* and *The Jungle Book*. When *Bambi* was released, numerous critics opposed its "G" rating because of the violent death of Bambi's mother. A collection of essays entitled *From Mouse to Mermaid: The Politics of Film, Gender, and Culture,* edited by Elizabeth Bell, Lynda Haas, and Laura Sells, takes issue not only with the concerns already mentioned but also with Disney's ideological agenda.

4. A representative example of psychoanalytic literary criticism is found in Frye's *Anatomy of Criticism: Four Essays*. Psychoanalytic film criticism is discussed in Bordwell's *Making Meaning: Inference and Rhetoric in the Interpretation of Cinema* and in *Approaches to Popular Film*, ed. Hollows and Jancovich.

5. At first glance this may appear to be more a reference to baptism than to paradise. The theme of baptism is also here and will be discussed further below.

6. Specific references to dialogue are cited from Gina Ingoglia's *Disney's The Lion King* and have been confirmed on the videotaped release of the film.

7. At this point, the story appears to draw more from African than biblical myth. Susan Feldmann observes that the loss of paradise is also a frequent myth in African tales (25–26) and that most of these myths have a passive god who is ultimately removed from the earth to the sky. In *The Lion King,* Mufasa too is removed to a passive sky position.

8. See, for example, Rushing, "Evolution of 'The New Frontier' in *Alien* and *Aliens:* Patriarchal Co-optation of the Feminine Archetype"; Rushing and Frentz, "The Frankenstein Myth in Contemporary Cinema"; and Rushing and Frentz, "Integrating Ideology and Archetype in Rhetorical Criticism."

9. In addition to the articles cited in note 1, see also Osborn's articles, which began the interest in archetypes: "Archetypal Metaphor in Rhetoric: The Light-Dark Family" and "The Evolution of the Archetypal Sea in Rhetoric and Poetic." See also Chesebro, Bertelsen, and Gencarelli, "Archetypal Criticism"; Davies, Farrell, and Matthews, "The Dream World of Film: A Jungian Perspective on Cinematic Communication"; and Sillars, "Psychoanalytic Criticism: The Interaction of the Conscious and the Unconscious."

10. Osborn has identified light and darkness as a particularly powerful archetype. He states: "Such metaphors express intense value judgments and may thus be expected to elicit significant value responses from an audience" ("Archetypal Metaphor" 117).

11. Although the intention may have been to draw on archetypes of light and dark for rhetorical force, the hyenas' use of "black slang" and apparent darkness has raised cries of racism and stereotyping. See, for example, Foster, "The 'Lion King' Falls Prey to Howls of Sexism, Racism." Perhaps the reason many critics responded so negatively to the film is their awareness of the power of *The Lion King* as myth. By drawing on archetypes of light and dark, good and evil within the "people" without acknowledging cultural change, the movie comes dangerously close to stereotyping.

12. For extended analysis of the archetype as frontier, see Rushing, "Evolution of 'The New Frontier' in *Alien* and *Aliens:* Patriarchal Co-optation of the Feminine Archetype" and "Mythic Evolution of 'The New Frontier' in Mass Mediated Rhetoric."

13. James L. Hoban Jr. discusses rebirth as an archetype that forms a critical part of rhetorical ritual, in "Rhetorical Rituals of Rebirth."

14. Much has been written about pilgrimages or sacred journeys as found in a variety of cultures, as well as pilgrimages as metaphorical. For specific case studies in anthropology, see *Sacred Journeys: The Anthropology of Pilgrimage,* ed. Morinis; for an example in the rhetorical literature, see Stelzner, "The Quest Story and Nixon's November 3, 1969 Address." For discussion of pilgrimage as metaphor, see Graves, "Functions of Key Metaphors in Early Quaker Sermons, 1671–1700"; Graves, "Stephen Crisp's *Short History* as Spiritual Journey"; or Roppen and Sommer, *Strangers and Pilgrims: An Essay on the Metaphor of Journey.*

CHAPTER 3. *POCAHONTAS:* THE SYMBOLIC BOUNDARIES OF MORAL ORDER

1. A particularly powerful critique comes from Disney's Native American consultant, Shirley Custalow McGowan, also called Little Dove. Disney found her when they were doing research at Jamestown and even used her for some of the sketches of Pocahontas. For her, changes in the story were an affront to her people and a historical lie. The storytelling tradition of the Mattaponi people, direct descendants of the Powhatan Indians (Vincent, "Disney Vs. History" E5), is what preserves their culture, and changes to the stories destroy it (Faiola A1). McGowan contends, "This is a great story of respect and honor that has been lost in favor of just a romance. The real story is one of respect—the respect a child held for those new settlers. It was not a worldly love that bridged that gap" (Vincent, "Disney Vs. History" E1). McGowan laments the story that was not told: "John Smith was not the important force in her life. When she accepted Jesus Christ as her savior was the most important moment. She was the first of our people" (Vincent, "Disney Vs. History" E5).

2. Prior to the public release of *Pocahontas* in June 1995, Disney found itself involved in a different historical battle. The company announced plans to put a historical theme park in Virginia, promising to work closely with historians. They believed that the theme park would stimulate further interest in history, so that those who came to Disney would then seek out actual historical sites in the area. There was a strong negative response to these plans, and ultimately Disney was forced to abandon the project. But Disney's surprise at the reaction against it is itself quite amazing. That it sees little difference between what it does and "real" history offers a rationale for cultural critiques that engage more of Disney texts.

3. In discussing cultural analysis, Robert Wuthnow elucidates the strengths and weaknesses of various sociological approaches for uncovering meaning and moral order. He organizes the history of sociological research on culture into three subgroups: classical, represented by Marx, Weber, and Durkheim; neoclassical, represented by Berger, Bellah, and Geertz; and poststructuralist, represented by Douglas, Foucault, and Habermas. These traditional categories blur for Wuthnow as he examines moral order, and he finds them inadequate. Consequently, he proposes a different classification system, based on levels of cultural analysis: subjective, structural, dramaturgic, and institutional (10). This categorization allows him to focus on the question of meaning and of moral order.

For my purposes, rather than focusing on the distinctions among these categories, I draw from them the common application of the moral dimension. As a rhetorical critic, I bring the subjective dimension into my interpretation of the text. I also employ structural methods (as described below) with the dramaturgical purpose of seeking to explore how "cultural forms [in *Pocahontas*] dramatize (articulate, clarify, reaffirm) the character of moral obligations" (Wuthnow 344). Concurrently, I look for how ideology both "articulates ideas about moral obligations" and "reinforces" them (345).

For example, Edgerton and Jackson's analysis is ideological and serves to reveal how Disney's ideology is played out in the film. Wuthnow clearly relates cultural analysis to moral order, the very dimension I wish to explore more deeply. Thus his research is particularly useful in this rhetorical, textual exploration of the *Pocahontas* text.

4. For example, see Mary Douglas's *Natural Symbols,* in which she examines bodily symbolism in the context of group social relations and ego-centered relations. While the symbolism can serve several purposes, "it can serve as a philosophy of being, by distinguishing the forces of good from the forces of evil" (viii–ix).

5. Interestingly, Frances Mossiker, historian of Pocahontas, begins her first chapter with the quote from explorer Sir Walter Raleigh, "To seek new worlds for gold, for praise, for glory" (7).

6. The concept of collective innocence applies only in part to the Indians. They are collectively innocent in that they are the victims of white colonialism. However, in that they have not been willing to talk before going to war, they bear some of the responsibility and guilt. Thus, there is still need for Powhatan to be converted to the wisdom of Pocahontas.

7. Another extension of the light-dark metaphor—unrelated to morality, however—is the setting for the film. Given the historical nature of the material, Virginia is the setting, but Disney had a choice of seasons in which to set the action. Historically, the Virginia Company landed in Virginia on April 26 in the height of spring (Mossiker 7). *Pocahontas* takes place in the late summer and early fall, when the Indians are harvesting their crops. That the rhythm of the seasons is important to the Indians is emphasized in their singing in "Steady as the Beating Drum." The reference to the changing seasons suggests the balance in their lives.

By using only the fall season, Disney creates an allusion to the Indian's future. For around the corner is winter, a season of darkness. Osborn observes, "The variations in light and darkness from one season to another, the different qualities of sunlight, the extreme variations in heat and cold, all give seasonal contrasts a complex and powerful potential for symbolizing value judgments rising from hope and despair, fruition and decay" ("Archetypal Metaphor" 124). By setting the encounter with the Europeans in the fall, Disney implies that the Indians have a good life now, but their future will soon be marred by the coming "winter" of colonists.

8. Several examples of rhetorical scholarship involving the conversion narrative include Brown's "Logics of Discovery as Narratives of Conversion: Rhetorics of Invention in Ethnography, Philosophy, and Astronomy"; Griffin's "The Rhetoric of Form in Conversion Narratives"; Gregg's "A Rhetorical Re-examination of Arthur Vandenberg's 'Dramatic Conversion,' January 10, 1945"; and Frentz and Farrell's "Conversion of America's Consciousness: The Rhetoric of *The Exorcist.*" See also the two articles cited in the text following.

9. For example, consider some of the central characters from several other Disney films: Pinocchio of *Pinocchio,* Ariel of *The Little Mermaid,* Jasmine of *Aladdin,* or Simba of *The Lion King.*

10. It is not surprising that John Smith has no culpability for his earlier actions and attitudes toward the land and toward Native Americans. Susan Jeffords, in a critique of Disney's *Beauty and the Beast,* makes an interesting observation that may apply in this case as well:

> In contrast to the commanding, sophisticated, and intelligent Beasts that frequent the other tales and that finally make them so deserving of Beauty's love, this Beast seems childish, blustering, "clumsy," petulant, and untutored. As with his upbringing and his initial acquisition of his selfish personality, the Beast does not have to take responsibility for his behavior. It is the work of other people, especially women, to turn this childish Beast into a loving man. This message is clear: if the Beast has not changed before, it is not his fault, but that of those around him who failed to show him otherwise. (169)

Disney's male characters are patronized by women. But the fact that the women willingly put up with the male chauvinism and patiently teach the men more enlightened attitudes (another example includes Nala and Simba's relationship in *The Lion King*) may reflect contemporary values and demonstrates a Disney moral order that wants to allow women equality but is not willing to hold men responsible for uncooperative attitudes.

CHAPTER 4. *THE HUNCHBACK OF NOTRE DAME:* COMICALLY FRAMING VIRTUE AND VICE

1. A select group of scholars have taken up the concept of "frame" to analyze a variety of rhetorical situations, yielding insights regarding comedy and tragedy in public discourse (see Brummett's "Burkean Comedy and Tragedy, Illustrated in Reactions to the Arrest of John DeLorean"); the comic frame at work in social movements (see Carlson's "Gandhi and the Comic Frame: 'Ad Bellum Purificandum,'" as well as Carlson's "Limitations on the Comic Frame: Some Witty American Women of the Nineteenth Century," which demonstrated how the comic can change to the satirical and the burlesque); the application of the burlesque frame to political cartoons (see Bostdorff's "Making Light of James Watt: A Burkean Approach to the Form and Attitude of Political Cartoons"); the comic and tragic in apocalyptic rhetoric (see O'Leary's "A Dramatistic Theory of Apocalyptic Rhetoric"); the comic as an argument frame (see Madsen's "The Comic Frame as a Corrective to Bureaucratization: A Dramatistic Perspective on Argumentation"); the comic and the vice presidency (see Bostdorff's "Vice-presidential Comedy and the Traditional Female Role: An Examination of the Rhetorical Characteristics of the Vice Presidency"); and the comic as a response to the exigencies of social conditions (see Christiansen and Hanson's "Comedy as Cure for Tragedy: Act Up and the Rhetoric of AIDS").

2. Specific references to dialogue are cited from the movie itself unless otherwise noted.

3. Expectations for *The Hunchback* to bring in strong box office numbers were high. Industry analysts predicted: "Walt Disney Co.'s animated film *The Hunchback of Notre Dame* is expected to gross $150 million or more in domestic box-office receipts." That the analysts expected much from this film is no surprise, given Disney's track record. The foreign market was also a major consideration: "'*Hunchback* will also play well overseas, and generate as much as $150 million in additional revenue from video sales,' said Dave Davis, senior associate with investment banking firm Houlihan Lokey Howard and Zukin in Los Angeles." The Disney Company itself believed the film would do well: "'We have very high hopes for this film,' Disney spokesman Tom Deegan said" ("Disney's *Hunchback* Seen Grossing" 1).

However, reality did not live up to expectations. By August 2, 1996, the film had grossed $91.4 million and was being bumped from the charts by megahit *Independence Day* (Backlot). Disney was pleased by the film's strong showing outside the United States. Michael Eisner says, "*The Hunchback of Notre Dame* opened with extraordinary results in 12 territories, including France, Germany, Belgium, Switzerland and Holland" (Walt, "Letter," *1996* I:1). Nevertheless, the film was not generating the high box office numbers that Disney had hoped for. Vincent confirms that the studio was concerned about the box office numbers: "[If the film] takes in anything less than $100 million at the box office, it will be a disappointment. Studio pundits are predicting a $200 million take, but admit that this one is a risk" ("Will" E1). That it never quite took $100 million says something about this film in comparison with earlier Disney films.

4. Burke speaks of attitudes of acceptance and rejection as symbolic frames for looking at the world, for transcendence. He defines the positive thus: "By 'frames of acceptance' we mean the more or less organized system of meanings by which a thinking man gauges the historical situation and adopts a role with relation to it" (*Attitudes* 5).

Elsewhere Burke speaks of "terministic screens" (*Language* 44 ff.), a concept related to framing perspectives. The terministic screen of a particular choice of language directs the responding attention or attitude to correspond with that particular screen. Similarly, "Each frame enrolls for 'action' in accordance with its particular way of drawing the lines. Out of such frames we derive our vocabularies for the charting of human motives" (*Attitudes* 92). Logically a discussion of worldview should follow here. I prefer to leave it for the last chapter, in which I can more readily draw from the work of earlier chapters for examples.

5. Although Burke identifies a number of poetic forms (epic, tragedy, comedy, elegy, satire, burlesque, and the grotesque) as expressions of attitudes of acceptance and rejection (*Attitudes* Chap. 2), he focuses on the tragic and comic frames, which may incorporate these other forms. In more explicit terms, Northrop Frye contrasts the motivational perspectives, or "existential projections," inherent in the tragic and comic genres. He says, "It is natural . . . for tragedy and comedy to throw their shadows, so to speak, into philosophy and shape there a philosophy of fate and a philosophy of providence respectively" (64).

6. Although Burke also suggests a "didactic" frame (*Attitudes* 75 tff.), it does not fit *The Hunchback*—perhaps because of the complexity of Victor Hugo's original story and characterizations. Disney does take a didactic tone overall, but also includes ambivalence in its central character, Quasimodo. And the fact that there is much more emphasis on the "upward turn"—on the providential rather than fateful freeing of the hero—places this film in the comic frame.

7. Robert B. Louden asserts, "It is common knowledge by now that recent philosophical and theological writing about ethics reveals a marked revival of interest in the virtues" (227). One often-cited representative of the contemporary revival of virtue ethics is Alasdair MacIntyre, particularly his *After Virtue.* He "has argued in the Aristotelian tradition that the modern morality of rules (Utilitarian or Kantian) must be rejected unless it fits into a larger scheme in which the virtues are central" (Albert, Denise, and Peterfreund 386). However, MacIntyre's discussion of virtue ethics is in the context of a broader concept of ethics. As Vernon Cronen observes, MacIntyre is trying "to construct a rational and universal basis for ethical thought" based on the three ideas of "practice, the unity of an individual life, and the concept of virtue" (30) and rejecting the trend toward emotivism.

Theologian Stanley Hauerwas, who builds on MacIntyre's work to include the centrality of narrative to conceptions of virtue, wisely notes that "no ethic is formulated in isolation from the social conditions of its time" (48). Disney, too, is influenced by its surrounding culture, and its perspective on virtues and vices reflects that influence. For example, although many of our immediate ancestors lived in a world where duty was an expected ingredient in life, our society is one that places value on freedom and individuality. The result is that, for many, ethics has become a matter of situation rather than a principle or rule. Virtue ethics is an emphasis that allows for the advocating of morality in such a way as to get beyond every situation. (Whether or not Disney actually advocates virtue ethics or emotivism will be discussed in Chapter 7.)

8. Compare this language with the following passages from the Bible: "The Lord will smite him" (1 Sam. 26:10). "The angels will come out and separate the evil from the righteous, and throw them into the furnace of fire" (Matt. 13:50). "Then Death and Hades were thrown into the lake of fire" (Rev. 20:14).

CHAPTER 5. *HERCULES:* A CELEBRITY-HERO

1. Specific references to dialogue are cited from the movie itself unless otherwise noted.

2. According to Wells, Walt Disney was known for his desire for realism in the animation: "[Walt] Disney . . . insisted on verisimilitude in his characters, contexts and narratives. He wanted animated figures to move like real figures and be informed by a plausible motivation" (23).

3. The mixed critical response was reflected in the box office numbers. This Disney film brought in only $97 million domestically, less than *The*

Hunchback of Notre Dame ($100 million) and far less than *Pocahontas* ($142 million) and *The Lion King* ($313 million) (Corliss, "There's Tumult" 90). The less than enthusiastic response reflects the disparate elements of the film.

In addition to mixing myth stew, there are so many visual distractions. Scenes bombard the eye with detail, adding complexity to the stew. Multiple mythological characters appear throughout, mixing the original stories. Fast-paced quick cuts change scenes at the blink of an eye. Stylistic changes in music multiply the mix from Gospel to Broadway, love song, and postmodern phrase songs with narrative interruptions (e.g., "Go the Distance"). One moment the audience is steeped in myth, fighting monsters; the next, it is laughing at a Disney spoof of its own marketing with an emphasis on contemporary consumerism. The film offers a buffet of myths, images, ideas, and music. And what happens at a buffet? The food gets mixed together on one's plate into tastes of this and that, bits of unappetizing globs that leave one feeling overfull and aesthetically dissatisfied.

4. *Time's* film editor, Richard Corliss, declares *Hercules* to be a success that harkens back to the "form and formula" of musical comedy. Acknowledging that it does not adhere to the original myth, Corliss believes that the return to the Disney standard theme of "adolescent self-discovery" with the "shtick" tie-ins to popular culture "proves that Walt's art form is still sassy and snazzy" ("Hit" 76). Similarly, Janet Maslin of the *New York Times* raved about it as "divine" with "cleverness to spare" even though "the legend of Hercules has been trivialized and shoehorned into a familiar mold" ("Review" C1). Michael Wilmington, film critic for the *Chicago Tribune,* describes the film as "another scintillating Disney display of modern animation technique, and an often hilarious satire of super-action movies and the modern celebrity sports media machine" (D–E).

5. Another critic, Desson Howe, also expressed dislike of the film: "In the Disney movie, the dark material [of Greek myth] has been airbrushed out of existence. This is understandable, but in its place, the mouse factory has inserted narrative mush that's ineptly conceived, woefully performed by the off-screen actors and badly animated."

6. For an excellent discussion of Burke's contributions to the field of rhetoric, see Foss, Foss, and Trapp's "Kenneth Burke." Cheney's "The Rhetoric of Identification and the Study of Organizational Communication" includes numerous references to sources that discuss and apply the concept of "identification."

7. Disney's myth reflects a Western value that emphasizes individualism—the thing that motivates and provides rationalizations for self-centered behavior. Yet hand in hand with individualism is the need to feel accepted, to belong. Ironically, being an individual often means standing alone, apart from the group.

8. For a discussion of emotive meaning, see Stevenson's *Ethics and Language,* Chap. 2.

9. In fact, according to codirector John Musker, "The film intends to be, for lack of a better term, a 'boy's movie'" (Tucker 38).

10. A number of important dimensions have been highlighted in studies about the rhetoric of form in music (Irvine and Kirkpatrick, "The Musical Form in Rhetorical Exchange: Theoretical Considerations"; Rasmussen, "Transcendence in Leonard Bernstein's Kaddish Symphony"); music and power (Jones and Schumacher, "Muzak: On Functional Music and Power"); and music as a resistance strategy (Carter, "The Industrial Workers of the World and the Rhetoric of Song"; Knupp, "A Time for Every Purpose Under Heaven: Rhetorical Dimensions of Protest Music"; Sanger, "Slave Resistance and Rhetorical Self-definition: Spirituals as a Strategy"); as well as studies of the rhetoric of specific styles (Holmberg, "Toward the Rhetoric of Music: Dixie"; Francesconi, "Free Jazz and Black Nationalism: A Rhetoric of Musical Style"; LeCoat, "Music and the Three Appeals of Classical Rhetoric"; Rybacki and Rybacki, "The Rhetoric of Song") or of specific musicians (Beebe, "Ballad of the Apocalypse: Another Look at Bob Dylan's 'Hard Rain'"; Gonzalez and Makay, "Rhetorical Ascription and the Gospel According to Dylan"; Makay and Gonzalez, "Dylan's Biographical Rhetoric and the Myth of the Outlaw Hero").

Despite my limitations on the analysis of music in this study, it is valuable to remember that music's power as rhetoric does extend beyond the written word. An excellent article that discusses the history of rhetoric as applied to music and asks how far a "linguistic system" can be extended to an "aesthetic system" is Vickers's "Figures of Rhetoric/Figures of Music?" *Rhetorica* 2 (1984): 1–4. He concludes by reminding us that although there may be overlap between the two arts, music remains outside linguistic symbolism; much of what and how music expresses itself is outside of the naming process. Music yields "insight," whereas "rhetoric is inalienably about communication" (44).

11. It is more like Disney is "proclaiming" itself the hero. In 1997 it renovated the New Amsterdam Theater in the heart of Times Square sleaziness and served as the anchor for a cleaned-up, family-friendly 42nd Street. Disney acted the part of the hero in "saving" the heart of New York City (Handy).

CHAPTER 6. *MULAN:* EAST MEETS WEST

1. The oriental influence can be seen particularly in the visuals and in the musical instruments. According to Disney, "The artistic approach is based on the Chinese 'sing' style of 'negative,' or empty spaces balanced by 'positive' detail—almost a 'yin and yang' concept" (Walt, "*Mulan* Fun Facts"). Artistically, Disney also creates contrasts in the color palette, employing colors that suggest a Chinese watercolor for the majority of the film and interspersing brights for the dramatic moments (*Mulan Press Kit* 16). Musically, Disney tried to incorporate some traditional Chinese instruments (20). The Eastern influence wanes, however, in some of the songs, which the musicians created from their "sensibilities for Western music and pop" (20–21), and in the content of the narrative itself, which often reflects Western values.

2. Rather than examine how Disney's version deviates from the original tale, I will take the film at face value, as if it weren't based on a well-loved legend. In so doing, I focus on how this film mixes both Eastern and Western values. For a good source on its deviations from "The Song of Mulan," see Mo and Shen's "A Mean Wink at Authenticity: Chinese Images in Disney's *Mulan.*"

3. Note that these concepts are not necessarily opposite and may coexist within the same culture. However, the generalization that Eastern cultures are more collectivist-oriented than are Western, and vice versa, holds true (Kagitçibasi 55–56).

4. See, for example, Chen et al.; Chu and Ju, *The Great Wall in Ruins: Communication and Cultural Change in China;* Gao and Ting-Toomey, *Communicating Effectively With the Chinese;* and Kim et al., *Individualism and Collectivism: Theory, Method, and Applications.*

5. Specific references to dialogue are cited from the movie itself unless otherwise noted

6. See, for example, the pop psychology book by John Gray, *Men Are From Mars, Women Are From Venus,* Deborah Tannen's *You Just Don't Understand: Women and Men in Conversation,* or Tannen's more scholarly work, such as *Gender and Discourse.* Tannen's work cites John Gumperz's research on interethnic communication, which is the scholarly foundation for the cross-cultural concept.

7. Pan et al., in *To See Ourselves: Comparing Traditional Chinese and American Cultural Values,* argue that the Cultural Revolution in China negatively affected the acceptance of traditional values (216). It is only now, in contemporary society, that the younger generation is readapting some of the traditional values. Furthermore, the findings of this research suggest that there are more similarities in values between Chinese and Americans than once thought, due in part to cultural change as well as to historical events (212–213).

8. Generalizations about values can be helpful but can also be dangerous. Although I contrast Chinese and American values below, please keep in mind that there are "three distinct and competing influences . . . operating in contemporary China: traditional Chinese cultural orthodoxy, Marxism and Maoism, and Western influences" (Pan et al. 25). Marxist propagandizing has been strong, and some of its values are in direct opposition to Confucianism. Pan et al.'s study found that some elements of Confucian values remain strong, but others, such as a woman's inferiority and obedience to her husband, have declined.

9. In intercultural communication a similar concept is used: value homophily (Dodd 179).

CHAPTER 7. A DISNEY WORLDVIEW: MIXED MORAL MESSAGES

1. Condit addresses these potential limitations of a text when she argues for the term *polyvalence* over *polysemy:* "polyvalence occurs when audience members share understandings of the denotations of a text but disagree

about the valuation of those denotations to such a degree that they produce notably different interpretations" ("Rhetorical" 106).

2. Codirector of *The Hunchback,* Kirk Wise, speaks of the concerns the studio had with this film: "To make it work in the genre we're in—the Disney animated musical—we knew that we were going to have to leaven it with humor" (Dretzka, *Hunchback* 8). Commenting on Disney director Wise's concern for balancing the darkness of *The Hunchback,* Dretzka observes that the "balance of good and evil is nothing new for Disney filmmakers" (8). And the president of Walt Disney Feature Animation, Peter Schneider, contends: "In *Pocahontas,* I think maybe we were a little bit too politically correct." But *The Hunchback* was a more freeing, "joyous" film to work on because of the balanced treatment of sensitive issues: "We felt the message that Quasimodo doesn't have to transform to be accepted was so powerful in the disabled community—with all of us—that it would be extremely successful" (Dretzka, *Hunchback* 9).

3. The concept of an "open" text is developed in the work of John Fiske. For example, see his "Television: Polysemy and Popularity." Another example of an application of the open text to film is Solomon and McMullen's *"Places in the Heart:* The Rhetorical Force of an Open Text."

4. Worldview discussions have addressed these fundamental questions from a variety of descriptions. Walsh and Middleton, for example, use four questions to organize a worldview discussion: "Who am I? Where am I? What's wrong? and What is the remedy?" (35). The two-volume work *Building a Christian World View,* ed. W. Andrew Hoffecker, is organized around the following themes: God, man, knowledge, the universe, society, and ethics. Arthur Holmes, arguing that a worldview begins at the "prephilosophical level," suggests that a worldview should address issues of the "whole person" and will incorporate theological, philosophical, and scientific questions (*Contours* 31–53).

5. In "Furthering the Kingdom in Psychology," Kirk Farnsworth discusses worldview as a "conceptual framework" composed of "components" or "control beliefs."

6. The ending of the film is extremely weak. The implication that the only way Smith would live is to make the long voyage back to England is irrational unless the assumption is that only "white man's" medicine will work. He is wounded and weak. The Indians have their own medicine, and it may be more effective to treat him immediately. Pocahontas even gives him powdered bark from Grandmother Willow to help with the pain.

7. Another dimension of the gender bias in Disney's worldview is the role of the mother. The mother, if one is in the picture, is never given a significant role in the story. In *The Lion King,* Simba's mother is shown giving him a bath and later is shown in failing strength under Scar's reign. Whereas the father/son relationship is central to the story, the mother/son relationship is insignificant. At least Simba had a mother, however. Of the main characters in recent Disney films (*The Little Mermaid, Beauty and the Beast, Aladdin, The Lion King, Pocahontas, The Hunchback of Notre Dame, Tarzan,* and *Dinosaur*), Simba was the only one to be so blessed. As Toscano observes,

Disney has a penchant for removing mothers from the picture (4). In *The Hunchback*, for example, Hugo's novel does not include a mother at all, but Disney creates one, only to kill her off immediately. The role of the mother in a Disney world is not significant, character shaping, or central to the narrative. What kind of role model is that for young children?

8. Some critics have argued that Disney is antidemocratic and that the ideal world would be structured as a monarchy. (See Foster, "The 'Lion King' Falls Prey to Howls of Sexism, Racism.") Monarchy is not advocated in all of these films; however, male authority is presented as the norm.

9. This is not to say, however, that community has no significance. Nevertheless, it is individual actions and emotions, not communal experiences, that yield insight. Simba is able to save the Pride Land community because he has gained the knowledge of who he is. He arrives at that knowledge with encouragement from Nala and from his father's spirit telling him to look inside himself, but he knows what is right and is able to finally act on that knowledge only because he finally listens to his heart. He was not convinced by Nala's rhetoric nor by a sense of duty; rather, he knows because he experiences his father's reminder. Likewise, Pocahontas comes to know what her right path is because she follows her heart. Her heart is the ultimate source of truth, not her father's wisdom or tribal tradition. Quasimodo is encouraged to look inside himself to see the truth that he is not a monster. Hercules comes to see himself as a hero when he rescues Meg. Mulan comes to know her own strength when she stands up to Shan-Yu and claims the credit for taking away his victory. To know is to "feel" that something is right, and what one person feels or experiences is as valid as what another feels. Emotivism, rooted in individualism, provides the justification and motivation for decisions and actions.

10. Alasdair MacIntyre labels this approach "emotivism" and says that emotivism "lacks rational criteria for evaluation" (31) and that moral action is based on individual desire because of the value of individual freedom (10). After diagnosing the cultural problem as emotivism, MacIntyre offers a solution to this type of ethics by reviving Aristotelian virtue ethics and anchoring them in narrative. But as Thomas Frentz reveals, this turn toward virtue and narration is also emotiveness at base: "For when the telos for humanity is a quest plus humanly derived moral concepts, all that can follow is a humanly grounded morality, and those are at base emotiveness, no matter how persistent the protests to the contrary" (15). Thus, Disney's use of stock virtues and vices to clearly proffer a vision of good and evil is still rooted in an "emotivist" worldview.

11. Margaret Miles argues: "Movies cannot replace religion in its traditional capacity to define and encourage love. The media's secular imagination relies on caricatures of religion while strenuously trying to fill religion's shoes. Yet popular film contributes to identifying and engaging issues of how to live even in its failure to provide richly imagined pictures of human life and relationships" (156). While in reality religion may be irreplaceable, Disney may be becoming the substitute for a voice of moral authority.

12. For example, see Trujillo, "Hegemonic Masculinity on the Mound: Media Representations of Nolan Ryan and American Sports Culture"; Lewis, "Making Sense of Common Sense: A Framework for Tracking Hegemony"; Condit, "Hegemony in a Mass-mediated Society: Concordance About Reproductive Technologies."

13. Disney is well aware of its target audience. Michael Eisner says: "We know our audience, and predominantly it is a family audience. We should not lament that others appeal more strongly to the disenfranchised teenage audience. They always come back when they become re-enfranchised adults with children" (Walt, "Letter," 1995, 5).

14. The call for the boycott was motivated by Disney's decision to extend its benefit coverage to homosexual partners (Price 9A). Several organizations have expressed dismay and fear that this action, combined with some of Disney's other products (e.g., Hyperion Books' publication of pro-gay books; the release of the film *Priest*, in which a priest has a homosexual relationship; and the adult themes in other films financed or produced by Disney), means that Disney is abandoning its commitment to family values. The American Family Association has been particularly vocal in calling for a Disney boycott. James Dobson's Focus on the Family has criticized Disney extensively but stops short of calling for an organized boycott. For examples of some of the criticism by Donald Wildmon and the American Family Association, see "Disney's Moral Plunge Continues." There have been a variety of articles criticizing Disney, beginning in the monthly *AFA Journal* issues from August 1996 on. Focus on the Family's magazine, *Citizen*, is also a source for a number of critical articles; see Buss, "Mickey's New Friends" or "Disney's Latest Blunder."

"ABC: Disney's Kingdom." *Business Week* 14 August 1995: 30–35.

Albert, Ethel M., Theodore C. Denise, and Sheldon P. Peterfreund, eds. *Great Traditions in Ethics*. 6th ed. Belmont, Calif.: Wadsworth, 1988.

Alleva, Richard. "The Beasts of Summer: 'Lion King' and 'Wolf.'" *Commonweal* 19 August 1994: 18–20.

Aristotle. *Nichomachean Ethics*. Trans. Martin Ostwald. Indianapolis: Bobbs-Merrill Educational Publishing, 1962.

Arnold, Gary. "Movies." *Washington Times* 20 June 1996: M20.

Atlantis: The Lost Empire. Dir. Gary Trousdale and Kirk Wise. Walt Disney Pictures, 2001.

Aubry, Jack. "Latest Disney Hit a Hit With Indians: *Pocahontas* Gives Canadian Children Positive Image, Say Native Viewers." *Ottawa Citizen* 23 June 1995: A1.

Backlot Box Office. "U.S. Box Office (August 2–4, 1996)." Accessed 18 February 1997. <http://www.film.com:80/backlot/boxoffice/archive/box.office.aug2.4.htm>.

Bakhtin, M. M. *The Dialogic Imagination: Four Essays*. 1981. Ed. Michael Holquist. Trans. Caryl Emerson and Michael Holquist. Austin: University of Texas Press, 1988.

Barber, Benjamin R. "From Disney World to Disney's World." *New York Times* 1 August 1995: A15.

Beauchamp, Tom L. *Philosophical Ethics: An Introduction to Moral Philosophy*. New York: McGraw-Hill, 1982.

Beebe, Thomas O. "Ballad of the Apocalypse: Another Look at Bob Dylan's 'Hard Rain.'" *Text and Performance Quarterly* 11 (1991): 18–34.

Bell, Elizabeth, Lynda Haas, and Laura Sells, eds. *From Mouse to Mermaid: The Politics of Film, Gender, and Culture*. Bloomington: Indiana University Press, 1995.

Bellah, Robert N., et al. *The Good Society*. 1991. New York: Vintage Books, 1992.

———. *Habits of the Heart: Individualism and Commitment in American Life*. 1985. New York: Harper and Row, 1986.

Bennett, William, ed. *The Book of Virtues: A Treasury of Great Moral Stories*. New York: Simon and Schuster, 1993.

Benson, Thomas W. "The Study of American Rhetoric." *American Rhetoric: Context and Criticism*. Ed. Thomas W. Benson. Carbondale: Southern Illinois University, 1989. 1–17.

Berland, David I. "Disney and Freud: Walt Meets the Id." *Journal of Popular Culture* 15 (1982): 93–103.

Bernard, Jamie. "Disney's 'Lion King' Roars Out of Africa." *New York Daily News* 12 June 1994, NewsBank, Art, 16: G3–G5.

Bettelheim, Bruno. *The Uses of Enchantment: The Meaning and Importance of Fairy Tales*. New York: Random House, 1977.

Bird, S. Elizabeth. "Gendered Construction of the American Indian in Popular Media." *Journal of Communication* 49.3 (1999): 61–83.

Biskind, Peter. "American Beauty." *Premiere* July 1995: 84–85.

———. "Win, Lose—But Draw." *Premiere* July 1995: 81–86, 108.

Bitzer, Lloyd F. "The Rhetorical Situation." *Philosophy and Rhetoric* 1 (1968): 1–14.

Boje, David M. "Stories of the Storytelling Organization: A Postmodern Analysis of Disney as 'Tamara-land.'" *Academy of Management Journal* 38.4 (1995): 997–1035.

Booth, Mark. "The Art of Words in Song." *Quarterly Journal of Speech* 62 (1976): 242–249.

Bordwell, David. "The Bounds of Difference." *The Classical Hollywood Cinema: Film Style and Mode of Production to 1960*, by David Bordwell, Janet Staiger, and Kristin Thompson. New York: Columbia University Press, 1985. 70–84.

———. *Making Meaning: Inference and Rhetoric in the Interpretation of Cinema*. Cambridge: Harvard University Press, 1989.

Bostdorff, Denise M. "Making Light of James Watt: A Burkean Approach to the Form and Attitude of Political Cartoons." *Quarterly Journal of Speech* 73 (1987): 43–59.

———. "Vice-presidential Comedy and the Traditional Female Role: An Examination of the Rhetorical Characteristics of the Vice Presidency." *Western Journal of Speech Communication* 55 (1991): 1–27.

Bowers, Detine L. "Afrocentrism and *Do the Right Thing*." *Rhetoric in Popular Culture*, by Barry Brummett. New York: St. Martin's Press, 1994. 199–221.

———. "The Blackness of Weakness, Meekness, and the Voice of the Signifying Monkey: Issues and Controversies in Disney's *The Lion King*." Speech Communication Association Convention paper. San Antonio, Texas, November 1995.

"Box-Office Statistics in Millions of U.S. Dollars." Accessed 1 June 1999. <http://www.vex.net/~odin/Gross/>.

Brandt, Richard B. "Emotive Theory of Ethics." *The Encyclopedia of Philosophy.* 1972 ed.

Branham, Robert James. "The Role of the Convert in *Eclipse of Reason* and *The Silent Scream.*" *Quarterly Journal of Speech* 77 (1991): 407–426.

Brown, Corie, and Laura Shapiro. "Woman Warrior." *Newsweek* 8 June 1998: 64.

Brown, Richard Harvey. "Logics of Discovery as Narratives of Conversion: Rhetorics of Invention in Ethnography, Philosophy, and Astronomy." *Philosophy and Rhetoric* 27 (1994): 1–34.

Brown, William J., and Arvind Singhal. "Ethical Issues of Promoting Prosocial Messages Through the Popular Media." *Journal of Popular Film and Television* 21.3 (Fall 1993): 92–99.

Brummett, Barry. "Burkean Comedy and Tragedy, Illustrated in Reactions to the Arrest of John DeLorean." *Communication Studies* 35 (1984): 217–227.

Buescher, Derek T., and Kent A. Ono. "Civilized Colonialism: *Pocahontas* as Neocolonial Rhetoric." *Women's Studies in Communication* 19 (1996): 127–153.

Burke, Kenneth. *Attitudes Toward History.* 1937. 3rd ed. Berkeley: University of California Press, 1984.

———. *A Grammar of Motives.* 1945. Berkeley: University of California Press, 1969.

———. *Language as Symbolic Action: Essays on Life, Literature, and Method.* 1966. Berkeley: University of California Press, 1968.

———. *Permanence and Change: An Anatomy of Purpose.* 1935. 3rd ed. Berkeley: University of California Press, 1984.

———. *The Philosophy of Literary Form: Studies in Symbolic Action.* 1941. New York: Vintage Books, 1957.

———. *A Rhetoric of Motives.* 1950. New York: Prentice-Hall, 1952.

Buss, Dale D. "Mickey's New Friends." *Citizen* 16 October 1995: 1–3.

Campbell, John Angus. "Between the Fragment and the Icon: Prospect for a Rhetorical House of the Middle Way." *Western Journal of Speech Communication* 54 (Summer 1990): 346–376.

Campbell, Joseph. "The Historical Development of Mythology." *Myth and Mythmaking.* 1959. Ed. Henry A. Murray. Boston: Beacon Press, 1968. 19–45.

Carassavas, Anthee. "*Hercules* Film Raises Greek Chorus of Protest." *USA Today* 2 October 1997: 10D.

Carlson, A. Cheree. "Gandhi and the Comic Frame: 'Ad Bellum Purificandum.'" *Quarterly Journal of Speech* 72 (1986): 446–455.

———. "Limitations on the Comic Frame: Some Witty American Women of the Nineteenth Century." *Quarterly Journal of Speech* 74 (1988): 310–322.

Carson, Frances. "Motion Pictures and Our Youth." *Quarterly Journal of Speech* 28 (1942): 186–189.

Carter, David A. "The Industrial Workers of the World and the Rhetoric of Song." *Quarterly Journal of Speech* 66 (1980): 365–374.

Carter, Stephen L. *Integrity*. New York: Basic Books, 1996.

Chen, Chao C., James R. Meindl, and Raymond G. Hunt. "Testing the Effects of Vertical and Horizontal Collectivism: A Study of Reward Allocation Preferences in China." *Journal of Cross-Cultural Psychology* 28 (1997): 44–70.

Chen, Ling. "Chinese and North Americans: An Epistemological Exploration of Intercultural Communication." *Howard Journal of Communications* 4.4 (1993): 342–357.

Cheney, George. "The Rhetoric of Identification and the Study of Organizational Communication." *Quarterly Journal of Speech* 69 (1983): 143–158.

Chesebro, James W., Dale A. Bertelsen, and Thomas F. Gencarelli. "Archetypal Criticism." *Communication Education* 39 (1990): 257–274.

Christiansen, Adrienne E., and Jeremy J. Hanson. "Comedy as Cure for Tragedy: Act Up and the Rhetoric of AIDS." *Quarterly Journal of Speech* 82 (1996): 157–170.

Chu, Godwin C., and Yanan Ju. *The Great Wall in Ruins: Communication and Cultural Change in China*. Albany: State University of New York Press, 1993.

Cochran, Connor Freff. "Hans Zimmer and the Music of *The Lion King*." *Roland Users Group* 12.2 (1994): 30–37.

Cochrane, J. Scott. "*The Wizard of Oz* and Other Mythic Rites of Passage." *Image and Likeness: Religious Visions in American Film Classics*. Ed. John R. May. Mahwah, N.J.: Paulist Press, 1992. 79–86.

Coles, Robert. *The Moral Life of Children*. Boston: Atlantic Monthly Press, 1986.

———. *The Spiritual Life of Children*. Boston: Houghton Mifflin, 1990.

Condit, Celeste Michelle. "Crafting Virtue: The Rhetorical Construction of Public Morality." *Quarterly Journal of Speech* 73 (1987): 79–97.

———. "Hegemony in a Mass-mediated Society: Concordance About Reproductive Technologies." *Critical Studies in Mass Communication* 11 (1994): 205–230.

———. "The Rhetorical Limits of Polysemy." *Critical Studies in Mass Communication* 6 (1989): 103–122.

Connell, Joan. "Pocahontas: Whose Myth Is It Anyway?" *Port St. Lucie (Fla.) News* July 1995: D1, D7.

Cooks, Leda M., Mark P. Orbe, and Carol S. Bruess. "The Fairy Tale Theme in Popular Culture: A Semiotic Analysis of *Pretty Woman*." *Women's Studies in Communication* 16 (1993): 86–104.

Corliss, Richard. "A Grand Cartoon Cathedral." *Time* 24 June 1996: 73.

———. "A Hit from a Myth." *Time* 23 June 1997: 76.

———. "The Lion Roars." *Time* 20 June 1994: 58–60.

———. "An Ode to Martial Smarts." *Time* 22 June 1998: 69.

———. "Princess of the Spirit." *Time* 19 June 1995: 59.

———. "There's Tumult in Toon Town: Rival Studios Challenge Disney's Monopoly." *Time* 17 November 1997: 88–90.

Crandall, Christian S., Jo-Ann Tsang, Susan Goldman, and John T. Pennington. "Newsworthy Moral Dilemmas: Justice, Caring, and Gender." *Sex Roles: A Journal of Research* 40 (February 1999): 187–300 (2). Ebsco host.

Trinity Christian College Library, Palos Heights, Ill. Accessed 1 June 1999. <http://ioweb.uiuc.edu>.

Crazy Horse, Chief Roy. "The Pocahontas Myth." Accessed 22 January 1997. <http://www.powhatan.org/pocc.html>.

Cronen, Vernon E. "Coordinated Management of Meaning Theory and Post Enlightenment Ethics." *Conversations on Communication Ethics.* Ed. Karen Joy Greenberg. Norwood, N.J.: Ablex, 1991. 21–53.

Daily Variety. "Film Box Office Top 100 of 1995." Accessed 8 July 1996. <http://www.Leonardo.net/aasen/top1995.html>.

Damon, William. *The Moral Child: Nurturing Children's Natural Moral Growth.* New York: Free Press, 1988.

Davies, Robert A., James M. Farrell, and Steven S. Matthews. "The Dream World of Film: A Jungian Perspective on Cinematic Communication." *Western Journal of Speech Communication* 46 (1982): 326–343.

Davis, Sandi. "Disney Strives for Accuracy Bringing *Pocahontas* to Screen." *Daily Oklahoman* 18 June 1995, Travel: 8.

Day, Aidan. *Jokerman: Reading the Lyrics of Bob Dylan.* New York: Basil Blackwell, 1988.

"Deluxe Inks Deal With Disney." *Associated Press Online* 16 January 2001. Newspaper source. Ebsco host. Trinity Christian College Library, Palos Heights, Ill. Accessed 20 July 2001. <http://ioweb.uiuc.edu>.

Dinosaur. Dir. Ralph Zondag and Eric Leighton. Walt Disney Pictures, 2000.

Disney Lover's Web Ring. 13 August 2001. <http://nav.webring.yahoo.com/hub?ring=disneylover&list>.

"Disney Plans Cutbacks in Animation." *Associated Press Online* 24 April 2001. Newspaper source. Ebsco host. Trinity Christian College Library, Palos Heights, Ill. Accessed 20 July 2001. <http://ioweb.uiuc.edu>.

"Disney's Deal with ABC Develops Deep Domain." *AFA Journal* (August 1996): 9.

Disneyseek.com. Search engine. Accessed 13 August 2001. <http://disneyseek.com>.

Disney's Hercules. Dir. John Musker and Ron Clements. Walt Disney Pictures, 1997.

"Disney's *Hercules* Is a Breezy Romp Through Greek Mythology." *Chicago Tribune* 10 July 1997, 2: 4.

Disney's Hercules: Press Kit. May 1997.

Disney's The Hunchback of Notre Dame. Dir. Gary Trousdale and Kirk Wise. Walt Disney Pictures, 1996.

Disney's The Hunchback of Notre Dame: Press Kit. Burbank, Calif.: Walt Disney Pictures. 1996.

"Disney's *Hunchback* Seen Grossing More Than $150 Million." *Nando Times.* Nando.net. Accessed 18 February 1997. <http://xenocide.nando.net/newsroom/ntn/enter/062096/entert_191.html>.

"Disney's Latest Blunder." *Citizen* 19 June 1995: 5.

"Disney's Moral Plunge Continues." *AFA Journal* 20.9 (1996): 1, 22–23.

Disney's Mulan. Classic Storybook. Mouseworks, Disney Enterprises, 1998.

Dodd, Carley H. *Dynamics of Intercultural Communication.* 4th ed. Madison, Wisc.: Brown and Benchmark, 1995.

Dorfman, Ariel, and Armand Mattelart. *How to Read Donald Duck: Imperialist Ideology in the Disney Comic.* 1971. Trans. David Kunzle. New York: International General, 1991. 4th ed.

Douglas, Mary. *Natural Symbols: Explorations in Cosmology.* 1970. New York: Pantheon Books, 1982.

———. *Risk and Blame: Essays in Cultural Theory.* London: Routledge, 1992.

Douglas, Susan. *Where the Girls Are: Growing Up Female With the Mass Media.* New York: Times Books, 1994.

Dretzka, Gary. *"Hunchback* for the '90s." *Chicago Tribune* 16 June 1996, 7: 1, 8–9.

———. "Rocking Disney." *Chicago Tribune.* 14 June 1998, 7: 14.

Duncan, Hugh Dalziel. *Communication and Social Order.* 1962. New Brunswick, N.J.: Transaction Publishers, 1989.

Ebert, Roger. "A Victory in Battle: *Mulan* to Win Adults, Too." *Chicago Sun-Times* 19 June 1998: 27.

Edgerton, Gary, and Kathy Merlock Jackson. "Redesigning Pocahontas: Disney, the 'White Man's Indian,' and the Marketing of Dreams." *Journal of Popular Film and Television* 24 (1996): 90–98.

Eliade, Mircea. *Cosmos and History: The Myth of the Eternal Return.* 1949. Trans. Willard R. Trask. New York: Harper and Row, 1959.

———. *Myths, Dreams, and Mysteries: The Encounter Between Contemporary Faiths and Archaic Realities.* 1957. Trans. Philip Mairet. New York: Harper Torchbooks, 1960.

———. *The Sacred and the Profane.* Trans. Willard R. Trask. New York: Harcourt, Brace, 1959.

Eliot, Marc. *Walt Disney: Hollywood's Dark Prince.* New York: Birch Lane Press, 1993.

Elliott, Stuart. "Disney and McDonald's Become Double Feature." *New York Times* 24 May 1996: C1, D1.

Elson, Mary. *"Hunchback* Disney-Style." *Chicago Tribune* 21 July 1996, 2: 1, 8.

Faiola, Anthony. "Little Dove Vs. *Pocahontas:* To Virginia Tribe's Keeper of History, Disney Got It Wrong." *Washington Post* 25 May 1995: A1.

Farnsworth, Kirk E. "Furthering the Kingdom in Psychology." *The Making of a Christian Mind: A Christian World View and the Academic Enterprise.* Ed. Arthur Holmes. Downers Grove, Ill.: InterVarsity Press, 1985. 81–103.

Fasching, Darrell J. "Where Mass Media Abound, The Word Abounds Greater Still: Reflections on Robert Cole's Study of Children, Movies, and Ethics." *Ellul Studies Forum* 9 (1992): 6–8.

Feldmann, Susan. *African Myths and Tales.* New York: Dell, 1963.

Felperin, Leslie. "*Pocahontas.*" *Sight and Sound* 5 (1995): 57–58.

"Film Censors; Child-minders." *Economist* 13 August 1994: 78.

Fisher, Walter R. *Human Communication as Narration: Toward a Philosophy of Reason, Value, and Action.* 1987. Studies in Rhetoric/Communication. Columbia: University of South Carolina Press, 1989.

Fiske, John. "Television: Polysemy and Popularity." *Critical Studies in Mass Communication* 3 (1986): 391–408.

Fjellman, Stephen M. *Vinyl Leaves: Walt Disney World and America.* Boulder, Colo.: Westview Press, 1992.

Flowers, Betty Sue, ed. *Joseph Campbell: The Power of Myth, With Bill Moyers.* New York: Doubleday, 1988.

Foss, Sonja K., Karen A. Foss, and Robert Trapp. "Kenneth Burke." *Contemporary Perspectives on Rhetoric,* 2nd ed. Prospect Heights, Ill.: Waveland Press, 1991. 169–207.

Foster, David. "The 'Lion King' Falls Prey to Howls of Sexism, Racism." *Chicago Tribune* 26 July 1994, North Sports Final ed.: 3.

Francesconi, Robert. "Free Jazz and Black Nationalism: A Rhetoric of Musical Style." *Critical Studies in Mass Communication* 3 (1986): 36–49.

Frankena, William K. *Ethics.* 2nd ed. Englewood Cliffs, N.J.: Prentice-Hall, 1973.

Frentz, Thomas S. "Rhetorical Conversation, Time, and Moral Action." *Quarterly Journal of Speech* 71 (1985): 1–18.

Frentz, Thomas S., and Thomas B. Farrell. "Conversion of America's Consciousness: The Rhetoric of *The Exorcist.*" *Quarterly Journal of Speech* 61 (1975): 40–47.

Frentz, Thomas S., and Janice Hocker Rushing. "Integrating Ideology and Archetype in Rhetorical Criticism, Part 2: A Case Study of *Jaws.*" *Quarterly Journal of Speech* 79 (1993): 61–81.

Friends of Disney Alliance. Accessed 13 August 2001. <http://www.disney corner.com>.

Frye, Northrop. *Anatomy of Criticism: Four Essays.* 1957. Princeton, N.J.: Princeton University Press, 1973.

Gamble, Debra Lynn. "A Content Analysis of Romantic Love in Disney's Animated Video Cassette Tapes." *MAI* 30.1 (1992): 59.

Gans, Herbert J. Preface. *Cultivating Differences: Symbolic Boundaries and the Making of Inequality.* Eds. Michele Lamont and Marcel Fournier. Chicago: University of Chicago Press, 1992. vii–xv.

Gao, Ge, and Stella Ting-Toomey. *Communicating Effectively With the Chinese.* Communicating Effectively in Multicultural Contexts 5. Thousand Oaks, Calif.: Sage, 1998.

Garanzini, Michael. "Matching the Inner World With Outer Reality: Moral Development Domains and the Role of the Media." *Mass Media and the Moral Imagination.* Eds. Philip J. Rossi and Paul A. Soukup. Communication, Culture, and Theology. Kansas City, Mo.: Sheed and Ward, 1994. 85–106.

Geertz, Clifford. *The Interpretation of Cultures: Selected Essays.* New York: Basic Books, 1973.

Geist, Kenneth. "Aladdin." Rev. of *Aladdin. Films in Review* (April 1993): 127–128.

Gilligan, Carol. *In a Different Voice.* Cambridge: Harvard University Press, 1982.

Giroux, Henry A. "Animating Youth: The Disneyfication of Children's Culture." *Socialist Review* 24.3 (1994): 23–55.

———. *Disturbing Pleasures: Learning Popular Culture.* New York: Routledge, 1994.

———. "Memory and Pedagogy in the 'Wonderful World of Disney': Beyond the Politics of Innocence." *From Mouse to Mermaid: The Politics of Film, Gender, and Culture.* Eds. Elizabeth Bell, Lynda Haas, Laura Sells. Bloomington: Indiana University Press, 1995. 46–61.

———. "When You Wish Upon a Star It Makes a Difference Who You Are: Children's Culture and the Wonderful World of Disney." *International Journal of Educational Reform* 4 (1995): 79–83.

Gleiberman, Owen. "The Hunchback of Notre Dame: Towering Achievement." *Entertainment Weekly* 21 June 1996: 43–44.

Goldberger, Paul. "Cuddling Up to Quasimodo and Friends." *New York Times* 23 June 1996, 2: 1, 26, 27.

Golden, James L., Goodwin F. Berquist, and William E. Coleman. "Secular and Religious Conversion." *The Rhetoric of Western Thought,* 5th ed. Dubuque, Iowa: Kendall/Hunt, 1992. 447–475.

Gonzalez, Alberto, and John J. Makay. "Rhetorical Ascription and the Gospel According to Dylan." *Quarterly Journal of Speech* 69 (1983): 1–14.

Grant, Myrna Reid. "Mass Media and the Enlargement of Moral Sensibility." *Mass Media and the Moral Imagination.* Eds. Philip J. Rossi and Paul A. Soukup. Communication, Culture, and Theology. Kansas City, Mo.: Sheed and Ward, 1994. 242–248.

Graves, Michael P. "Functions of Key Metaphors in Early Quaker Sermons, 1671–1700." *Quarterly Journal of Speech* 69 (1983): 364–378.

———. "Stephen Crisp's *Short History* as Spiritual Journey." *Quaker Religious Thought* 26 (1993): 5–23.

Gray, John. *Men Are From Mars, Women Are From Venus.* New York: Harper Collins, 1992.

Gregg, Richard B. "A Rhetorical Re-examination of Arthur Vandenberg's 'Dramatic Conversion,' January 10, 1945." *Quarterly Journal of Speech* 61 (1975): 154–168.

Griffin, Charles J. G. "The Rhetoric of Form in Conversion Narratives." *Quarterly Journal of Speech* 76 (1990): 152–163.

Grover, Ron. *The Disney Touch: Disney, ABC, and the Quest for the World's Greatest Media Empire.* Rev. ed. Chicago: Irwin Professional Publishing, 1997.

Gudykunst, William B., Yuko Matsumoto, Stella Ting-Toomey, Tsukasa Nishida, Kwangsu Kim, and Sam Heyman. "The Influence of Cultural Individualism-Collectivism, Self Construals, and Individual Values on Communication Styles Across Cultures." *Human Communication Research* 22 (June 1996): 510–543.

Gumperz, John. *Discourse Strategies.* Cambridge: Cambridge University Press, 1982.

Günther, Susanne. "The Construction of Gendered Discourse in Chinese-German Interactions." *Discourse and Society* 3 (1992): 167–191.

Habermas, Jürgen. "Discourse Ethics: Notes on a Program of Philosophical Justification." *Moral Discourse and Practice: Some Philosophical Approaches.* Eds. Stephen Darwall, Allan Gibbard, and Peter Railton. New York: Oxford University Press, 1997. 287–302.

———. *Moral Consciousness and Communicative Action.* Trans. Christian Lenhardt and Shierry Weber Nicholsen. Cambridge: MIT Press, 1990.

———. *The Theory of Communicative Action.* Vol. 1: *Reason and the Rationalization of Society.* Trans. Thomas McCarthy. Boston: Beacon Press, 1987.

Hall, Lee. "The Story Disney Dared Not Tell." *Chicago Tribune* 12 August 1997: 11.

Hamilton, Edith. *Mythology: Timeless Tales of Gods and Heroes.* 1940. New York: New American Library, 1963.

Handy, Bruce. "Miracle on 42nd Street." *Time* 7 April 1997. Accessed 5 February 2000. <http://www.pathfinder.com/time/magazine/1997/dom/970407/ashow.miracle_on_42.htm>.

Hart, Roderick P. *Modern Rhetorical Criticism.* Glenview, Ill.: Scott, Foresman and Co., 1990.

Hauerwas, Stanley. *Vision and Virtue: Essays in Christian Ethical Reflection.* Notre Dame, Ind.: Fides Publishers, 1974.

Hauerwas, Stanley, and L. Gregory Jones, eds. *Why Narrative? Readings in Narrative Theology.* Grand Rapids, Mich.: Wm. B. Eerdmans, 1989.

Hearne, Betsy. "Disney Revisited, Or, Jiminy Cricket, It's Musty Down Here!" *Horn Book* 73.2 (1997): 137–146.

Henke, Jill Birnie, Diane Zimmerman Umble, and Nancy J. Smith. "Construction of the Female Self: Feminist Readings of the Disney Heroine." *Women's Studies in Communication* 19 (1996): 229–249.

Henry, Carl F. H. "Postmodernism: The New Spectre?" *The Challenge of Postmodernism: An Evangelical Engagement.* Ed. David S. Dockery. Wheaton, Ill.: BridgePoint Books, 1995.

"Heracles." *The Oxford Classical Dictionary,* 2nd ed. Eds. N. B. L. Hammond and H. H. Scullard. Oxford: Clarendon Press, 1970.

"Hermes." In *The Oxford Classical Dictionary,* 2nd ed. Eds. N. B. L. Hammond and H. H. Scullard. Oxford: Clarendon Press, 1970.

Hersh, Richard H., Diana Pritchard Paolitto, and Joseph Reimer. *Promoting Moral Growth: From Piaget to Kohlberg.* New York: Longman, 1979.

Hettrick, Scott. "'Lion King' to Video March 3." *Hollywood Reporter* 27–29 January 1995: 1, 58.

Hiestand, Tess. "Disney to Offer Television Station for Preschoolers." *Los Angeles Daily News* 22 June 2001. Newspaper source. Ebsco host. Trinity College Library, Palos Heights, Ill. Accessed 20 July 2001. <http://ioweb.uiuc.edu>.

Hoban, James L., Jr. "Rhetorical Rituals of Rebirth." *Quarterly Journal of Speech* 66 (1980): 275–288.

Hoerrner, Keisha L. "Gender Roles in Disney Films: Analyzing Behaviors From Snow White to Simba." *Women's Studies in Communication* 19 (1996): 213–228.

Hoffecker, W. Andrew. *Building a Christian World View*. Vol. 1: *God, Man, and Knowledge*. Vol. 2: *The Universe, Society, and Ethics*. Phillipsburg, N.J.: Presbyterian and Reformed Publishing Company, 1986.

Hoffner, Cynthia. "Children's Wishful Identification and Parasocial Interaction With Favorite Television Characters." *Journal of Broadcasting and Electronic Media* 40:3 (1996): 389–402.

Hofmeister, Sallie. "Disney to Put 'Lion King' Into Early Hibernation." *New York Times* 13 August 1994, Late ed., 1: 37.

Hofstede, Geert. *Culture's Consequences: International Differences in Work-Related Values*. 1980. Abridged ed. Cross-Cultural Research and Methodology Series 5. Beverly Hills, Calif.: Sage, 1984.

Hollows, Joanne, and Mark Jancovich, eds. *Approaches to Popular Film*. Manchester, U.K.: Manchester University Press, 1995.

Holmberg, Carl Bryan. "Toward the Rhetoric of Music: Dixie." *Southern Communication Journal* 51 (1985): 71–82.

Holmes, Arthur F. *Contours of a World View*. Grand Rapids, Mich.: Wm. B. Eerdmans, 1983.

———. *Ethics: Approaching Moral Decisions*. Contours of Christian Philosophy. Downers Grove, Ill.: InterVarsity Press, 1984.

Holmquest, A. "The Rhetorical Strategy of Boundary Work." *Argumentation* 4 (1990): 235–258.

Honeycutt, Kirk. "Oscars Reward 'Gump'-tion." *The Hollywood Reporter* 28 March 1995: 1, 6–7, 10, 13.

hooks, bell. *Killing Rage: Ending Racism*. New York: Henry Holt and Co., 1995.

Hoover's Online. "The Walt Disney Company." Accessed 13 August 2001. <http://www.hoovers.com>.

Howe, Desson. "Disney's Myth Conception." *Washington Post* 27 June 1997. Accessed 1 June 1999. <http://www.washingtonpost.com/wp-srv/style/longterm/movies/review97/herculeshowe.htm>.

Howells, Richard. "Pc, History, and Film." Online posting, H-Film/H-Net discussion list, 13 June 1995. Availability: H-Film@msu.edu.

Hugo, Victor. *The Hunchback of Notre Dame*. Trans. Lowell Blair. New York: Bantam Books, 1963.

Huxley, Aldous. *Brave New World*. Garden City, N.Y.: Doubleday, Doran, and Co., 1932.

"The Indian Romance." *American Enterprise* 6.5 (1995): 74–75.

Ingoglia, Gina. *Disney's Hercules*. Illustrated Classic. New York: Disney Press, 1997.

———. *Disney's The Hunchback of Notre Dame*. Illustrated Classic. New York: Disney Press, 1996.

———. *Disney's The Lion King*. Illustrated Classic. New York: Disney Press, 1994.

———. *Disney's Pocahontas*. Illustrated Classic. New York: Disney Press, 1995.

Internet Movie Database. "Box Office." Accessed 13 September 1999, 1 June 1999, 1 February 2000. <http://us.imdb.com/Charts/worldtopmovies>.

Irvine, James R., and Walter G. Kirkpatrick. "The Musical Form in Rhetorical

Exchange: Theoretical Considerations." *Quarterly Journal of Speech* 58 (1972): 272–284.

Ivie, Robert L. "Where Are We Headed?" *Quarterly Journal of Speech* 79 (1993): 384.

Jackson, Kathy Merlock. *Walt Disney, A Bio-Bibliography.* Westport, Conn.: Greenwood Press, 1993.

Jaffe, Aniela. "Symbolism in the Visual Arts." *Man and His Symbols,* 1964. Eds. Carl G. Jung and M. L. von Franz. New York: Dell, 1968. 255–322.

Jameson, Fredric. "Postmodernism and Consumer Society." *Studying Culture: An Introductory Reader.* Eds. Ann Gray and Jim McGuigan. New York: Edward Arnold, 1993. 192–205.

Jeffords, Susan. "The Curse of Masculinity: Disney's *Beauty and the Beast.*" *From Mouse to Mermaid: The Politics of Film, Gender, and Culture.* Eds. Elizabeth Bell, Lynda Haas, and Laura Sells. Bloomington: Indiana University Press, 1995. 161–172.

Jensen, J. Vernon. "Values and Practices in Asian Argumentation." *Argumentation and Advocacy* 28 (1992): 153–166.

Johnston, Ollie, and Frank Thomas. *The Disney Villain.* New York: Hyperion, 1993.

Jolson-Colburn, Jeffrey. "Grammy Buzz Boosts Boyz." *Hollywood Reporter* 2 March 1995: 1, 5.

Jones, Simon C., and Thomas G. Schumacher. "Muzak: On Functional Music and Power." *Critical Studies in Mass Communication* 9 (1992): 156–169.

Jung, Carl G., and M. L. von Franz, eds. *Man and His Symbols.* 1964. New York: Dell, l968.

Kagitçibasi, Çigdem. "A Critical Appraisal of Individualism and Collectivism: Toward a New Formulation." *Individualism and Collectivism: Theory, Method, and Applications.* Eds. Uichol Kim, Harry C. Triandis, Çigdem Kagitçibasi, Sang-Chin Choi, and Gene Yoon. Vol. 18, Cross-Cultural Research and Methodology Series. Thousand Oaks, Calif.: Sage, 1994.

Kempley, Rita. "Disney's *Hercules:* Myth for the Masses." *Washington Post* 27 June 1997. Accessed 1 June 1999. <http://www.washingtonpost.com/wp-srv/style/longterm/movies/review97/herculeskemp.htm>.

Keogh, Tom. "*Mulan:* Chinese Mythology, With Jokes." *Film.com* 1998. Accessed 1 June 1999. <http://www.film.com/film-review/1998/10632/23/default-review.html>.

Kershaw, Sarah. "Coming to Classrooms: The Real Pocahontas Story." *New York Times* 12 July 1995: B6.

Kilpatrick, Jacquelyn. "Disney's 'Politically Correct' *Pocahontas.*" *Cineaste* 21 (1995): 36–37.

Kim, Albert. "A Whole New World?" *Entertainment Weekly* 23 June 1995: 22–25.

Kim, Uichol, Harry C. Triandis, Çigdem Kagitçibasi, Sang-Chin Choi, and Gene Yoon, eds. *Individualism and Collectivism: Theory, Method, and Applications.* Vol. 18, Cross-Cultural Research and Methodology Series. Thousand Oaks, Calif.: Sage, 1994.

Klass, Perri. "A Bambi for the 90's, via Shakespeare." *New York Times* 19 June 1994, Late ed., sec. 2: 1.

Kluckhohn, Clyde. "Recurrent Themes in Myths and Mythmaking." *Myth and Mythmaking,* 1959. Ed. Henry A. Murray. Boston: Beacon Press, 1968. 46–60.

Knapp, Patricia-Ann Goodnow. "Rhetoric, Animation, and the Iconic Image: Ultimate Persuasion by Bugs Bunny and Donald Duck in Government-Sponsored World War II Animation." *DAI* 54/07-A (1993): 2386. University of Pittsburgh.

Knupp, Ralph E. "A Time for Every Purpose Under Heaven: Rhetorical Dimensions of Protest Music." *Southern Speech Communication Journal* 46 (1981): 377–389.

Koenig, David. *Mouse Under Glass: Secrets of Disney Animation and Theme Parks.* Irvine, Calif.: Bonaventure Press, 1997.

Kohlberg, Lawrence. "The Child as a Moral Philosopher." *Moral Education.* 1973. Eds. Barry I. Chazan and Jonas F. Soltis. New York: Teachers College Press, 1979. 131–143.

Larson, Charles. "Pocahontas Animated." *World and I* 11 (1996): 328–335.

LeCoat, Gerard G. "Music and the Three Appeals of Classical Rhetoric." *Quarterly Journal of Speech* 62 (1976): 157–166.

Lee, Jennifer Gin. "*Mulan.*" *Austin (Texas) Chronicle* 17 August 1998. Accessed 15 October 2001. <http://www.auschron.com/issues/vol17/issue49/xtra.mulan.html>.

Lee, Philip. "Film in Culture—Holding Up a Mirror to Imagination." *Media Development* 60 (1993): 21–24.

Leeming, David Adams. *The World of Myth: An Anthology.* New York: Oxford University Press, 1990.

Leff, Michael. "Textual Criticism: The Legacy of G. P. Mohrmann." *Quarterly Journal of Speech* 72 (1986): 377–389.

Leff, Michael, and Andrew Sachs. "Words the Most Like Things: Iconicity and the Rhetorical Text." *Western Journal of Speech Communication* 54 (Summer 1990): 252–273.

Lewis, Charles. "Making Sense of Common Sense: A Framework for Tracking Hegemony." *Critical Studies in Mass Communication* 9 (1992): 277–292.

Linyong, Zhu. "Legendary Figure Favoured." *China Daily* 17 August 1998. Accessed 4 June 1999. <http://www.chinadaily.net/cndy1998/08/d9-198.h17.html>.

The Lion King. Dir. Rob Minkoff and Roger Allers. Walt Disney Pictures, 1994.

The Lion King Press Kit. Burbank, Calif.: Walt Disney Pictures, 1994.

Lipson, Edna Ross. "A Better Reason to Fear *The Lion King.*" *New York Times* 10 July 1994, Late ed., 4: 2.

Louden, Robert B. "On Some Vices of Virtue Ethics." *American Philosophical Quarterly* 21 (1984): 227–236.

Lu, Xing. "An Interface Between Individualistic and Collectivistic Orientations in Chinese Cultural Values and Social Relations." *Howard Journal of Communications* 9.2 (1998): 91–107.

Lucas, Stephen E. "The Renaissance of American Public Address: Text and Context in Rhetorical Criticism." *Quarterly Journal of Speech* 74 (May 1988): 243–262.

Luckett, Moya. "*Fantasia:* Cultural Constructions of Disney's 'Masterpiece.'" *Disney Discourse: Producing the Magic Kingdom.* Ed. Eric Smoodin. New York: Routledge, 1994. 214–236.

MacIntyre, Alasdair. *After Virtue: A Study in Moral Theory.* 2nd ed. Notre Dame, Ind.: University of Notre Dame Press, 1984.

Madsen, Arnie J. "The Comic Frame as a Corrective to Bureaucratization: A Dramatistic Perspective on Argumentation." *Argumentation and Advocacy* 29 (1993): 164–177.

Makay, John J., and Alberto Gonzalez. "Dylan's Biographical Rhetoric and the Myth of the Outlaw Hero." *Southern Communication Journal* 52 (1987): 165–180.

Maltin, Leonard. *The Disney Films.* 3rd ed. New York: Hyperion, 1995.

Martin, Thomas M. *Images and the Imageless: A Study in Religious Consciousness and Film.* 2nd ed. London: Associated University Presses, 1991.

Maslin, Janet. "The Dancing Gargoyles Romp and Wisecrack." *New York Times* 21 June 1996: C14.

———. "The Hero Within the Child Within." *New York Times* 15 June 1994, Late ed.: C11.

———. "*Mulan:* Female Warrior Takes on Huns and Stereotypes." *New York Times* 2 June 1999. Accessed 19 June 1999. <http://www.nytimes.com/library/film/061998mulan-film-review.html>.

———. "*Pocahontas:* Romantic and Revisionist." *New York Times* 23 June 1995: C6.

———. Rev. of *Hercules. New York Times* 13 June 1997: C1.

May, John R., ed. *Image and Likeness: Religious Visions in American Film Classics.* Mahwah, N.J.: Paulist Press, 1992.

Mbiti, John S. *African Religion and Philosophy.* New York: Praeger, 1969.

McGee, Michael Calvin. "The 'Ideograph': A Link Between Rhetoric and Ideology." *Quarterly Journal of Speech* 66 (1980): 1–16.

———. "Text, Context, and the Fragmentation of Contemporary Culture." *Western Journal of Speech Communication* 54 (Summer 1990): 274–289.

McGreal, Jill. Review of *Mulan. Sight and Sound* 8.10 (1998): 47–48.

Mechling, Elizabeth Walker, and Jay Mechling. "The Sale of Two Cities: A Semiotic Comparison of Disneyland With Marriott's Great America." *Rhetorical Dimensions in Media: A Critical Casebook.* Eds. Martin J. Medhurst and Thomas W. Benson. Dubuque, Iowa: Kendall/Hunt, 1984. 400–413.

Medhurst, Martin J. "*Hiroshima, Mon Amour:* From Iconography to Rhetoric." *Rhetorical Dimensions in Media: A Critical Casebook.* Eds. Martin J. Medhurst and Thomas W. Benson. Dubuque, Iowa: Kendall/Hunt Publishing Co., 1984, 112–143.

Miles, Herbert J. *Movies and Morals.* Grand Rapids, Mich.: Zondervan Publishing House, 1947.

Miles, Margaret R. *Seeing and Believing: Religion and Values in the Movies.* Boston: Beacon Press, 1996.

Mitchell, Alice Miller. *Children and Movies.* Chicago: University of Chicago Press, 1929. Chicago: Jerome S. Ozer, 1971.

Mo, Weimin, and Wenju Shen. "A Mean Wink at Authenticity: Chinese Images in Disney's *Mulan.*" *New Advocate* 13.2 (2000): 129–142.

Morinis, Alan, ed. *Sacred Journeys: The Anthropology of Pilgrimage.* Foreword Victor Turner. Contributions to the Study of Anthropology 7. Westport, Conn.: Greenwood Press, 1992.

Mosley, Leonard. *Disney's World: A Biography.* New York: Stein and Day, 1985.

Mossiker, Frances. *Pocahontas: The Life and the Legend.* New York: Alfred A. Knopf, 1976.

Movieweb. "Box Office Totals for the Weekend Ending June 30." Accessed July 8, 1996. <http://www.movieweb.com/movie/top25.html>.

Mulan. Dir. Barry Cook and Tony Bancroft. Walt Disney Pictures, 1998.

"Mulan Debut Stalls at the Box Office." *South China Morning Post* 18 March 1999. Accessed 5 October, 1999. <http://www.geocities.com/Tokyo/Towers/2038/990317.txt>.

Mulan Press Kit. Burbank, Calif.: Walt Disney Pictures. 1998.

"Mulan Wins Battle for Young Hearts." *South China Morning Post* 19 February 1999. Accessed 5 October, 1999. <http://www.geocities.com/Tokyo/Towers/2038/990217.txt>.

Murphy, Patrick D. "'The Whole Wide World Was Scrubbed Clean': The Androcentric Animation of Denatured Disney." *From Mouse to Mermaid: The Politics of Film, Gender, and Culture.* Eds. Elizabeth Bell, Lynda Haas, Laura Sells. Bloomington: Indiana University Press, 1995. 125–136.

Murray, Noel. Rev. of *Mulan.* In "Striking Distance." *Nashville Scene* 6 July 1998. Accessed 1 June 1999. <http://archives.nashvillescene.com>.

Nadel, S. F. *Nupe Religion: Traditional Beliefs and the Influence of Islam in a West African Chiefdom.* 1954. New York: Schocken Books, 1970.

Noddings, Nel. *Caring: A Feminine Approach to Ethics and Moral Education.* Berkeley: University of California Press, 1984.

Oberholtzer, Ellis P. *The Morals of the Movie.* Philadelphia: Penn Publishing Co., 1922.

O'Leary, Stephen D. "A Dramatistic Theory of Apocalyptic Rhetoric." *Quarterly Journal of Speech* 79 (1993): 385–426.

Ono, Kent A. "Deciphering Pocahontas: Unpackaging the Commodification of a Native American Woman." Paper. NCA Convention, Chicago, 6 November 1999.

Oosthuizen, Gerhardus Cornelis. "The Place of Traditional Religion in Contemporary South Africa." *African Traditional Religions in Contemporary Society.* Ed. Jacob K. Olupona. New York: International Religious Foundation, Paragon House, 1991. 35–50.

Osborn, Michael. "Archetypal Metaphor in Rhetoric: The Light-Dark Family." *Quarterly Journal of Speech* 53 (1967): 115–126.

———. "The Evolution of the Archetypal Sea in Rhetoric and Poetic." *Quarterly Journal of Speech* 63 (1977): 347–363.

Owens, Jennifer. "Kellogg Sponsors Minisite for Disney Animated Film." *Media Week* 21 May 2001. Newspaper source. Ebsco host. Trinity Christian

College Library, Palos Heights, Ill. Accessed 20 July 2001. <http://ioweb
.uiuc.edu>.

Pan, Zhongdang, Steven H. Chaffee, Godwin C. Chu, and Yanan Ju. *To See
Ourselves: Comparing Traditional Chinese and American Cultural Values.*
Boulder, Colo.: Westview Press, 1994.

Patterson, Philip, and Lee Wilkins. *Media Ethics: Issues and Cases.* 3rd ed. Boston: McGraw-Hill, 1998.

Payne, David. *"The Wizard of Oz:* Therapeutic Rhetoric in a Contemporary
Media Ritual." *Quarterly Journal of Speech* 75 (1989): 25–39.

Peng, Foo Choy. "Mulan Sinks at Box-office as Heroine Fails to Charm Pa-
trons." *South China Morning Post* 19 March 1999. Accessed 4 June 1999.
<wysiwyg://Main.230/http://business.scmp.com/search/SearchArticles
.idq>.

Philibert, Paul. "The Formation of Moral Life in a Mass-Mediated Culture."
Mass Media and the Moral Imagination. Communication, Culture, and The-
ology. Eds. Philip J. Rossi and Paul A. Soukup. Kansas City, Mo.: Sheed and
Ward, 1994. 71–84.

Pinsent, John. *Greek Mythology.* London: Paul Hamlyn Publishing, 1969.

Pinsky, Mark I. "In Walt's World, No Churches on Main Street or on Screen:
Disney Films Have Given Lessons on Good and Evil to Millions of Children, With No Mention of Religion." *Orlando Sentinel* 16 July 1995: A1.

Pocahontas. Dir. Mike Gabriel and Eric Goldberg. Walt Disney Pictures. 1995.

Pocahontas: Press Kit. Burbank, Calif.: Walt Disney Pictures, 1995.

Powers, William F. "Eeek? Disney Is Big and Getting Much Bigger. Should We
Be Afraid of the Mouse?" *Washington Post* 6 August 1995: G1.

Price, Deb. "Baptists Vs. Disney." Editorial. *Des Moines Register* 22 June 1996: 9A.

Rafferty, Terrence. "No Pussycat." *New Yorker* 20 June 1994: 86–89.

Rasmussen, Karen. "Transcendence in Leonard Bernstein's Kaddish Symphony." *Quarterly Journal of Speech* 80 (1994): 150–173.

Rasmussen, William M. S., and Robert S. Tilton. *Pocahontas: Her Life and Legend.* Richmond: Virginia Historical Society, 1994.

Real, Michael R. "The Disney Universe: Morality Play." *Mass-Mediated Culture.* Englewood Cliffs, N.J.: Prentice-Hall, 1977. 44–89.

———. *Exploring Media Culture: A Guide.* Thousand Oaks, Calif.: Sage, 1996.

———. "The Expressive Face of Culture: Mass Media and the Shape of the
Human Moral Environment (2)." *Mass Media and the Moral Imagination.*
Eds. Philip J. Rossi and Paul A. Soukup. Communication, Culture, and
Theology. Kansas City, Mo.: Sheed and Ward, 1994. 25–33.

———. *Mass-Mediated Culture.* Englewood Cliffs, N.J.: Prentice-Hall, 1977.

Rest, James R., Stephen J. Thomas, Yong Lin Moon, and Irene Getz. "Different Cultures, Sexes, and Religions." *Moral Development: Advances in Research and Theory.* Ed. James R. Rest. New York: Praeger, 1986. 89–132.

Rich, John Martin, and Joseph L. DeVitis. *Theories of Moral Development.*
Springfield, Ill.: Charles C Thomas, 1985.

Rickey, Carrie. "Filmmakers, Historians, and Indians Talk About *Pocahontas.*"
Philadelphia Inquirer 19 June 1995. CD NewsBank Comprehensive: 00843-
19950619-05157.

Rojek, Chris. "Disney Culture." *Leisure Studies* 12.2 (1993): 121–135.

Romine, Linda. "*Hunchback* Rife With Adult Themes." *Nashville Business Journal* 8 July 1996: 15.

Roppen, George, and Richard Sommer. *Strangers and Pilgrims: An Essay on the Metaphor of Journey.* New York: Humanities Press, 1964.

Rossi, Rosalind. "Schools on Values Bandwagon." *Chicago Sun-Times* 3 February 1997: 8.

Roth, Matt. "In the End: Deconstructing Disney." *In These Times* 11 November 1996: 40–49.

Rozen, Leah. "*Pocahontas.*" *People* 19 June 1995: 21.

Rubenstein, Carin. "Parent and Child: Debating the Violence in 'Lion King.'" *New York Times* 14 July 1994, Late ed.: C8.

Rudnick, Paul. "Pocahontas." *Esquire* August 1995: 67.

Rushing, Janice Hocker. "*E.T.* as Rhetorical Transcendence." *Quarterly Journal of Speech* 71 (1985): 188–203.

———. "Evolution of 'The New Frontier' in *Alien* and *Aliens*: Patriarchal Co-optation of the Feminine Archetype." *Quarterly Journal of Speech* 75 (1989): 1–24.

———. "Mythic Evolution of 'The New Frontier' in Mass Mediated Rhetoric." *Critical Studies in Mass Communication* 3 (1986): 265–296.

Rushing, Janice Hocker, and Thomas S. Frentz. "The Frankenstein Myth in Contemporary Cinema." *Critical Studies in Mass Communication* 6 (1989): 61–80.

———. "Integrating Ideology and Archetype in Rhetorical Criticism." *Quarterly Journal of Speech* 77 (1991): 385–406.

———. "Integrating Ideology and Archetype in Rhetorical Criticism, Part 2: A Case Study of *Jaws.*" *Quarterly Journal of Speech* 79 (1993): 61–81.

Rybacki, Karyn, and Donald Rybacki. "The Rhetoric of Song." *Communication Criticism: Approaches and Genres.* Belmont, Calif.: Wadsworth, 1991. 275–307.

Sanger, Kerran L. "Slave Resistance and Rhetorical Self-definition: Spirituals as a Strategy." *Western Journal of Communication* 58 (1995): 177–192.

Schama, Simon. "The Princess of Eco-Kitsch." Editorial. *New York Times* 14 June 1995: A21.

Schechner, Richard. *The Future of Ritual: Writings on Culture and Performance.* London: Routledge, 1993.

Schickel, Richard. *The Disney Version: The Life, Times, Art, and Commerce of Walt Disney.* New York: Simon and Schuster, 1968.

Schillaci, Anthony. *Movies and Morals.* Notre Dame, Ind.: Fides Publishers, 1968.

Schrader, Paul. *Transcendental Style in Film: Ozu, Bresson, Dreyer.* New York: Da Capo Press, 1972.

Schrag, Robert L. "Sugar and Spice and Everything Nice Versus Snakes and Snails and Puppy Dogs' Tails: Selling Social Stereotypes on Saturday Morning Television." *Television Criticism: Approaches and Applications.* Eds. Leah R. Vande Berg and Lawrence A. Wenner. New York: Longman, 1991. 220–232.

Schuetz, Janice. *"The Exorcist:* Images of Good and Evil." *Western Journal of Communication* 39 (1975): 92–101.

Schwartz, Wendy. "A Guide to Communicating With Asian American Families." *Eric Clearinghouse on Urban Education: Parent Guide.* Accessed 24 September 1999. <http://eric-web.tc.columbia.edu/guides/pg2.html>.

Schweizer, Peter, and Rochelle Schweizer. *Disney The Mouse Betrayed: Greed, Corruption, and Children at Risk.* Washington, D.C.: Regnery Publishing, 1998.

Sellnow, Deanna D., and Timothy L. Sellnow. "John Corigliano's 'Symphony No. 1' as a Communicative Medium for the AIDS Crisis." *Communication Studies* 44 (1993): 87–101.

Sells, Laura. "'Where Do the Mermaids Stand?': Voice and Body in *The Little Mermaid.*" *From Mouse to Mermaid: The Politics of Film, Gender, and Culture.* Eds. Elizabeth Bell, Lynda Haas, and Laura Sells. Bloomington: Indiana University Press, 1995. 175–192.

Seno, Alexandra A. "Woman Warrior: An Unconventional Chinese Heroine Who Stays True to Disney Tradition." *Asia Week.* Accessed 5 June 1998. <http://www.pathfinder.com/asiaweek/98/0605/feat7.html>.

Shapiro, Laura. "Beyond Tiger Lily." *Newsweek* 19 June 1995: 77.

Sharkey, Betsy. "Beyond Teepees and Totem Poles." *New York Times* 11 June 1995, sec.2: 2.

Shreve, Jenn. "Honor Thy Daughter." *Salon* 19 June 1998. Accessed 1 June 1999. <http://www.salon.com/ent/movies/reviews/1998/06/19reviewb .html>.

Sillars, Malcolm O. *Messages, Meanings, and Culture: Approaches to Communication Criticism.* New York: Harper Collins, 1991.

Silverstone, Roger. *The Message of Television: Myth and Narrative in Contemporary Culture.* London: Heinemann, 1981.

Sisenwine, Joel. *"Aladdin, The Lion King,* and Jewish Values." *Jewish Spectator* 59.3 (1995): 9–11.

Smoodin, Eric. *Animating Culture: Hollywood Cartoons from the Sound Era.* New Brunswick, N.J.: Rutgers University Press, 1993.

―――, ed. *Disney Discourse: Producing the Magic Kingdom.* New York: Routledge, 1994.

Solomon, Martha. "Villainless Quest: Myth, Metaphor, and Dream in *Chariots of Fire.*" *Communication Quarterly* 31.4 (1983): 274–281.

Solomon, Martha, and Wayne McMullen. *"Places in the Heart:* The Rhetorical Force of an Open Text." *Western Journal of Speech Communication* 55 (1991): 339–353.

Spark, Ronald. "The Disney Super Hit These Cranks Don't Want You to See: Entertainment, Crackpot Critics Give the 'Sexist and Racist' *The Lion King* a Mauling." *Mail on Sunday* 7 August 1994: 44.

"Special Issue on Rhetorical Criticism." *Western Journal of Speech Communication* 54 (1990).

Stamper, Chris. "Film: Formula Super-Heroes." *World* 12–19 July 1997. Accessed 7 January 1999. <http://www.worldmag.com/world/issue/07-12-97/cultural_1.asp>.

Stelzner, Hermann G. "The Quest Story and Nixon's November 3, 1969 Address." *Quarterly Journal of Speech* 57 (April 1971): 163–172.

Stevenson, C. L. *Ethics and Language*. New Haven, Conn.: Yale University Press, 1944.

Storey, John, ed. *What Is Cultural Studies? A Reader*. London: Arnold, 1996.

Strong, Pauline Turner. Review of *Pocahontas*. Online posting, H-Film/H-Net discussion list, 1 July 1995. Availability: H-Film@msu.edu.

Sykes, Charles J. *A Nation of Victims: The Decay of the American Character*. New York: St. Martin's Press, 1992.

Tannen, Deborah. *Gender and Discourse*. New York: Oxford University Press, 1994.

———. *You Just Don't Understand: Women and Men in Conversation*. New York: William Morrow and Co., 1990.

Tarzan. Dir. Chris Buck. Walt Disney Pictures, 1999.

Taylor, Charles. "Myth-Conceived." *Salon* 27 June 1997. Accessed 1 June 1999. <http://www.salon.com/june97/entertainment/hercules970627.html>.

Taylor, Charles Alan. "Defining the Scientific Community: A Rhetorical Perspective on Demarcation." *Communication Monographs* 58 (1991): 402–420.

Taylor, John. *Storming the Magic Kingdom: Wall Street, the Raiders, and the Battle for Disney*. New York: Alfred A. Knopf, 1987.

"The Ten Most Popular Cartoon Characters Among 6-to-11-Year-Olds." *Time* 4 November (1996): 20.

Thompson, Anne. "*The Hunchback of Notre Dame:* Playing a Hunch." *Entertainment Weekly* 21 June 1996: 28–33.

Tilton, Robert S. *Pocahontas: The Evolution of an American Narrative*. Cambridge: Cambridge University Press, 1994.

Tonkin, Boyd. "*The Hunchback of Notre Dame*." *New Statesman* 12 July 1996: 40.

"The Top Grossing Movies of All Time at the USA Box Office." Accessed 18 January, 2000. <http://us.imdb.com/Charts/usatopmovies>.

Toscano, Siobhan Fergus. "What Does Disney Have Against Mothers?" *Chicago Tribune* 8 September 1996, WomenNews: 4.

Trites, Roberta. "Disney's Sub/Version of Andersen's *The Little Mermaid*." *Journal of Popular Film and Television* 18 (1991): 145–152.

Trujillo, Nick. "Hegemonic Masculinity on the Mound: Media Representations of Nolan Ryan and American Sports Culture." *Critical Studies in Mass Communication* 8 (1991): 290–308.

Tucker, Ernest. "Herc Goes Hollywood: But Movie's Animated 'Stew" Has Local Flavor." *Chicago Sun-Times* 27 June 1997: 38.

Turner, Kathleen J., ed. *Doing Rhetorical History: Concepts and Cases*. Tuscaloosa: University of Alabama Press, 1998.

Turner, Victor. *From Ritual to Theatre: The Human Seriousness of Play*. 1982. New York: PAJ Publications, 1992.

Turner, Victor, and Edith Turner. *Image and Pilgrimage in Christian Culture: Anthropological Perspectives*. Lectures on the History of Religions 11. New York: Columbia University Press, 1978.

Van Gennep, Arnold. *The Rites of Passage*. 1908. Trans. Monika B. Vizedom and Gabrielle L. Caffee. Chicago: University of Chicago Press, 1960.

Van Wert, William F. "Disney World and Posthistory." *Cultural Critique* 32 (1995–1996): 187–214.

Veith, Gene Edward, Jr. *Postmodern Times: A Christian Guide to Contemporary Thought and Culture*. Wheaton, Ill.: Crossway Books, 1994.

Verburg, Peter. "In the Maw of the Mouse." *Alberta Report/Western Report* 22 July 1996: 26 ff. Academic Abstracts, item 9608217737: 1–8.

Vickers, Brian. "Figures of Rhetoric/Figures of Music?" *Rhetorica* 2 (1984): 1–44.

Vincent, Mal. "Disney Vs. History . . . Again." *Virginia Beach Virginian-Pilot* 20 June 1995: E1, E5.

———. "History: Separating the Facts from Movie Fiction." *Virginia Beach Virginian-Pilot* 20 June 1995: E1, E5.

———. "*Hunchback* Is an Instant Classic With Something for All." *Virginia Beach Virginian-Pilot* 25 June 1996: E1, E3.

———. "Will Disney's Hunch Pay Off?" *Virginia Beach Virginian-Pilot* 20 June 1996: E1, E3.

Wainer, Alex. "Reversal of Roles: Subversion and Reaffirmation of Racial Stereotypes in *Dumbo* and *The Jungle Book*." *Sync* 1 (1993): 50–57.

Wall, James M. "The Lost World of Children's Films." *Media Development* 41 (1994): 11–13.

Walsh, Brian J., and J. Richard Middleton. *The Transforming Vision: Shaping a Christian World View*. Downers Grove, Ill.: InterVarsity Press, 1984.

"Walt Disney Biography." Accessed June 7, 1996. <http://www.disney.com>.

Walt Disney Company. "Fourth Fiscal Quarter 1995." Accessed 8 July 1996. <http://www.disney.com/investors/annual/yirq495.html>.

———. "Letter From the Chairman." *1995 Annual Report*. Accessed 22 January 1997. <http://www.disney.com/investors/annual/chairman.html>.

———. "Letter From the Chairman." *1996 Annual Report,* parts I–III: 1–4, 1–3, 1–4. Accessed 19 February 1997. <http://www.disney.com/investors/annual96/_letter.htm>.

———. "Year in Review." *1995 Annual Report:* 1–2. Accessed 22 January 1997. <http://www.disney.com/investors/annual/yir.html>.

Walt Disney Pictures. "A Brief History of *The Hunchback of Notre Dame*": 1–2. Accessed 1 July 1996. <http://www.disney.com/DisneyPictur . . . e_Dame/the_film/brief.html>.

———. "The Directors": 1–3. Accessed 1 July 1996. <http://www.disney .com/DisneyPictur . . . e_Dame/the_film/the_directors.html>.

———. "*Mulan* Fun Facts." Accessed 30 November 1998. <http://disney .com/disneypictures/mulan/filmfacts/index.html>.

———. "The Producers": 1–2. Accessed 1 July 1996. <http://www.disney .com/DisneyPictur . . . e_Dame/the_film/the_producers.html>.

———. "The Writers": 1–3. Accessed 1 July 1996. <http://www.disney .com/DisneyPictur . . . e_Dame/the_film/writers.html>.

Ward, Annalee R. "*The Lion King*'s Mythic Narrative: Disney as Moral Educator." *Journal of Popular Film and Television* 23.4 (1996): 171–178.

Warner, W. Lloyd. *The Family of God: A Symbolic Study of Christian Life in America*. New Haven, Conn.: Yale University Press, 1961.

Wasko, Janet. *Understanding Disney: The Manufacture of Fantasy*. Malden, Mass.: Blackwell Publishers, 2001.

Watson, Denise. "Pocahontas Hits Stores With Big Expectations." *Virginia Beach Virginian-Pilot* 20 June 1995: E5.

Watts, Steven. "Walt Disney: Art and Politics in the American Century." *Journal of American History* 82.1 (1995): 84–110.

Weaver, Richard M. *The Ethics of Rhetoric*. South Bend, Ind.: Regnery/Gateway, 1953.

Wells, Paul. *Understanding Animation*. London: Routledge. 1998.

White, Hayden. "The Narrativization of Real Events." *On Narrative*. Ed. W. J. T. Mitchell. Chicago: University of Chicago Press, 1981. 249–254.

———. "The Value of Narrativity in the Representation of Reality." *On Narrative*. Ed. W. J. T. Mitchell. Chicago: University of Chicago Press, 1981. 1–24.

White, Susan. "Split Skins: Female Agency and Bodily Mutilation in *The Little Mermaid*." *Film Theory Goes to the Movies*. Eds. Jim Collins, Hilary Radner, and Ava Preacher Collins. New York: Routledge, 1993. 182–195.

Williams, Raymond. *Marxism and Literature*. New York: Oxford University Press, 1977.

Wilmington, Michael. "Hercules Rocks." *Chicago Tribune* 20 June 1997, Friday: D–E.

Wirt, John. "Delightful *Pocahontas* Is Entertainment, Not History." *Baton Rouge (La.) Advocate* 23 June 1995: 20a.

Wolfe, Alan. *Moral Freedom: The Search for Virtue in a World of Choice*. New York: W. W. Norton and Co., 2001.

Wolters, Albert M. *Creation Regained: Biblical Basics for a Reformational Worldview*. Grand Rapids, Mich.: Wm. B. Eerdmans, 1985.

"Worldwide Box Office." Accessed 2 August 2001. <http://www.worldwideboxoffice.com>.

Wuthnow, Robert. *Meaning and Moral Order: Explorations in Cultural Analysis*. Berkeley: University of California Press, 1987.

Yearley, Lee H. "Recent Work on Virtue." *Religious Studies Review* 16 (1990): 1–9.

Zarefsky, David. "The State of the Art in Public Address Scholarship." *Texts in Context: Critical Dialogues on Significant Episodes in American Political Rhetoric*. Eds. Michael C. Leff and Fred J. Kauffeld. Davis, Calif.: Hermagoras Press, 1989. 13–27.

Zipes, Jack. "Breaking the Disney Spell." *From Mouse to Mermaid: The Politics of Film, Gender, and Culture*. Eds. Elizabeth Bell, Lynda Haas, and Laura Sells. Bloomington: Indiana University Press, 1995. 21–42.